K. HOFFMAN
947-2455

A NATURAL HISTORY
Guide to the
COAST

A NATURAL HISTORY
Guide to the
COAST

TONY SOPER

Foreword by HRH The Duke of Edinburgh

Gazetteer by Brian Le Messurier

Bloomsbury Books
London

First published in Great Britain in 1984 by
Webb & Bower (Publishers) Limited
9 Colleton Crescent, Exeter, Devon EX2 4BY
in collaboration with the National Trust
and in association with
Michael Joseph Limited
27 Wright's Lane, London W8 5SL

Designed by Peter Wrigley for the National Trust,
36 Queen Anne's Gate, London SW1H 9AS
and Webb & Bower (Publishers) Limited

Production Nick Facer

Picture research by Anne-Marie Ehrlich

Second impression 1986

This edition published 1993 by
Bloomsbury Books, an imprint of
The Godfrey Cave Group,
42 Bloomsbury Street, London WC1B 3QJ,
under licence from Webb & Bower Ltd 1992.

ISBN 1-85471-064-8

Typeset in Great Britain
by August Filmsetting, Haydock, St Helens

Printed and bound in Great Britain by
BPCC Hazells Ltd
Member of BPCC Ltd

PRECEDING PAGES: Duckpool Sands, Cornwall.

Page 6: Rhossili Bay and Worms Head from Rhossili Down on the Gower peninsula in South Wales.

Contents

Foreword *7*
Enterprise Neptune *9*
Introduction *11*
Spring *19*
Summer *47*
Autumn *79*
Winter *97*
Gazetteer of National Trust Coastal Properties *127*

ENGLAND

Avon:
Sand Point and Middle Hope *128*

Somerset:
Brean Down *128*
Selworthy Beacon and North Hill *128*

Devon (north):
Countisbury, Glenthorne and the Foreland *129*
Woody Bay, Heddon's Mouth and the Great and Little Hangman *130*
Ilfracombe to Croyde Bay *132*
The Hartland Coast *133*
Lundy *133*

Cornwall:
Morwenstow *133*
Sandy Mouth, Duckpool and Maer Cliff *134*
Dizzard Point *136*
Castle Point to Rusey Cliff *136*
Boscastle *136*
Bossiney Haven, Tintagel to Tregardock *137*
Port Gaverne, Port Quin and Pentire *138*
Porthcothan, Park Head and Bedruthan *140*
The Gannel, Crantock Beach to Kelsey Head and Holywell Bay *141*
The St Agnes area *141*
Portreath to Godrevy *142*
Trencrom Hill *144*
The Penwith Coast from St Ives to Zennor, Gurnard's Head, Bosigran and Rosemergy *144*
Levant Cornish Beam Engine *146*
Polpry Cove, Chapel Carn Brea and the cliffs between Sennen Cove and Land's End *147*
The South Coast of Penwith *147*
The Egyptian House, Chapel Street, Penzance *148*
Trengwainton Garden, Penzance *148*
St Michael's Mount *148*

Cudden Point *150*
Rinsey Cliff *150*
The Loe *151*
Gunwalloe to Poldhu *151*
The Marconi Memorial, Mullion and Predannack *154*
Kynance Cove *154*
Bass Point (the Lizard), Cadgwith to Poltesco *154*
Beagles Point and Chynalls Cliff *155*
Lowland Point *158*
The Helford River *158*
Rosemullion Head *159*
Trelissick *159*
The Fal Estuary *160*
St Anthony in Roseland *160*
Porthmellin Head and the St Mawes Estuary *161*
Percuil *162*
Portscatho, Treluggan Cliff, Pendower Beach, Nare Head and Portloe *162*
The Dodman *162*
The Gribbin and the west side of the Fowey River *166*
Pont Pill *166*
Polruan to Lansallos *166*
Polperro *167*
Hore Point *167*
Looe to Rame Head *167*

Devon (south):
Wembury and the Yealm Estuary *168*
Bolt Tail to Overbecks *170*
Snapes Point *171*
East Portlemouth to Prawle Point *171*
Little Dartmouth and Gallants Bower *171*
Kingswear to Brixham *173*
Orcombe Point *173*
Salcombe Regis to Branscombe Mouth *173*

Dorset:
The Spittles and Black Venn *173*
Golden Cap – Charmouth to Eype Mouth *174*
Burton Cliff *175*
Lime Kiln Hill *175*
Burning Cliff and White Nothe *175*
St Aldhelm's Head to Poole Harbour *175*
Brownsea Island *176*

Isle of Wight:
Newtown *178*
West Wight – the Needles Headland eastward to Chilton Chine *179*
St Catherine's *181*
Ventnor *181*
Bembridge *181*

West Sussex:
East Head *182*

East Sussex:
Crowlink *182*

Kent:
Dover, Great Farthingloe *182*
Dover, St Margaret's Bay *182*

Essex:
Northey Island *183*
Ray Island *183*

Suffolk:
Dunwich Heath *183*

Norfolk:
4 South Quay, Great Yarmouth *183*
Horsey *183*
Gramborough Hill *185*
Blakeney Point *185*
Morston and Stiffkey Marshes *186*
Scolt Head Island *186*
Brancaster *187*

North Yorkshire:
Newbiggin Cliff *187*
Cayton Bay and Knipe Point *187*
Hayburn Wyke and Staintondale *187*
Robin Hood's Bay *187*
Saltwick Nab, Whitby *190*

Northumberland:
Druridge Bay and Buston Links *190*
Dunstanburgh, Low Newton and Beadnell *190*
The Farne Islands *191*
St Aidan's and Shoreston Dunes *193*
Lindisfarne Castle *194*

Cumbria:
Solway Commons and Burgh Marsh *195*
Sandscale Haws *195*

Lancashire:
Bank House Farm *195*
Jack Scout Land *197*

Merseyside:
Formby Point *198*
The Wirral *198*

WALES

Gwynedd:
Aberconwy House, Conwy *198*
Conwy Suspension Bridge *198*
Penrhyn Castle, Bangor *199*
Dinas Gynfor, Anglesey *199*
Cemaes, Anglesey *199*
Cemlyn, Anglesey *199*
Clegir Mawr (Mynydd-y-Garn), Anglesey *200*
Plas Newydd, Anglesey *200*
Cae Glan-y-Mor, Anglesey *201*
Glan Faenol *201*
Segontium *201*
Port Gwylan *201*
The tip of the Lleyn *202*
The Plas-yn-Rhiw Estate *202*
Tywyn-y-Fach *202*
Ynysgain *202*
Y Maes, Llandanwg *202*
Dinas Oleu *203*

Dyfed:
Coybal, Cwm Soden, Cwmtydi *203*
Lochtyn, Llangranog *203*
Penbryn *203*
Mwnt *203*
Ceibwr Bay *203*
Barry Island Farm *203*
St David's Head *204*
St Bride's Bay (north side) *207*
The Marloes Peninsula *207*
Kete *208*
Freshwater West *208*
Stackpole *208*
Lydstep Headland and Manorbier *209*
The Tudor Merchant's House, Tenby *209*
The Colby Estate, Amroth *210*

West Glamorgan:
The South Gower Coast *210*
The West Gower Coast *210*
The North Gower Coast *211*

NORTHERN IRELAND

Co. Londonderry:
Mussenden Temple, Black Glen, Bishop's Gate, Downhill Castle ruins and Bar Mouth *211*

Co. Antrim:
The Giant's Causeway and the North Antrim Coast *212*
Fair Head, Murlough Bay and Torr Head *215*
Cushendun and Layde *215*

Belfast:
Crown Liquor Saloon, Great Victoria Street *217*

Co. Down:
Belfast Lough *217*
Kearney and Knockinelder *217*
Strangford Lough Wildlife Scheme *217*
Mount Stewart *218*
Castle Ward *218*
Murlough Nature Reserve, Dundrum *219*
The Mourne Coastal Path *219*
Blockhouse Island and Green Island *220*

National Trust Headquarters and Regional Offices *220*
Acknowledgements *221*
Index *222*

Foreword

BUCKINGHAM PALACE.

On 11th May 1965 I launched 'Enterprise Neptune' at the Mansion House in London. The purpose was to raise funds for the National Trust to acquire 900 miles of unspoilt coastline of England, Wales and Northern Ireland. So far, half that target has been achieved and following the publication of this 'Guide to the Coast' the Trust is re-launching 'Enterprise Neptune' in an effort to acquire the unspoilt coastline which remains as part of the original target.

In many ways the achievements of 'Enterprise Neptune' have made it possible for this Guide to be written. I very much hope that it will now help to achieve the final target.

The days when we could take it for granted that we would always have beautiful stretches of coast around our islands are long since past. If we want future generations to share our enjoyment of the wildness and variety of our coastal scenery, we must make a determined effort now to help the National Trust to give it proper and lasting protection.

1984

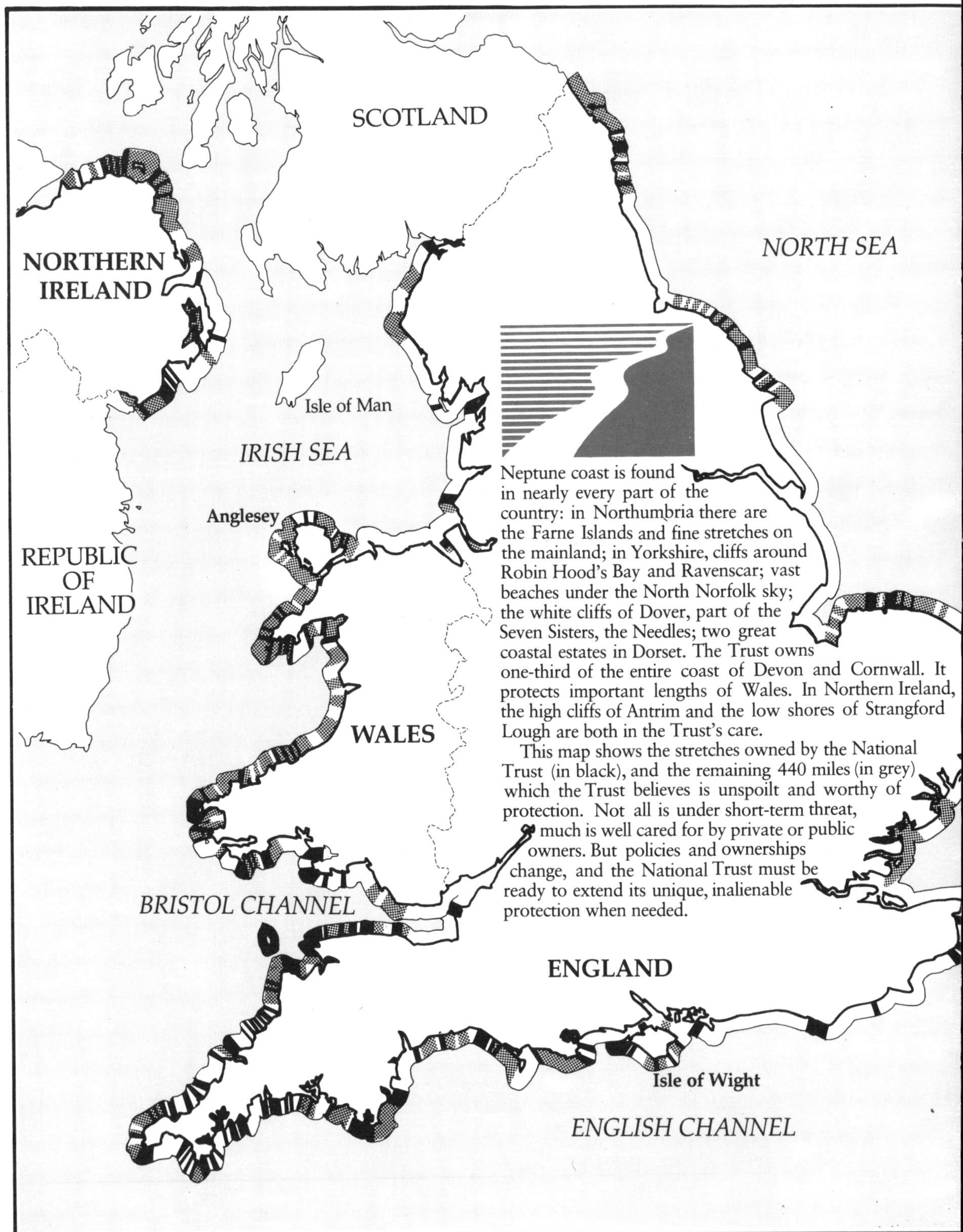

Neptune coast is found in nearly every part of the country: in Northumbria there are the Farne Islands and fine stretches on the mainland; in Yorkshire, cliffs around Robin Hood's Bay and Ravenscar; vast beaches under the North Norfolk sky; the white cliffs of Dover, part of the Seven Sisters, the Needles; two great coastal estates in Dorset. The Trust owns one-third of the entire coast of Devon and Cornwall. It protects important lengths of Wales. In Northern Ireland, the high cliffs of Antrim and the low shores of Strangford Lough are both in the Trust's care.

This map shows the stretches owned by the National Trust (in black), and the remaining 440 miles (in grey) which the Trust believes is unspoilt and worthy of protection. Not all is under short-term threat, much is well cared for by private or public owners. But policies and ownerships change, and the National Trust must be ready to extend its unique, inalienable protection when needed.

Enterprise Neptune

Britain has one of the most varied and beautiful coastlines in the world; high cliffs and great headlands, tiny coves and sweeping sands, lonely salt marshes, intricate sand-dunes, and long banks of shingle. Colours range from the white cliffs of Dover to the red rocks of Devon, from the black basalt of the Giant's Causeway in Antrim to the pale grey of Stackpole Head in South Wales. Our coastlands offer beauty and open space, which should be accessible to all. They are places where people live and work, and where wild animals, plants, and birds can survive. They are also under constant threat of development.

Perhaps it all began when King George III entered the water at Weymouth, and established our love of the seaside, or possibly when Brunel raised his great bridge at Saltash, and brought the railway into Cornwall. Let's just say that it was during the early part of the nineteenth century that Britain's coastline ceased to be of interest only to those travellers, traders, fishermen who had business on the sea, and became a place of resort for millions. If the steam train brought the visitors, the steam ship caused many port towns to expand out of all recognition. A pattern was set that is still with us; the coasts of our densely-populated island felt the twin pressures of leisure and industry.

Back in 1897, two years after the foundation of the National Trust, the building of a great hotel at Tintagel caused an outcry, and a group of people subscribed to buy the neighbouring headland and to put it into the care of the Trust. The arrival of the motor car, combined with the lack of adequate planning controls between the wars, intensified the pressure on remaining unspoilt coast. So, in 1965, the National Trust invited the Duke of Edinburgh to launch Enterprise Neptune – a campaign to raise funds to preserve the 900 remaining miles of coastline around England, Wales and Northern Ireland (Scotland has its own Trust).

This campaign has been a tremendous success: the Trust has raised more than £8 million; many fine stretches of coast have been donated; half our aim has been achieved, but the remaining vital 440 miles are still to go. That is why Enterprise Neptune was relaunched in 1985. The response showed how deeply we care about our coastline; £1 million was raised in the next twelve months. Every penny of that was needed and spent on coastal preservation, adding over ten miles.

Neptune rarely has time to appeal for a specific piece of coast, rather we aim to have funds available for the time when a property comes onto the market. Each gift ensures that yet another stretch of our precious coastline stays a reality for future generations, not a fading memory.

Introduction

Tony Soper at home on the Salcombe Estuary in South Devon.

The coast is more than the edge of our country. It is our frontier with life in a different medium. But there is no hard and fast divide. Instead, the land and sea interact with each other and the inhabitants of both venture back and forth across the boundary, often making this narrow frontier strip their permanent home.

The joint forces of both land and sea working upon the marvellously varied geological structure of our country have bestowed upon the coast a great range of maritime habitats from the truly marine to the faintly salt-tinged; each forms a special type of country peopled by particular plants and animals as determined by the character of the land, from sheer cliff to sandy bay, rocky shore to estuary mud. The work of the sea as destroyer and builder of the land is of vital importance, but if the land were uniform – a high wall of uniform rock – the results would be predictable and unvaried. Instead we find our gloriously varied geology displayed at the coast where the sea can get its teeth into every kind of rock, hard or soft, ancient or modern. The mix is as varied as a fruit cake and, like cutting a slice of cake to reveal the interior, a visit to the coast is a revelation, an insight into the structures which usually lie hidden beneath our feet. It is this variety of

Erosive forces at work. Weaker materials have been storm-blasted away, leaving an arch of carboniferous limestone. Green Bridge of Wales at Flimston, Dyfed.

rocks, worked on by the unceasing energy of the sea, that provides the varied wealth of our coastal landscape.

The sea has immense power to erode, but it does not work alone. On a cliff, for example, the sea can only do its work when high tide allows it to reach the base of the cliff and gnaw away at the rocks. By contrast, rain, wind and frost can do their damage at any time, enlarging cracks, exploiting weaknesses and washing away protective debris. So the sea works hand in hand with the land-based agents of erosion; when, for example, the expanding power of frost cleaves the rock to cascade fragments to the beach below, the sea seizes these rough stones and adds them to its erosive armoury.

The sea would be powerless without its wind-generated waves, but with them it can act in several ways. It can hurl a great weight of water against a cliff, trapping air in a crevice until the pressure creates explosive power which loosens rocks and further exploits the weakness of a joint or fault. It can batter the cliff with an array of abrasive stones and rocks eroded from the cliff itself, adding insult to injury. Sheer weight of water beating wave on wave, acts as a battering ram. So develops the architecture of our cliffs, the most dramatic features being the produce of

Sand dunes are susceptible not only to the forces of the sea but to the trampling of human feet. When the fragile covering of vegetation is destroyed it may be necessary to fence areas in order to discourage access while tough pioneer plants like marram grass (*Ammophila arenaria*) begin the stabilizing process again.

Battering waves reveal the complexities of the earth's crust. Drag fold associated with an overthrust at Saundersfoot beach, Dyfed.

An intimate wilderness. In the comparatively sheltered estuaries, tidal forces persuade mudbanks to rise. In due course they are colonized by salt-marsh plants. Newtown estuary, Isle of Wight.

erosion; stacks separated from their parent cliff, blow holes and arches, caves and islands.

The sea is never still and with the movement of the water there goes a mass movement of beach material – sand, shingle, pebbles – transported by the action of the waves. This transport can be to a destructive end, raking down protective shingle from the foot of a cliff to allow further bouts of erosion, but it is often a positive deed, building our much loved beaches, spits and bars. The process by which this transport is achieved is known as 'longshore drift' – a gradual shifting of material with the direction of the prevailing wind made possible by the oblique approach of waves as they run up the beach and the subsequent return of the backwash at ninety degrees to the shore. Beach material is thus shifted along until it meets an obstacle: a rocky headland or, in places where sand is a prized asset for the holiday industry, an artificial groyne. Where the configuration of the coast allows it – in a sheltered bay for example – the beach builds up as a permanent feature, albeit one which changes its mood, maybe adding storm ridges of high-flung boulders or losing sand to the neighbours. For although the sea may appear all powerful, it is dependent on the wind to determine these moods which vary

Most coastal processes are slow, but shingle banks may alter their shape in response to the building or destroying forces of a single storm. Dunwich, Suffolk.

from monstrous 'Earth Shaker' screaming with white horses to innocent mill pond.

Sometimes you can see the work of the sea going on – crashing waves dragging shingle away from a bank during a storm, cliff sections slumping during heavy rain, sand piling up against stout marram grass as the searing wind carries its load. But mostly the processes of coastal development and change are slow, rooted in the geological time scale and refined through centuries, and so we trust scientific and historical observations to tell us how things have happened and are content ourselves to enjoy and cherish the happy results.

Plants enjoy the coast as home, staking their claim, as in every other type of country, according to the physical environment and the extent of the competition. Animals, birds especially, do the same, with visiting as an extra dimension: to forage for feed, to breed or just to rest after the rigours of migration. Like the animals, we use the coast for a great variety of reasons, but unlike the birds which are constant in their desires – breeding grounds, particular food requirements and so on – our use of the coastline has changed, often dramatically, according to our agricultural and industrial fortunes, our military and cultural aspirations.

At different times our coastline has been important to us as a springboard for inland exploration and settlement, for defence, as a base from which to harvest the riches of the sea,

Cliffs show the scars of a never-ending battle between the forces of land and sea. To keep a foothold here, plants and animals need to be hardy and well adapted.

a place to colonize for industry and for holiday fun . . . the emphasis has changed with changing times. It wasn't until the coming of the railways in the middle of the last century that people flocked to the coast for health and recreation, but since that Victorian discovery of the glorious freedom of the seaside the coast has remained as popular as ever. It has become a magnet for residential development and all kinds of water-based sport and recreation. In our times this is where the emphasis lies, on the coast as a playground and place for pleasurable pursuits.

It is true that the coast – our frontier country between land and sea – provides more variety of opportunity for our many pursuits than any other kind of countryside because the bones of the land are so varied and are complemented by the coming and going of the sea. It is a land of opportunity for wildlife, too, and one of the greatest pleasures is to observe and understand other creatures as they live their lives. The different seasons bring their own highlights, be they the first wheatear to arrive in spring, the extra-high tides of the equinoxes, or a particularly well remembered sunset. Different parts of the coast have their high spots too. Picturesque harbours, outstanding natural beauty, sea-bird cities . . . the British coastline has them all and with the National Trust as one of its guardians we can all enjoy and learn about its bounty.

Spring

A westerly view from the rocky foreshore of Crackington Haven, North Cornwall.

One of the more astonishing sights at the coast in springtime is that of the arrival of vast quantities of insects. It is convenient to think of migration in terms of birds, but small creatures like hoverflies or ladybirds sometimes home in on our shores in such numbers that they make flocks of migrant birds seem insignificant.

Ladybirds crowding on a sandy beach. These insects sometimes arrive from the continent in huge numbers. This is the most common species, the 7-spot ladybird (*Coccinella 7-punctata*), gathered about a washed-up cork float.

Closely packed ladybirds may practically cover a beach, or a convenient boat, until they obliterate it from view. From March onwards, butterflies may be commonly seen by yachtsmen and seamen as they flutter their insubstantial but resolute way across the Channel, having wintered in the warmth of the continent. Some are irregular visitors, spurred on by population excesses or by capricious winds, so that, for instance, we may enjoy 'clouded yellow' years. Monarch butterflies may be diverted on their journey from California to southern Canada to be blown ashore along the coast of the south-west. Red admirals and painted ladies regularly fly to the south coast, colonizing our splendid British stinging nettles, there to mate and lay eggs which produce offspring which in their turn will fly south in the autumn. The parents, our spring migrants, are unlikely to survive for that journey. An influx of large white butterflies from southern Scandinavia braves the North Sea to increase the numbers of our residents. Occasionally there is a welcome immigration of the Camberwell beauty, also along the east coast.

The fact of migration has been known for millennia, but because the phenomenon is so difficult to pin down by observation there have always been plenty of rival hypotheses to explain the seasonal movements of animals, especially in the case of birds. Until comparatively recently, it seemed a great deal easier to believe that swallows spent the winter having a quiet sleep in muddy ponds than to accept the possibility that they might cross seas and continents to enjoy the warmth and insect harvests of faraway places. But over a period of time the accumulating information on bird distribution and movements together with arrival and departure times showed the truth of the existence of seasonal movements.

Apart from the conclusive evidence of ringing, diligent observation at the coast has provided a mass of data. From the string of observatories strategically placed on islands, headlands and natural landing points, the character of the patterns of bird movements has emerged.

We tend to think of migration in terms of a mass movement between latitudes, with birds moving south in autumn to return in spring. But there is also a marked movement longitudinally, with Scandinavian and continental European birds moving west to winter in the comparative mildness of the Atlantic seaboard. And this says nothing of local movements which, while not covering great distances, may bring birds down from high altitudes in the mountains to a sea-level winter.

Migration has close links with climate, in that animals have learned to take advantage of seasonal changes. But the practical act of travelling is determined by weather in its day-to-

Wheatears winter in southern Africa, returning either to breed or as passage-migrants in March, or even February.

day manifestations. Dark skies and gale-force winds will reduce enthusiasm for movement. Settled weather, clear skies and rising temperatures will trigger the action on a particular day in spring. Swallows pass over the coast at any time by day, but most of the army of advancing songbirds migrate under cover of darkness, taking advantage of the safety it provides from the attention of predators. Early morning at coastal observatories can be an exciting time, with the carefully nurtured bushes and scrub harbouring countless numbers of newly arrived, tired and hungry warblers.

One of the band of migrants is the wheatear, whose striking white rump is one of the welcome sights of spring. The first birds normally arrive on the south coast about the middle of March, though they have been seen as early as February. Wintering in southern Africa, one of the races of this attractive bird faces a tough journey taking it all the way to Greenland. It is a slightly larger bird than the wheatear which breeds in Britain, and it needs the extra weight to carry enough fuel to power its open Atlantic passage of over 1500 miles. Ringing recoveries – before and after – have shown the marked loss of weight which birds suffer on these ocean crossings.

Cuckoos are characteristic birds of passage at the coast, normally arriving in early April, though there are plenty of earlier records. They are late arrivals for the simple reason that they have no nest to build and can afford a leisurely journey while the warblers or pipits which they are going to parasitize are doing all the work.

While by far the greater proportion of our summer visitors perform these time-proven migration journeys, there are some cases where individuals have broken the pattern by sitting it out through the winter in Britain, possibly pioneering a new way of life, if for instance climatic change encourages the behaviour to continue. Even swallows have been known to overwinter in West Cornwall, where mild winters can provide just enough flies to sustain them. The marshes and weedy beaches inshore of St Michael's Mount are likely places for these unusual sightings. But it is best to be fairly sceptical of records of overwintering swallows, since there are plenty of mid-December sightings which relate to birds which are simply late on migration. A few wheatears overwinter, but chiffchaffs and blackcaps seem to do it more and more frequently, presumably as a response to the general amelioration in climate. If mild winters persist, doubtless we shall be seeing more of these birds staying on to become residents instead of summer visitors.

Relatively few small birds are resident at the coast. The plump-headed stonechat is one of them, particularly well established in the coastal areas of Scotland, western Wales and the south and south-west of England. Severe winters in the past have reduced its numbers inland, but it is abundant along western coasts, nesting in heather and gorse, and feeding over rough

N.W.CUSA.

CLIFF FACE

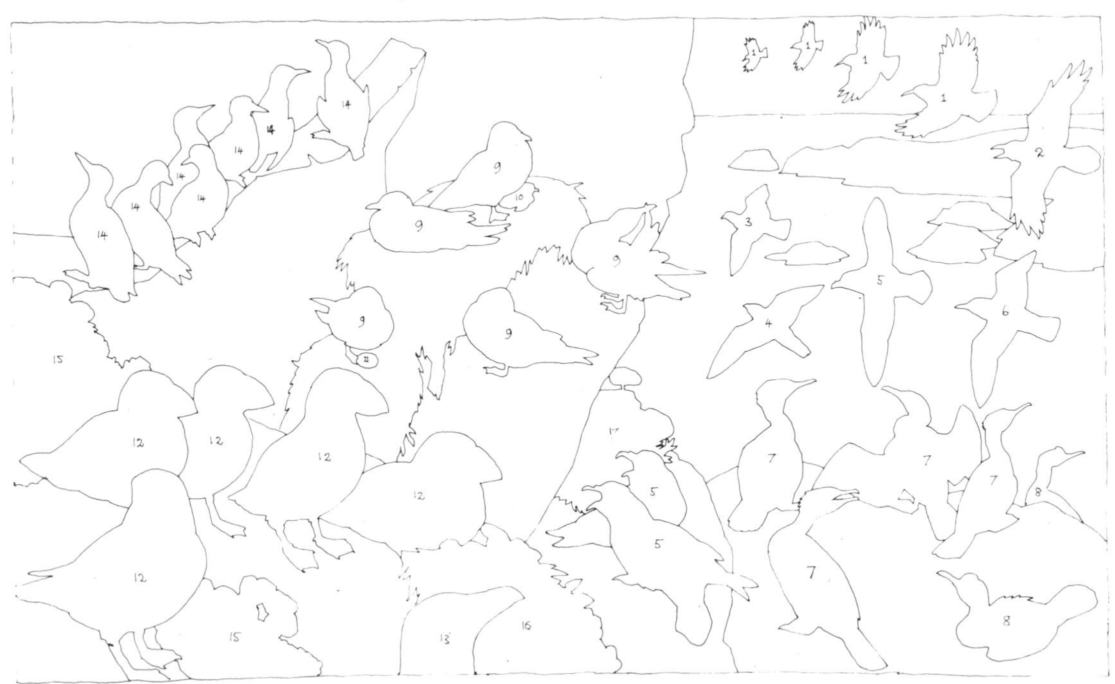

Spring at the cliff face. It is the height of the breeding season for the colonies of sea-birds. Just below us a group (12) of puffins (*Fratercula arctica*) rests on a lichen-covered rock among (15) thrift, or sea-pink (*Armeria maritima*) and (16) sea-campion (*Silene maritima*) while (13) a razorbill (*Alca torda*) stands almost at our feet. Below, on a cliff ledge where (17) samphire (*Crithmum maritimum*) grows, a pair (5) of fulmars (*Fulmarus glacialis*) bills and coos. On the cliff face beyond there is a colony (9) of kittiwakes (*Rissa tridactyla*). One bird rests, another preens, a third broods, one has (11) an egg and another (10) a single downy chick. Higher up the cliff, on a narrow ledge a line (14) of guillemots (*Uria aalge*) is noisily busy with its communal arrangements. Below us, on a rocky islet (7) cormorants (*Phalocrocorax carbo*) and (8) shags (*Phalacrocorax aristotelis*) share breeding territory, the cormorants however gathering and nesting on the exposed summit of the rock while the shags favour ledges and crannies lower down. Over the sea (4) a peregrine (*Falco peregrinus*) pursues (3) a pigeon (*Columba livia*) which, although it has the markings of a rock dove, is probably a domestic pigeon gone wild. Disturbed no doubt by the falcon, (3) a raven (*Corvus corax*) and (1) four choughs (*Pyrrhocorax pyrrhocorax*) have left their cliff perches and will circle noisily until danger is past. A third fulmar glides by below us on rigid wings and further away (6) a herring gull (*Larus argentatus*) exhibits its contrasting manner in the air.

ground, especially when there is some reed-fringed water nearby. Walking the coastal paths in spring, you'll see its jaunty upright figure clinging high on stems, and insisting that you notice its alarm call – the clicking sound of pebbles being struck against each other.

Cock cirl bunting in full cry.

A very much rarer, or rather more localized, coastal bird is the cirl bunting. Rather smaller than the closely related yellowhammer, the male bird at least is easy enough to distinguish by its more strikingly marked head. And the song is a truncated version of the 'little-bit-of-bread-and-no-cheese', rattled away from the early spring right through till autumn. The species was first discovered to be breeding in Britain by a Colonel Montagu, of Kingsbridge in South Devon, in 1800, and its main stronghold is still the narrow coastal strip between Salcombe and Exeter, and National Trust properties like Bolberry Down, Little Dartmouth and Coleton Fishacre are promising locations to listen for it. The cirl bunting is best looked on as the Mediterranean form of the yellowhammer; its natural home is the hot terraced valleys of the vineyards. The gorsy clifftop walks of Devon represent the extreme northern limit of its range and its very existence here as a breeding bird depends upon mild winters.

The black redstart is another rare breeding species which showed some signs of establishing itself on the coast. On the continent it nests in mountain scree and on sea cliffs, and range expansion first brought it to a tentative foothold in Sussex and Cornwall in the 1920s. Breeding sporadically in the south-east, it took unexpected advantage of the sudden increase in available nest sites in bomb-hit London in the 1940s. One of the more bizarre side effects of the conflict was the way in which these strikingly coloured birds began to establish themselves in the 'cliffsides' of bombed sites. There have been suggestions that their establishment in London was aided by the 'heat-island' effect which increases ambient temperature in big cities, but whatever the cause of their temporary success in London, the bomb sites are no longer available and the black redstarts have turned instead to coastal versions of these industrial sites; places like power stations. And they are now colonizing the more typical coastal cliffs. Over the last three decades some thirty pairs have succeeded in breeding each year, but there is a long way to go before they are firmly established as British breeding birds.

Some members of the crow family have taken to coastal life and, all year round, they liven up any coastal excursion. The largest, and most splendid, is the raven. Wherever it can live without persecution, from the mountainous high tops by way of woodland to sea level, the raven may not be common but it is typically a bird of western Britain. Its hoarse resonant calls are unmistakable, and the large size and wedge-shaped tail help to identify this welcome bird – welcome to the land-based birdwatcher, anyway. Ravens, like certain other creatures – for instance rabbits – are traditionally beasts of ill-omen for sailors.

Ravens inhabit wild places, so the very sound and sight of them is a passport to wilderness. The largest of our crows, they have stout arched black bills and a purple-green gloss to their all-black plumage. With a four-foot wingspan, they soar high in the up-draughts and have superb aerobatic capability. Where they have a chance to breed in reasonable numbers they are gregarious birds, flocking together to feed on carrion and roosting sociably on cliffs, sometimes in parties of a hundred or more. Restless birds, they seem always to be on the move, swinging about the sky, landing for a short time on precipitous crags. One of the places where you can be almost certain of seeing them is at St Michael's Mount, the superb National Trust island property in Mount's Bay, West Cornwall, where, because of the shortage of suitable precipitous cliffs, they build their nests, uncharacteristically, in places where it is fairly easy to see them. They have three ancestral sites on the north-west face of the Mount, and tend to patronize a different one each year. Astonishing structures, the nests are massive and solid. Both members of the pair collect material, piling it on to the foundations which become larger and larger as the years go by. A seeming jumble of large sticks forms the core, then earth and turves prepare a bed for the relative comfort of the cup which may be lined with sheep's wool and rabbit's fur. In Cornwall they will be renovating the nest site as early as January, when the young will be flying in May. A spring visit to St Michael's Mount will almost certainly be rewarded by some excellent raven-watching.

Jackdaws are very common around cliff sites. Although they take readily to town life when conditions favour them, they are equally at home on the wild open cliffs, foraging on the shore at low water and at all times on the open close-cropped sward of the cliff edge, in search of insects and seeds. There's no danger of mistaking them for ravens. Quite apart from their 'tchak' calls they are much smaller and generally quicker in their movements than their relatives. Given the chance, they will be quick to take advantage of other birds on the cliff faces. If, for example, an auk should leave its egg unattended for a moment a jackdaw will move in for a feast. At one time it was considered possible that jackdaw predation was responsible for the general decline in auk numbers, and on some islands the jackdaws were shot in large numbers in an attempt to reverse the trend. The activity had little effect on the jackdaw population. Since the easy feeding on islands is attractive to jackdaws, the moment a vacant niche became available, new blood arrived from the mainland to maintain the numbers by immigration.

The other crow which is characteristic of the coastal habitat is the chough, the red-billed crow. Known in the West Country as the Cornish chough, it is sadly no longer present in the south-west at all, not having bred in Cornwall since the early 1940s. Nowadays this exciting bird is restricted to western Scotland, the north and west coast of Wales, the Isle of Man and Ireland. The reasons for its decline are not obvious, but once again the jackdaw cannot be blamed, for although the two close relatives share a habitat they are not in competition for nest sites or food. The choughs' downfall has perhaps been their over-specialized and un-crowlike feeding habits; they prefer the restricting diet of ants and 'ants' eggs' (actually the insects' pupae or larvae) for which they probe in the rabbit-cropped turf. Sociable birds, they wheel and turn in wild extravagant aerobatics above the sea, but it's almost easy to pass them by without noticing the curved red beak and spread wing tips which distinguish them from the all-pervasive jackdaws. The musical call 'cho' may well be the signal which draws your attention, and it becomes immediately clear that their name is onomatopoeic, making it a nonsense that nowadays we pronounce them 'chuff'.

Although in Wales choughs often nest far inland on quarry faces, the more typical nest site is high up in a sea cave or on an inaccessible ledge or crevice. The deer park peninsula of Martin's Haven, near Marloes, is as good a place as any to walk the cliff path in the hope of seeing a passing chough. Just as in the case of the raven, the nest

Choughs—adults and young—at the nest in a sea cave. Nowadays these 'red-billed crows' are restricted to the wilder parts of coastal Scotland, Wales, the Isle of Man and Ireland.

is practically unreachable. It ought to be possible to attract choughs to artificial nest sites; in Ireland they have bred in disused lighthouses and in Martello towers and other derelict buildings.

The rock pipit is another resident bird which chooses to nest in cliff holes and crevices. Hunting for insects along the shoreline and amongst piles of rotting seaweed they are birds of the upper shore. In spring the unremarkable looking male bird indulges in a charming display flight, where he leaps a few yards into the air in order to glide down, singing as he goes, to land on top of an outcrop. But at any time of the year these 'rockets' are anticipated companions on a walk along the rocky shore.

Small brown birds like rock pipits don't fit the received image of longshore bird life, but the shags and cormorants which are widespread around our coast are surely everyone's idea of coastal species. Though they appear superficially similar it is fairly easy to become adept at distinguishing the two birds. Cormorants are larger, standing a good couple of inches higher. In the breeding season their glossy black plumage sports a white patch on either side behind the wing, and they always show a white face and chin patch. Shags have a rather more snake-like head and neck, and their plumage has more of an oily greenish tinge. At one time they were commonly called green cormorants. In the breeding season they have a distinct quiff to their heads, in which the feathers form a forward-curving crest.

Shags have rather more snake-like heads and necks than cormorants.

When it is time to breed, both cormorants and shags frequent inshore rocks and islands, enjoying the freedom from disturbance offered by coastal 'mewstones'. Both are colonial by preference, but whereas the cormorants nest close together and in the open, the shags choose rather more private ledges and dark crevices, and are more loosely associated with their kind. The nests of both species are quite elaborate, with seaweeds and various trifles picked from the surface of the sea forming a cup-lining inside a bulky base of twigs. Throughout the incubation period and even when the chicks are near to leaving the nest, the parents persist in decorating and improving the happy home, weaving plastic beach toys and other bric-à-brac around the rim of the cup.

Cormorants lay three or four bluish-white eggs and the parents share the duties of incubation for a month. Unusually for birds, they have no bare brood patch with which to warm the eggs, but their blood system provides for a rich supply to their feet. So the cormorant actually stands on its eggs, covering them with its warm paddles, before settling to incubate. The young are born blind and naked, and remarkably reptilian in aspect, but soon grow a dense black down which sheds as the juvenile plumage appears. A couple of times a day they're fed with a rich and thick soup of well digested fish which is regurgitated by the parent in response to the purposeful exploration of its gullet by the juvenile. They become independent at about ten weeks of age.

At one time cormorants were severely persecuted by ignorant fishermen, in the mistaken belief that they caused harm to fish stocks simply by being more efficient than the anglers in pursuit of fish. Even Water Authorities, which ought to know better but sometimes don't, used to offer rewards in exchange for dead cormorants. Of course, cormorants can do a lot of damage in a lake where a superabundance of fish is kept in unnatural conditions, but in the normal course of events in natural conditions they act simply as predators carrying out their allotted tasks of regulating animal numbers.

Both cormorants and shags are resident birds, remaining within a fairly short distance of their birthplace. Coastal plants could be said to display much the same fidelity, but, like the birds, they are merely well adapted to their habitat and way of life. Plants can't move, except in the sense that they can explore and colonize by means of their seeds. And coastal plants are by nature tough, designed to cope with a testing variety of conditions and sites. Exposed cliff faces may be unsympathetic places for plants to establish themselves, but the weathering processes of wind, rain and frost eventually produce cracks and crannies and debris enough to offer a foothold to some hardy plant. It is in the lower levels, where tolerance of salt spray is mandatory, that the maritime plants are seen at their hardiest. It is only the specialists which exist in these harsh conditions. They tend to be perennials, wind and salt hardened by an environment which favours maturity and discourages brash youth. The hopeful seed imported by the temporary visit of a bird to a crevice has all the odds stacked against it. Even if there is enough soil in the crevice to support germination, there is every chance of being blown away by the wind or suffering a lethal drying out in the hot sun. But if it can establish a toe-hold, then its very presence acts as a wind break, allowing more soil-forming detritus to pile up in the crevice, thus giving the youthful plant more of a chance. As it grows, its roots will probe deeply in the search for moisture and, growing woody and fibrous, they will serve as an anchor.

Exposure to a succession of gales reduces the range of competition amongst cliff plants. Unless there is a fair degree of shelter there will be few trees along the coast. Monterey pines were introduced to Britain from California in the 1830s with the object of providing coastal shelter belts. On the eastern side of the entrance to Dartmouth harbour, for instance, there is a most attractive stand of these trees. Impressively large, they display a dense foliage of vivid emerald green needles. The pines' rapid growth, as much as three feet a year, has made them useful for the timber trade in Australia and New Zealand, but they provide a rather coarse product which is regarded as non-commercial in Britain. But in the milder parts, for instance in the south-west, they serve well in their role of decorative shelter belt.

If a plant can tolerate the awkward gradients and soil sparsity of a cliff, it is able to benefit from the lack of competition. Where rabbits and sheep cannot graze plants may flourish, but different plants flourish in clearly defined zones which relate to their tolerance to the presence of salt seawater. In the areas below the higher reach of the big spring tides, you are in the region of the seaweeds, whose many forms are dictated by the duration of tidal submersion; from the air- and sun-tolerant green weeds of the upper zone by way of the medium-sized mid-shore brown wracks to the monstrous low-water kelps and the totally submerged red weeds. Above the reach of the tide, but within the sphere of influence of the saltwater spray, the 'splash zone' is characterized by the hardy lichens. Then come the ledge and crevice plants which are able to withstand a modicum of salt spray, and are thereby described as *halophytes*. Our only maritime fern, sea spleenwort, is one of these, a

Sea-spleenwort (*Asplenium marinum*). A common fern of south-western cliffs.

plant which hides itself in shady cracks on the cliffs of the west coast. Perhaps thrift is the best known and loved of these salt-tolerant plants. The dry and windy conditions of cliff faces and slopes are too exacting for most plants, and thrift thrives in spite of the salt rather than because of it.

Some of the cliffside plants are surprisingly large and impressive. The vigorous tree mallow grows practically to the height of a man's chest. With its large pink flowers, it is abundant in the far west of Devon and Cornwall at places like Berry Head, near Brixham, for instance. Often you will find it in profusion on the outskirts of sea-bird colonies, where it proves its ability to survive high levels of nitrogen and phosphorus, deposited as droppings by the roosting and socializing birds. Another astonishing plant

Typical limestone plants. LEFT: red valerian, viper's bugloss, sea carrot and wild cabbage.
ABOVE: tree mallow.

ABOVE: some terns fully deserve the nickname of 'sea swallow'.

which sometimes threatens to take over the steep cliffsides in the West Country is the Hottentot fig or ice-plant, *Carpobrotus edulis*, which has fleshy leaves and large yellow flowers. Originally introduced from South Africa as a garden plant, it has spread to establish itself in abundance. In the Isles of Scilly it was used, experimentally, along with marram grass, to stabilize sand dunes. Once it has a foothold it increases to cover large areas in a short time, successfully ousting the native plants. Indeed, in Scilly, the ice-plant is now well established all over the place, spread partly by man but also by the activities of the gulls which use pieces of the plant for their nests, thus affording an opportunity for yet more spread.

Almost as spectacular as the ice-plant in late spring are the massed yellow flowers and large blue-green leaves of the wild cabbage which spreads abundantly over steep cliff slopes. Like the sea-beet and sea-kale, the wild cabbage provided the stock for our cultivated varieties. Indeed many of our most important food plants have their ancestral roots back on the sea coast.

Sea-beet grows freely on shingle and on strand lines, as well as on the cliffs, and is happy to be nourished by a certain amount of bird droppings. A coarse perennial with fleshy roots, it straggles over the ground producing a delicious profusion of leaves. The younger ones taste excellent prepared as spinach, and indeed our garden spinach is a cultivated form. At one time its close relative, sea-kale, was grown extensively in Britain, but nowadays it is an uncommon vegetable. In times past people would blanch it *in situ* by covering the wild crowns with a foot or so of shingle.

There are other cliff plants with culinary value. The leaves of fennel are used for salad dressings and in fish sauces and soups. Rock samphire was once gathered in quantity to be sold as 'crest marine' on the streets of London, then used for pickling or as an iodine-rich zest. The large white roots and the tender green stalks have a hot and spicy taste. The aromatic fleshy young leaves used at one time to be salted, boiled and covered with spiced vinegar to form part of an old-fashioned pickle.

Red campion is a nitrogen-loving plant which benefits from the droppings of sea-birds, becoming especially prolific in those areas where lesser black-backed gulls have their nesting and courting grounds. Its luscious pink flowers are also typical of the slopes below gannet and puffin colonies, provided there's not too much wind-blown salt spray. Rabbits don't much like red campion, only eating it as a penance, another factor which encourages its growth. White sea-campion is a close relative, but more typical of warmer, drier climates and at the edge of its distribution range in Britain.

Once above or back from the ravages of salt spray, the plants of the cliff are less specialized. Grasses such as red fescue become commonplace, and stonecrop does well. As the gradients become less extreme you enter the regions which are grazed by rabbits, sheep and cattle. Indeed towards the top of a cliff the plant community becomes that typical of heath or scrubland. Back from the edge and out of the teeth of salt-laden winds heather and gorse begin to show their faces; there is altogether a greater profusion of species. The winds which are characteristic of cliff life make conditions unfavourable for flying insects, and the fauna tends to be recognizably terrestrial, grass-hoppers, snails and woodlice predominating. This is the kind of coastal habitat which favours the occasional family of badgers, who enjoy a well-drained sunny aspect, relatively undisturbed and well supplied with worms.

Of the dozen families of sea-birds which throng to the coast in spring, few are truly pelagic. The good feeding in British coastal waters encourages a great multitude to make this their home. The cold North Atlantic current brings a rich soup of plankton to support vast quantities of fish and, in turn, sea-birds. The seafaring life is hard, but relatively safe. Few predators and plenty of food make for great numbers and sea-birds are long-lived as individuals. They even tend to lay fewer eggs at longer intervals than land-based birds, but nevertheless they must come ashore to breed. Because land offers great danger to them, they tend to congregate in the safety of numbers in places as remote or undisturbed as possible – cliffs, headlands, islands and shingle banks.

The gulls and terns which nest colonially will think little of physically attacking intruders. Walk into one of their nest concentrations and you risk having the skin of your head split open and blood drawn. Terns, especially, always object strongly if anyone invades their nesting area, dive-bombing to express their displeasure. If seals should approach they will be given the same treatment, not because the seals would eat their eggs, but presumably because of the danger of crushing them.

Terns, most of which winter off the tropical west and south coasts of Africa and fly in to spend the summer with us, nest in close-packed groups, but sometimes on the open sward of cliff tops. Both the eggs and, subsequently, the chicks are well camouflaged in the simple scrape nest. In the case of roseate terns the scrape is not even

An adult sandwich tern flies in to bring a choice morsel to the juvenile.

lined, but the even rarer little terns line the saucer with a few small stones while common, arctic and sandwich terns make something of a nest with grasses. Terns clearly enjoy an advantage in breeding colonially. The stimulus of close company leads them to act almost as a single organism, courting and copulating as a group; their egg-laying is synchronized and the interest of the colony is always mutual. Predators can't cope with the embarrassment of riches placed in front of them, and the general rule of 'safety in numbers' applies.

The terns, however, face dangers peculiarly their own. An inconvenient spring gale may literally wash their settlement away. Eggs may be floated off by an exceptionally high tide to be abandoned and ignored by their parents. A thick blanket of spume may cover the nests to confuse and bemuse the owners. These fates may overwhelm the terns even at places like Blakeney Point, where the National Trust sets great store by the efficiency of its wardening service. Ringed plovers nest in the same habitat, and often suffer the same fate.

After the weather, one of the main problems facing the animals which colonize sandy beaches and sand dunes is the trample of enthusiastic human feet. For plovers, oystercatchers and terns, an ideal nesting place is a sand or shingle bank, out of reach of the waves yet within easy

Typical sand dune and shingle plants—sea-holly and samphire.

reach of sea feeding. Unfortunately, these are places which people find attractive too. The little tern, for instance, tends to nest just above high-water mark, just where holiday-makers like to explore. Furthermore, the birds lay small eggs, in barely recognizable scrapes, in widely scattered places on the shingle, not even benefiting from the protection and visibility of a noisy colony. On the Chesil Beach, for example, one of their former strongholds, they breed in pitifully small numbers because of the unwitting trampling by visitors who ignore or simply don't hear the distressed cries of the adult birds flying close to the nest.

The crowning irony is that as a species becomes rarer – and the little tern is one of our rarest breeding birds – the incentive for egg-collectors becomes intensified, so it is threatened by both deliberate and unintentional disturbance.

Shingle plants are specially adapted for life in this terrain, where shortage of humus, a drying wind and an abundance of salt water make things difficult. Their problem is to reduce water loss by evaporation. Sea-holly sports a thick leathery and waxy skin; the yellow-horned poppy sprouts hairs on its leaves to reduce the wind effect.

On these open sand and shingle beaches and in the dunes, terns, plovers and oystercatchers nest in a manner which makes them vulnerable to disturbance and predation. In fact the sustained losses have led the oystercatchers to experiment with breeding in unfamiliar habitats such as salt-marsh, where it may be they will have some success.

Apart from the terns, the vast majority of sea-going birds, as well as the coastal gulls, choose to breed on the safer cliffs and cliff slopes, especially favouring islands and remote places

ABOVE: kittiwakes nest on seemingly impossible cliffs by taking advantage of any ledge, or by simply plastering their nests to the rock face. Their nitrogen-rich droppings help the thrift and sea-campion to flourish. RIGHT: wing patterns of adult (left) and juvenile.

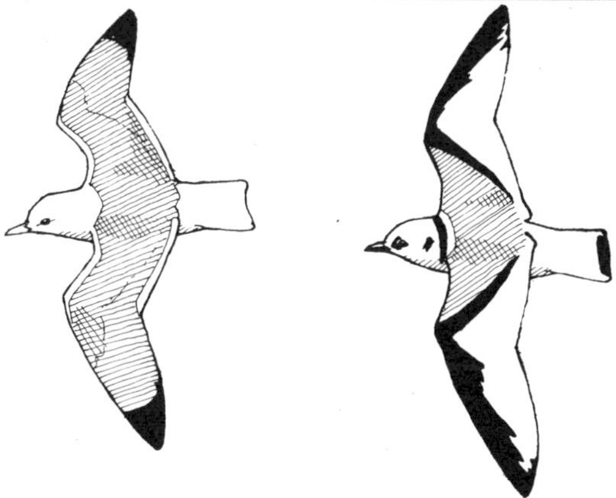

Sand martins excavate nest burrows. Coastal sandstone cliffs or blown-out compacted sand dunes often offer suitable sites.

where they are subject to less disturbance. From the Isles of Scilly by way of the superb National Trust islands in Wales, their breeding sites tend to be long-established, the criteria being safety from land-based predators and reasonable proximity to the food supply. It follows that the strongholds tend to be mainly on the west and north coasts of the British Isles, with a relatively poor showing in the south and east, where human disturbance is at its greatest, although the Farne Islands off the coast of Northumberland, administered by the National Trust, are a triumphant exception.

At first sight, a thriving sea-bird cliff is a vision of chaos, with birds flying everywhere and every ledge and cranny occupied in a bewildering jumble of bodies. But in reality that is a superficial view. The occupied cliff represents an ordered, structured society with complex and sophisticated life styles. The strongest and most aggressive birds get the best places. Mated pairs tend to remain faithful both to each other and to 'their' chosen nest site, though it is not clear whether returning birds are homing in on the presence of their partners or the actual ledge which is to be the cradle for their chicks each year.

Guillemots breed most successfully when they are concentrated in large numbers on remote cliff ledges or stack-tops.

N.W.CUSA.

SHINGLE BANK AND LAGOON

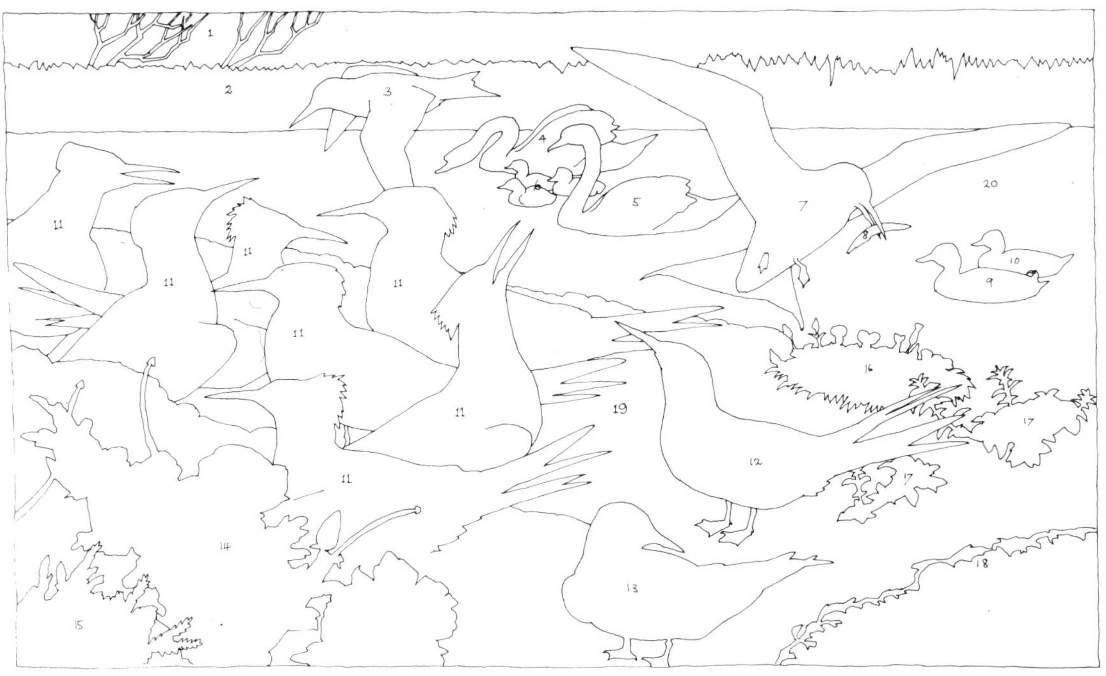

A shingle ridge and brackish lagoon in springtime. A colony (11) of sandwich terns (*Sterna sandvicensis*) is busy with family affairs. The colony also includes a few common terns (*Sterna hirundo*) of which one (7) is bringing (8) a lesser sand-eel (*Ammodytes tobianus*) to his mate (12). In the foreground there is (13) a single arctic tern (*Sterna paradisaea*) and (3) a little tern (*Sterna albifrons*) flies by. The weed (18) shows how high the tide can come and how perilously the tern colony is situated. The plants shown are among those that first colonize these shingle banks, namely (15) shrubby sea-blite (*Suaeda fruticosa*), (14) yellow horned poppy (*Glaucium flavum*), (16) sea-campion (*Silene maritima*) and (17) sea sandwort (*Honkenya peploides*). On the brackish lagoon beyond the bank a pair of mute swans (*Cygnus olor*) have hatched (6) a trio of cygnets and these are accompanied both by the male or 'cob' (4) and the female or 'pen' (5). Also on the pool is a pair of mallard (*Anas platyrhynchos*), drake (9) and duck (10) swimming side by side. On the far side of the lagoon is (2) a bed of reeds (*Phragmites australis*) and beyond are the dead branches of, perhaps, (1) goat willow (*Salix caprea*) killed when last a storm made the ground temporarily too salty for this shrub.

Though it is customary to think of sea-birds as spending the best part of their lives at sea, the fact is that many of them are patrolling the nest places for months before they occupy them. Fulmars, for instance, may well be keeping an eye on the home cliff before Christmas. Most of the gulls spend a fair part of their lives within commuting distance of the breeding place, though the pattern changes in winter. But kittiwakes are truly sea-going gulls, returning to the coast only because they must nest ashore. They build their nests on sheer cliff faces, plastering the grasses on to seemingly impossible sites, using the slight outcropping of a fault in the rock or a protruding pebble to form the basis for a nest which may be practically cantilevered out over the sea.

Whatever the character of the cliff, there will be a bird to colonize it. Should it be of soft sand then sand martins may take advantage, excavating tunnels that go back as much as a metre. Sadly, the number of sand martins breeding in natural sites is decreasing; nowadays they seem mostly to patronize man-made habitats such as gravel pits, but they are opportunists, always looking to take advantage of a situation. Sand martins are early arrivals, in April, and so are the storm petrels, although the petrels will have been fishing in British waters right through the year. In colonies from Scilly in the Western Approaches all the way up the west coast to furthest Shetland, they choose rocky islands. Some, like the martins, may excavate burrows, but most find a secret home under a rock or in a stone wall.

Auks spend the winter way down south, off the coast of the Iberian peninsula, or far out at sea – though birds from the east coast colonies may winter in the North Sea. In spring they make their way back to the breeding places, perhaps swimming a good deal of the journey; they are gregarious birds which do everything in a sociable manner. The nearest thing we have to a penguin in the northern hemisphere, auks have closely knit plumage and rounded contours, carrying plenty of warmth-retaining blubber. Their webbed feet are attached to legs which are set well back on the body, the ideal place for underwater propulsion, and the reason why they must stand upright when on land. One of the prime reasons for their popularity is this upright posture, reminiscent of the human figure. In other words, we like them because they resemble us.

Sometimes people ask why there are no real penguins in the north, and the answer is simple enough. They are confined to the southern hemisphere because they cannot tolerate life in warm seawater. So the extreme northern limit of their range coincides with a line linking places with a mean annual *air* temperature of 20°C. Oceanic currents bear a temperature which relates to air temperature, and the warm water effectively acts as a thermal barrier to any penguin seeking new seas to colonize. In 1936, a group of nine king penguins was introduced and released in the Norwegian Lofoten Islands. Two years later a number of macaroni and jackass penguins were imported. But the experiment was not a success, partly because the local people didn't take to the idea and used any excuse to kill the 'bogeymen'. Some survived for eighteen years, but none attempted to nest, probably for reasons which will become apparent when we consider the noisy sociability which is part and parcel of sea-bird breeding.

Auks, in a sense, are our northern penguins. Though they are not related they live the same lives; having a great deal in common they have come to resemble them, an example of what biologists call 'convergent evolution'.

The representatives of the auk family with which we are most familiar around British coasts are the guillemots, razorbills and puffins. All are characteristically numerous and noisy. Guillemots have slender, pointed bills, chocolate brown heads and upper parts. They are slightly larger than the bitter chocolate razorbills which also have, not surprisingly, a flatter, old-fashioned razor-shaped bill – somewhat deeper and thinner than that of the guillemot.

Guillemots choose to breed on rather exposed

ledges where they jostle together in astonishing numbers, whereas razorbills go for less sociable conditions – corners of ledges, under boulders and on rocky slopes. Like the guillemots, they make no nest, though there may sometimes be a small stone or a piece of vegetation alongside the single egg. The egg is laid directly onto the ledge. And while it is crudely true to say that all eggs are egg-shaped, there is quite a bit of variation. The typical hen's egg is oval, with a large end tapering to a narrow one; a shape convenient for rolling and turning in the interest of even distribution of warmth and, also important, comfortable to sit on and strong enough to take the strain. But guillemots' eggs are almost pear-shaped. Laid on an exposed ledge, with only inches between them and a fearsome drop to the sea below, their shape causes them to spin like a top if they are nudged, so saving them from disaster. In addition to this, they soon become coated with muck in the natural course of events, and thus are even more likely to stick tight. And as incubation proceeds, the air pocket inside the egg grows bigger, naturally accumulating at the blunt end of the egg, so that the weight and the centre of gravity moves to the sharp end, thus increasing the tendency to spin in tight circles.

Guillemots typically crowd together at their nest places, and their noisy sociability seems to be a prerequisite for successful pair formation. They encourage each other, yet keep a critical distance, just out of pecking range from a neighbour with whom they are prepared to be friendly, but not too friendly. The birds' eggs are laid synchronously, almost as if the colony were a single organism. But presumably this is all part and parcel of the over-riding requirement for defence of the colony, the common interest making for strength.

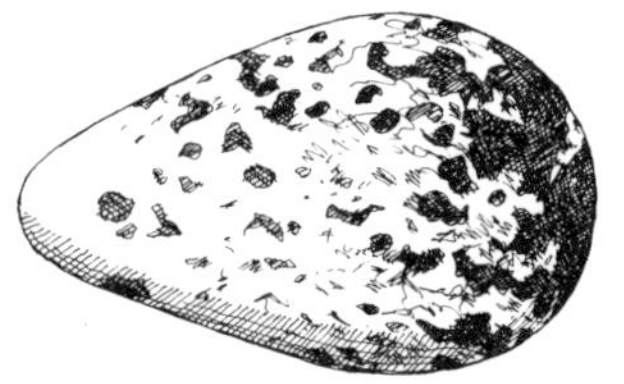
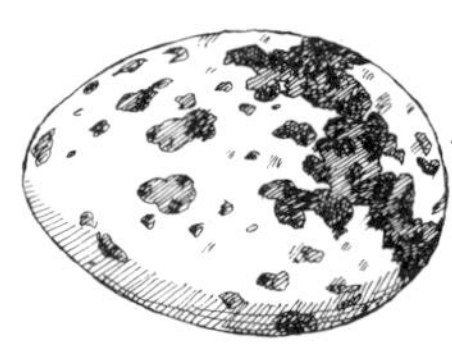

Egg of (left) guillemot (*Uria aalge*) and (right) egg of kittiwake (*Rissa tridactyla*). The guillemot's egg, laid in the open on a narrow cliff ledge, is near conical in shape so that when nudged it spins rather than rolls and so is less likely to fall. The kittiwake, nesting in similarly perilous localities, builds a rounded cup-shaped nest of seaweed and thus its eggs can be of the more usual shape.

In early April the first male puffins make a cautious landing on their breeding slopes, the horny sheaths on their bills at their most parrot-like and colourful. Breeding first at the age of four years, they must find a nest site and court a desirable female. As with the other auks, the heaviest and most successful puffin males bag the most desirable nest sites. Puffins nest underground in burrows either of their own making or in holes which rabbits have conveniently prepared for them. Laid in places where they cannot be seen, the eggs are white, at least for the first few hours! (Guillemot and razorbill eggs are strikingly patterned and coloured, to aid identification by the parents.)

The most desired burrows are on the steepest slopes, the advantage being that the emerging birds can become airborne with minimum effort. Returning with a payload of fish, they can fly straight into the entrance, thus avoiding harassment by the waiting gulls. The puffinry is decorated by huge cushions of thrift and luxuriant growths of red campion which flourishes mightily on the nutrient-rich bird dung flung liberally about by the socializing puffins. However, on some well manured and trampled patches the ground may be so rich in phosphates and nitrogen that no plants can survive at all.

The scourge of the auks' life is continual harassment by gulls which patrol on the lookout for an unguarded egg or an unwary adult or chick. Apart from man, their other major predator is the peregrine, which makes a comfortable living taking pigeons and sea-birds on the wing at the climax of a powerful aerial dive – the stoop. On top of a catastrophic decline due to human persecution, peregrines were

Peregrine falcons are at home on the coast where they take pigeons and auks as the climax of a fearsome power dive. Here, the female brings food to two-week-old chicks.

reduced almost to the verge of extinction in Britain because of the knock-on effect of agricultural pesticides, whose poisons were concentrated in the bodies of their prey, causing them to lay infertile or otherwise unsatisfactory eggs. But over recent decades the trend has been firmly reversed as a result of the partial ban on organo-chlorine pesticides, and now these superb birds are increasing again. Although the simple view has it that this must be bad news for pigeons and sea-birds, quite the opposite is the case, for the peregrine is acting out its entirely healthy function of encouraging its prey species to be quicker and more aware. The peregrines' coastal eyries are carefully chosen for their strategic positions, and it is known that some of them have been occupied at least as far back as the Middle Ages.

Like plenty of other bird populations, sea-birds suffer fluctuations in fortune. Their way of life is hard, and it is characteristic of them that their numbers rise and fall, sometimes violently, often as a result of equally violent changes in the status of fish stocks. The story of the fulmar is not untypical, and it is of special interest to us because its numbers have increased in the most astonishing way in our own times.

Until 1870 the only British breeding fulmars were established on the remote Atlantic island of St Kilda where they had been present for eight or nine centuries, but in that year they gained a foothold on the Shetland island of Foula. Since then they have spread steadily along the coasts of the whole of the British Isles, wherever there is a cliff suitable for their nest sites – a scrape in a 'blow-out' hole or a ledge fairly close to the steeply sloping top of a sheer face. This astonishing range of expansion has been fuelled by the enormous increase in activities of the whaling industry and, more recently, the increase in trawling which has provided masses of offal, though another relevant factor may be the gradual warming up of the North Atlantic waters which has been noted in the last hundred years or so.

The closely related manx shearwaters breed in rabbit burrows or hole crevices which they excavate on level ground back from the cliff tops, though on the Scottish island of Rhum they breed high up on a mountainside a couple of thousand feet above sea level. At the more typical, and accessible, site on Skomer Island their burrows, and their nocturnal activity, seem to permeate all island life in the late spring. Underground life serves to protect the chicks and adults from the gulls which so persistently harass them, and the birds come and go from their nests only by night, a further strategy to avoid their attentions. After wintering in the South Atlantic off the South American coast they migrate to the island colonies off the Scottish and Welsh coasts in April. At this time of year, and well into summer, they congregate in their tens of thousands in 'rafts' on the surface of the sea, socializing and waiting for the light to go before they pluck up courage to run the gull gauntlet and come ashore to the nest sites. At last light on a calm day, the spectacle of many thousand auks and shearwaters both on the sea and swirling around the cliffs is something to savour and remember with great pleasure during those periods of our lives when we are denied access to sea-bird haunts.

A large part of the world populations of the North Atlantic gannet is based in Britain, where there are eighteen breeding colonies. Most are stationed on the north and west coasts of Scotland, but there are spectacular sites at Bempton, the Bass Rock and off the Channel Island of Alderney. While the immature gannets are away at sea during the winter, the adults spend most of their time near the ancestral breeding places. The bulky nests of seaweed and assorted flotsam are sometimes on level areas at cliff tops, sometimes on the steepest slopes and precipitous ledges. The glutinous seaweed sticks tight to the rocks, the nest cup is decorated – very often with pieces of brightly coloured rope thrown overboard from fishing boats to drift in tidal currents till they end up on the beaches, snarled up in small boat propellors or, indeed, as nest adornments. Sadly, these scraps of netting often prove fatal to the gannet chicks which become entangled in them, and it is no unusual sight to see an adult or sub-adult gannet flying the oceans with a permanent necklace of long-lasting synthetic rope.

Gannets are sociable birds, feeding and breeding in close company. But each nest is carefully built at pecking distance from its neighbour.

Gannets suffered greatly from man's exploitation of their stocks in the nineteenth century, when their meat, eggs and skins were taken in enormous numbers; but changing attitudes spared them to show a steady increase in population during this century. Currently there is said to be a total population of some 150,000 breeding pairs in Britain and Ireland.

Both sea-birds and their eggs have provided a useful food source since prehistoric times. Fossil bones in caves have shown that Stone Age hunters ate auks as well as gannets. While on the mainland the birds have been used without regard to the long-term consequences, remote islanders took good care to husband their stock in the interest of future survival. Although a substantial proportion of the first laying of eggs was taken, they made sure that the birds were undisturbed with at least one full clutch. And only a sustainable proportion of fat young were taken. It was on islands that Neolithic man learnt the benefits of seasonal occupation, taking sea-bird eggs and fat chicks while their sheep and cattle grazed the rich summer pasture.

On St Kilda the exploitation of the natural resources was carried out with the greatest care and skill. The welfare of the human community relied on successful harvesting through at least fourteen centuries. A hundred people sustained themselves at a level above mere subsistence, and with a degree of happiness. Each year they took some two thousand each of the adult gannets and of the fat chicks, the gugas, providing meat, oil for lamps, feathers for beds and pillows, and they even used the skins for carpet slippers. The birds were taken either by nooses extended on poles or were simply clubbed on the head and thrown into the sea to be collected from boats waiting below.

In addition to the gannet catch, the islanders collected an average of 12,000 fulmars each year. Thomas Pennant wrote in 1776, 'no bird is of such use to the islanders as this: the fulmar supplies them with oil for their lamps, down for their beds, a delicacy for their wounds and a medicine for their distempers.' Puffins, too, were taken in enormous numbers. In the 1870s, for instance, something like 100,000 were killed for their feathers and meat, yet the population of birds was maintained.

Unfortunately the mainland colonies of sea-birds have been ruthlessly overexploited by men who have not had the long-term interests of their prey at heart, and birds have suffered accordingly. In the last century there were even shooting parties of so-called sportsmen which travelled to the cliffs in order to enjoy target practice with kittiwakes, gannets and auks.

In Tudor times puffins, as well as gulls, were much treasured as food items; it is said that the gulls were even grain-fed to make them more palatable. Gulls offered the convenience of habitually breeding in large numbers in places more easily accessible than the cliff-laying auks. Quite apart from that, they also lay a larger clutch, of three or four eggs, and, as with the domestic hen, they will continue laying when the eggs are taken from them. So, in years past, eggs were collected on a large scale; for instance 130,000 guillemot eggs were sent to Leadenhall market in London from the Bempton cliffs in 1884. In 1935 300,000 black-headed gull eggs suffered the same fate. But if the colonies are farmed intelligently, they are capable of supplying a sustained yield of great value. At Ravenglass, in Cumbria, for example, some 15,000 pairs of black-headed gulls nest on the sand dunes. In the mid nineteenth century similar gulleries were encouraged by the construction of suitable nesting islands, and one of the annual activities was the spring harvesting of gulls and their eggs.

Farmed sensibly, coastal colonies of sea-birds offer a useful source of good food, and the prudent farmer has the long-term health and interest of his charges at heart. Mile for mile, we play host to one of the richest world concentrations of sea-going birds. The coastline of Britain would be immeasurably the poorer without this population.

Summer

Caddow Combe, the Foreland, North Devon.

On calm nights in high summer the wavelets lapping on the shore mark a glistening line of curious pale green light. The water dripping from the paddles of a rowing boat flashes as if on fire. A magical experience. The watery fireworks are a display given by astronomical numbers of tiny creatures – dinoflagellates – which glow with phosphorescence when they are disturbed, a phenomenon known as bio-luminescence.

Stand on the cliff top during the day and if conditions are right you'll see streaks of foam which seem to divide whole stretches of the sea surface. These foam lines, too, are evidence of the uncountable numbers of plankton organisms, which, unable to move under their own steam, drift with the current and are concentrated together by a system of vortices in the water caused by wind activity. These swirling systems are known as 'langmuir circulations' and they serve to bring to our attention the extraordinary wealth of primary food available in the sea. Boil a bucketful of seawater over a beach fire, and you will produce an unappetizing grey rime of salts, mostly common sea salt, but containing small quantities of other chemicals and mineral traces. These nutrients, when in solution in the sea, maintain a flourishing growth of surface plant life, a floating pasture which derives benefit from the sunlight and produces oxygen to the benefit of the animal life which also co-exists with it. These minute plant and animal organisms, present in astronomic numbers, together represent the plankton, and they support the huge population of larger sea creatures.

Seals represent one of the higher animals which exist by virtue of the cornucopia of plankton life. Though fish are their staple diet they also eat cockles, which they pick daintily from the sandy shallows.

We have two species which inhabit our coast: grey and common seals. And though the grey seals are well in evidence along the rocky shores from the West Country to furthermost Shetland by way of the west coast, and breed in the autumn, the common seal is more characteristic of the sandy east coast, though it overlaps with grey seal distribution in Scotland, and it breeds in the summer. The common seal prefers sheltered, inshore waters. The largest colony is based on the Wash, in East Anglia, where there are some 6500, about a third of the total British population.

In these muddy places the common seals' own body colour is an effective camouflage while they are in the water, but their porpoising shapes and inquisitive stares usually give them away. Hauled out on remote sandbanks, they give birth to their pups in late May and June. On shore they are at a disadvantage, unable to move fast, but they are never far from the sea, where they are totally at home, fast, and superbly adapted. Even the new-born pups will swim, close to their mother, within a few hours of birth, when the incoming tide covers the sandbank where they were born. Well able to recognize its own mother by both smell and voice the pup may even climb on her back for a lift.

A seal's life has much to recommend it. Much of the time is spent basking on a convenient rock or a warm sandbank, and when it is hungry, the sea is full of fish. Seals are expert divers, with powerful hind flippers to propel them deep underwater in search of cockles, whelks and flounders. They have good vision, but an acute sense of smell and hearing is more important to them in these murky waters. In fact they are perfectly able to catch fish in total darkness. There is evidence that they employ an echo-location system in the manner of dolphins and bats.

Common seals are typically creatures of sandy places, enjoying the molluscs and fish which frequent this habitat. Sand is, on the face of it, an unlikely medium for life, being composed of hard fragments of rock. But in fact the accumulated mass of sand, in its relationship with the sea, provides a fruitful base for an astonishing variety of plant and animal life to flourish.

Pebbles and pebble banks are relatively devoid of life. Draining rapidly, without a protective coating of seawater, and grinding against each other, pebbles offer little comfort to an animal seeking shelter or a plant seeking a home. But sand grains, cushioned by a protective film of water, offer possibilities. The material from which the sand is formed is not of particular importance – whether it be ground from granite or mollusc shells – but the grain size matters a lot. Coarse grains hold less water around themselves than do fine grains.

A beach of fine grain sand is likely to hold a jungle of activity under its desert-like surface. While there will be no obvious fields of plants like seaweeds, which need something stable on which to grip, there will be animals colonizing the underground regions. Since there is nothing for them to hold on to at the surface, the animals burrow. By going below the surface the worms, crustaceans and shellfish achieve a certain stability, avoid the drying effects of wind and the extremes of surface temperature. Migrating upwards and downwards in the sand they may regulate their living conditions and yet emerge to take full advantage of the sea's bounty when the tide comes in.

It only needs a toy bucket and spade to explore the creatures of the surface sand, though most beaches will support a population of keen anglers, digging for bait ragworms and lugworms at low water.

One of the greatest pleasures of a beach for the longshore explorer is the strand line of a wide sandy bay. For the winds which create waves which in turn carry the sand particles to build up the beach also blow floating objects ashore in motley assemblages full of fascination. Torn-up seaweed, driftwood and all manner of wind and current-borne objects find themselves strewn along the strand line for our pleasure and enjoyment and the future benefit of many creatures. There is usually an endless line of seaweed fronds and stripes. Examine fresh specimens to find the various creatures which were rudely torn away from their homes along with the weed. There will be tufts of hydroids, sea-mats and sponges, sea-squirts and crabs, blue-rayed limpets and the rasp marks and depressions left by the grazing army of whelks and winkles. But there will also be cuttlefish 'bones' and the massed egg-cases of the common whelk looking like spongy tennis balls; the mermaid's purses of ray and skate eggs, and timber pit-props riddled with shipworm and gnawed by gribble. Split the soft wood of a beached pit-prop and it will most likely be riddled with the carefully bored galleries of *Teredo*, the shipworm. In fact the worm is a mollusc equipped with a pair of sharp valves at its head, the tools it uses to bore through the wood in search of its cellulose dinner.

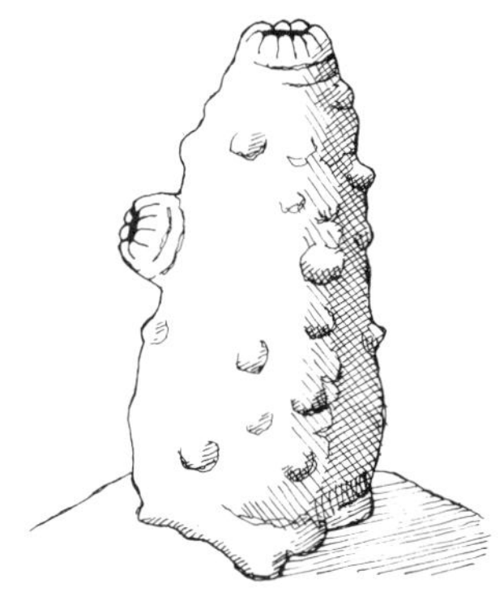

Sea squirt (*Ascidiella aspersa*), one of many kinds of sea squirt which have in common the bag-like structure with two openings or siphons. When squeezed, seawater is squirted from the bag from these orifices—hence the name. One of the orifices is an inlet for seawater from which nutriment is strained by the animal before the water leaves by the second, anal, orifice.

Pushed to the high-water mark of spring tides by the action of the sea, this mass of strand-line debris rots down and gives life to generations of kelp flies and sandhoppers. Many land creatures too will visit this meaty mix to take advantage, from foxes and hedgehogs to a whole list of birds which includes robins and sparrows, wagtails and starlings, while of course the specialist shore birds will exact their toll. Sandpipers and turnstones, plovers and rock pipits are all well aware of the value of the strand-line weed, yet the sandhoppers on which they feed thrive and multiply.

Behind the immediate region of a sandy beach, more often than not, man has colonized

N.W.CUSA.

DUNES AND DUNE SLACKS

Sand dunes and dune slacks, in late July or early August. Immediately adjacent to the beach is a line of new dunes (1) in process of stabilization mainly by marram grass (*Ammophila arenaria*), but also in the foreground by other plants, notably (5) sea-holly (*Eryngium maritimum*) and (6) sea bindweed (*Calystegia soldanella*). On the landward side of these dunes there is a relatively flat area, or 'low', between them and the more stable dunes that are off the picture to the right. In this low there are several pools (3) or dune 'slacks'. Growing on the edge of one of these slacks there is a plant (4) of creeping willow (*Salix repens*) already beginning to accumulate sand about its base, a process which, when continued, leads to the formation of the green hummocks or secondary dunes (2) in the middle distance. At our feet, by the foreground slack, (10) grass of Parnassus (*Parnassia palustris*) and (11) round-leaved wintergreen (*Pyrola rotundifolia*) are in bloom. Swimming in the pool there is (15) a black-headed gull (*Larus ridibundus*) in the brown juvenile plumage that is so rapidly lost. It comes no doubt from a nesting colony nearby. An adult (14) flies overhead. It still retains the dark brown hood of the breeding season. Beyond the pool a family of shelduck (*Tadorna tadorna*) makes its way across the low from the burrow nest where the ducklings (18) have recently hatched. The female (16) leads followed by the male (17), distinguished by his larger size, crimson knob at the base of his bill and lack of white on his face. An owl (13) patrols the dunes in daylight. It is a short-eared owl (*Asio flammeus*), probably one of a pair that has bred in the dunes nearby or on adjacent moorland. This owl frequently hunts by day. It is too early in the season for the influx of this species from the continent that occurs in the autumn. Among the vegetation in the foreground are (8) a natterjack (*Bufo calamita*) and (9) a smooth newt (*Triturus vulgaris*). These amphibians have laid their eggs in the pool below and have returned to a terrestrial life until the next breeding season. Caterpillars (7) of the shore wainscot moth (*Leucania littoralis*) feed on the marram grass. In the distance (12) there is a lark (*Alauda arvensis*) ascending.

the coast with a vengeance. Roads, promenades, embankments and car parks, backed by happy holiday villages and towns are the order of the day. But in nature, a sandy bay is often the frontier between the open sea and one of the most delightful of natural systems – the dunes. Studland Bay, by Poole in Dorset, Bosherston in Dyfed and Holkham in Norfolk are good examples.

The common, or viviparous lizard (*Lacerta vivipara*), frequently suns itself on sandy shores in the south.

The uppermost strand line is a place where, when conditions are right, a fragile plant community makes a tentative start at establishing itself. In the lee of an empty beer bottle or a fortuitous pile of debris, pioneer plants struggle to pave the way for a mighty colonization. Sea sandwort and prickly saltwort have succulent fleshy leaves and are well adapted to live in this difficult environment where there is a superabundance of salt. The major problem for these sand plants is to reduce water loss, and they have evolved various ways of solving it. In the case of sea-holly, for instance, the leaves have a secretion of wax on their surface. Other plants have hairy or downy leaves, devices which trap a layer of still air close to the leaf surface, helping to reduce water loss through transpiration.

The mere existence of a few plants provides an obstacle to the sand-laden wind and serves as a focus for a build-up of yet more sand and living materials. Insects arrive, a humus develops, birds build nests and the whole process of dune development begins. It is a fragile young community, vulnerable to trampling feet, and easily washed away by storms. But it may develop and mature into a complex community which will endure.

Trampling feet and breeding on sand or shingle are mutually exclusive, so for birds like terns, oystercatchers and plovers their best friend is an enlightened landowner. At Blakeney Point, for example, the teeming terneries benefit from the positive management of the National Trust, as is the case on the Farne Islands, and many thousands of people get the chance to see nesting sea-birds, but from a respectful distance. The result is that everyone benefits and the birds do well. The bird list at Blakeney Point is one of the longest for any part of Britain. Projecting into the North Sea from the Norfolk coast, the Point makes a convenient landfall for migrants, as well as being a stronghold for the tern cities. Apart from a few little terns, there are about a thousand pairs of common terns and variable numbers of sandwich terns. The glossy black and white oystercatcher breeds here freely, making an apology for a nest out of a few stones or bits of dead grass, decorated with a rabbit dropping or two. An excitable bird, the first to make its presence felt as you come into view, it flies around in wide circles, peep-peeping. With its long, strong orangey-red bill, it makes a living probing in the sand for cockles and shrimps. Sometimes several of the birds will join together for a curious performance in which they fly

Eggs of sandwich tern (*Sterna sandvicensis*) in a rudimentary nest in shingle, to show virtual invisibility.

Good country for breeding oystercatchers, terns and plovers, provided they are undisturbed!
Dunwich Heath, Suffolk.

Ringed plover with eggs in its 'nest', a rudimentary scrape in the sand. Try not to picnic here!

around in close company, then land on an undisturbed sandy place to continue an animated discussion, all of them piping at each other with as much power as they can muster.

Ringed plovers live in this kind of country too – small, plump waders with brown backs and white bellies, with a conspicuous black collar bordered with white. On hatching, the superbly camouflaged chicks desert the nest within a short time, to begin the process of learning how to fend for themselves in a difficult world, made more difficult by the fact that their chosen habitat is prime picnic country. If you stumble too close to them, the parent birds stage a masterly performance of feigned injury while the chicks crouch and freeze. Staggering about with a 'broken' wing, they lure you, or a marauding fox or stoat, to a comfortable distance away from the vulnerable chicks before taking off to rejoin the offspring as discreetly as may be.

Disturbance by holiday-makers was one of the factors which might have caused the rare Kentish plover to be lost as a British breeding bird in this century. A Mediterranean bird, it had a toe-hold on the Kentish coast, which lasted till the 1950s, but over the last couple of years very few pairs have bred again, this time on the Lincolnshire and south Humberside coast. As a regular migrant to the English coast, it only needs dry summers and a certain amount of peace and quiet to establish itself again, but those may both be optimistic requirements.

Shingle banks represent a very different habitat from sand and sand dunes. Where sand, by virtue of its capacity to retain a protective coating of seawater around the individual grains, offers a home to a whole community of creatures, a pebble beach offers little comfort. The pebbles are sea-worn by the grinding action of the waves, and that very grinding makes it well nigh impossible for any animal to find a home amongst them. Graded and transported by the action of the sea, the pebbles pile up to form the well known beaches, spits and bars, sculpted into ridges by the elements. The wind cannot blow the pebbles away, so over a period of time tidal debris accumulates and, to the extent that the shingle is stabilized, plants establish themselves and flourish. Although you might expect that a shingle ridge would be particularly well drained, the fact is that there is abundant fresh water a short distance under the surface, as can easily be checked by removing a few stones, so the plants are well watered.

Few plants are characteristic of shingle beaches, which is hardly surprising in so inhospitable an environment. Shrubby sea-blite is perhaps the most typical, growing up through pebbles to reach over three feet high when the shingle is more or less fixed and stable. But if the beach is mobile the stem keels over to be buried by pebbles, then shooting up new branches to keep its head above the stones which threaten to overwhelm it.

There is one insect which lives uniquely on the sea-shore, inhabiting crevices between the larger stones. The scaly cricket *Mogoplistes squamiger* is common in coastal regions of the continent and, since it is confined to the Chesil Beach in England, was presumably introduced.

Though the highly mobile sand and pebbles of the tidal regions of the beach provide scant comfort for plants, the story is very different when we come to rocky shores. And one of the great summer pleasures is to explore the seaweedy ledges and rock pools of any sheltered bay at low water, especially during spring tides when the deep-water kelps are revealed.

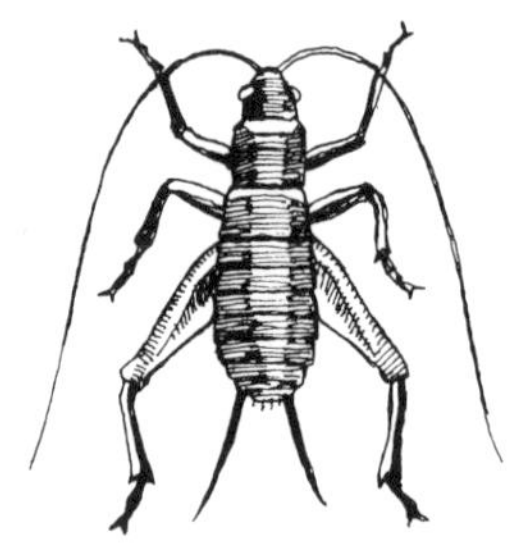

The chesil, or scaly, cricket (*Mogoplistes squamiger*), common on the continent but in Britain known only from Chesil Beach in Dorset.

The position on the shore, in relation to the reach of the tide, is most important when considering rock pools. Shallow pools, high up the beach, soon become overheated by the sun, and while they may be first choice for bathing children, they offer precious little to the naturalists. Rain dilutes the salt mix, sun evaporates and concentrates it; it is a difficult place to live. Shore crabs and the green *Enteromorpha* make most of the running. Lower down the shore the environmental extremes are less taxing and the list of inhabitants is more exciting. Nevertheless rock pools demand a high degree of tolerance on the part of their inhabitants. Quite apart from the fluctuations in salinity, there are violent changes in temperature. Only the periodic return of the flooding seawater restores 'normal' conditions.

Sometimes, the surface of a rock pool is

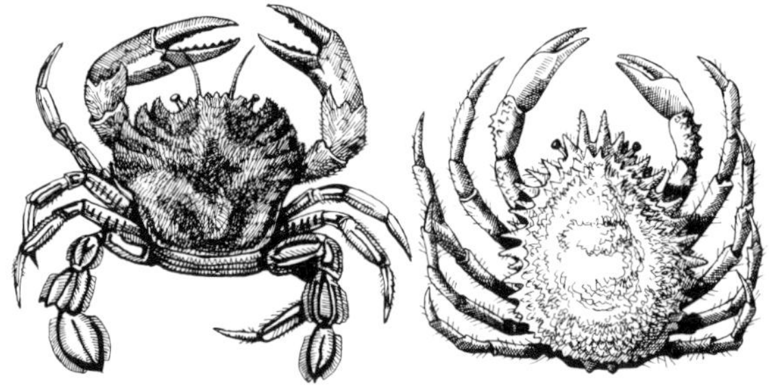

Above left: fiddler crab (*Portunus puber*). Note the hindmost limb which is more flattened than that of the shore crab and is an adaptation for swimming.
Above right: the spiny spider crab (*Maia squinada*) is a bottom-dwelling animal with rounded walking legs as in the edible crab.

swarming with crowds of small blue-black insects which move on the surface film in exactly the way pond-skaters enjoy the surface of a freshwater pond. These are maritime forms of the springtail, scavengers which hide in cracks and crevices when the returning waves pound the pools.

The fauna and flora of the lowest pools are the most extensive, with sponges, hydroids and polyzoans, worms, crabs, chitons, starfish,

ABOVE: Shore crabs can be scavengers, but given the chance they prefer fresh meat, as this lugworm.

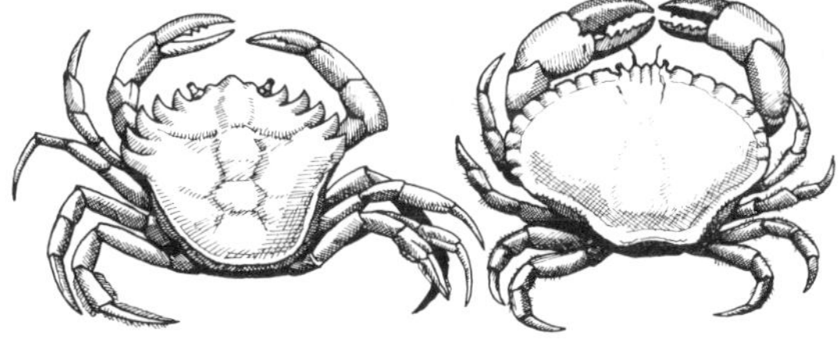

RIGHT ABOVE: (left) Shore crab (*Carcinus maenas*) and (right) edible crab (*Cancer pagurus*). Note the hindmost pair of legs of the shore crab is somewhat flattened in the terminal section as a paddle, whereas in the edible crab these legs are rounded exclusively for walking.

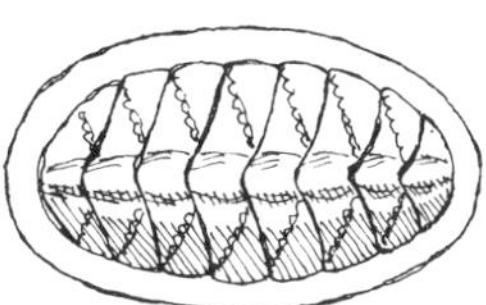

ABOVE: a chiton or coat-of-mail shell (*Lepidochiton cinereus*).

Some of the colourful inhabitants of rock pools.
LEFT: shrimp and fanworms.
ABOVE: leander prawn.
RIGHT: springtails feeding on an overturned limpet.

urchins and brittle stars all crowding the undersides of rocks and stones, while the seaweeds are at their most abundant and extravagant. In the open water the creatures tend to be difficult to see. Prawns may be pink when we peel them on the plate but they are practically transparent in the water. In winter they are in the open sea, but the warm weather of summer brings them close inshore, as scavengers and active hunters.

Unlikely though it always seems, the acorn barnacles which crowd the above-water surfaces of the rocks are closely related to the swimming prawns. Curiously, their life-span is directly related to their position on the shore gradient. Those inhabiting the low-water areas live only some three years while those which live nearer the extreme high-water mark may live more than five. These acorn barnacles are perfectly able to withstand long periods of exposure to the air, rain and sun, closing their protective plates to form a sealed unit when the food-providing tide retreats. As soon as they are covered by the incoming sea, those stout limy plates unfold to reveal feathery appendages which sample the water and grasp their plankton food.

The beautiful anemones, flower animals, are seen at their best in rock pools, when they are open. Their stout, muscular body columns are expanded at the upper end to reveal a disc mouth, surrounded by circles of hollow tentacles. Simple animals, they have no respiratory organs, their surface tissues taking in oxygen and releasing carbon dioxide. The many-coloured beadlet anemone is one of the commonest species, with its battery of stinging cells positioned at the base of each tentacle. Extended, these seize and enfold small prey animals. These anemones are firmly attached to their rock home but are perfectly able to slide about in order to achieve a more desirable site, or for the purposes of warfare.

Rock-pool fish are generally on the small side. They display remarkable adaptations to protect themselves from the danger of being damaged or swept away by the churning inshore water.

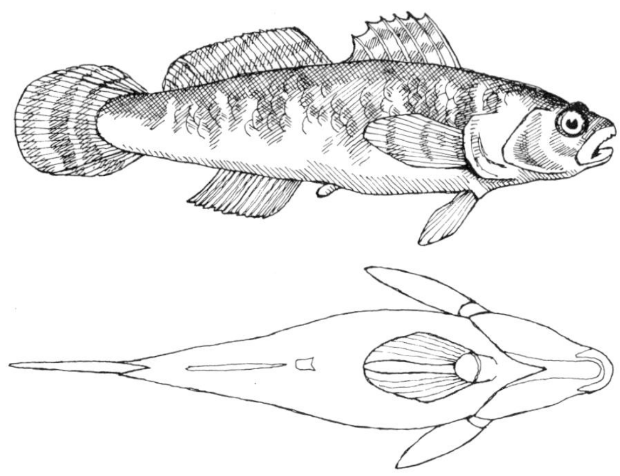

Rock goby (*Gobius paganellus*). The lower drawing shows how the pelvic fins are united to form a sucker used by the fish to attach itself to the bottom. This feature and the eyes, almost touching at the top of the head, constitute defining characteristics of the genus *Gobius*.

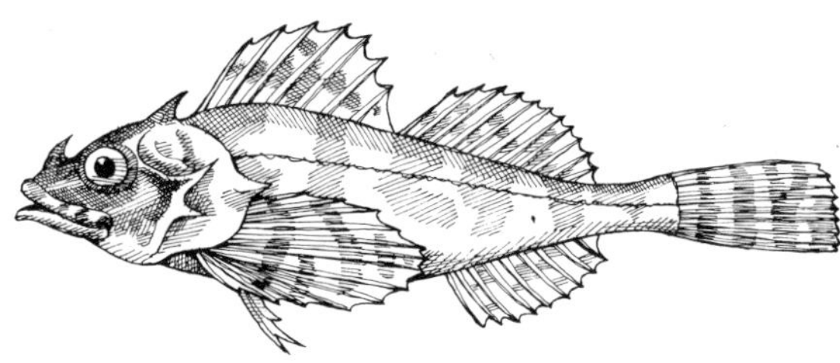

Sea scorpions either cling close to the rock face or hide in a crevice when the waves pound.

Gobies have fan-shaped suckers on the pelvic fins allowing them to grip tight to the rocks. Sea-scorpions have flattened bellies and are able to cling very close to a rock surface or slip into a narrow cranny for protection against pounding waves.

Winkles grip tight to the lee side of exposed rocks or on the waving fronds of seaweed, rolling to the punch of the sea rather than fighting it. Limpets are superbly shaped to deflect the force of the sea. Perhaps somewhat uninspiring at first sight, they are beautifully adapted to their way of life. When the incoming tide liberates them from their home base, where their perfect seal against the rock protects against desiccating effects of wind and sun, they move and graze the surrounding surface, rasping

Mussels cling to their rocks with mooring lines called byssus threads.

N.W.CUSA

SANDY FORESHORE

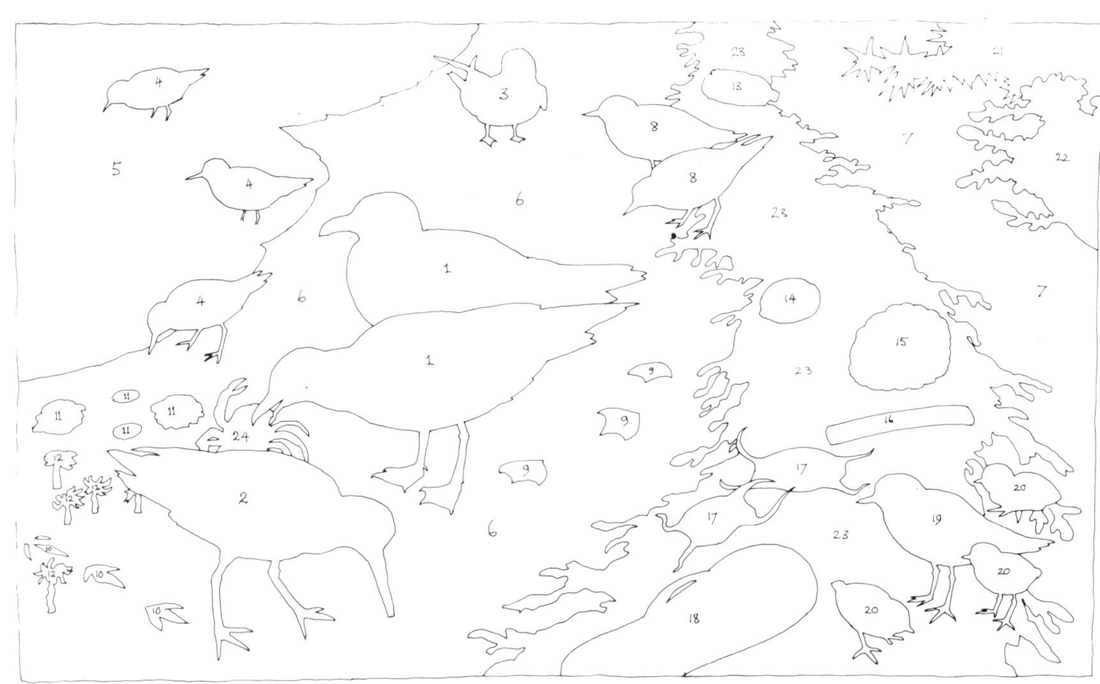

A sandy beach in late summer. The tide (5) has just begun to ebb from the strand line (23). Between tide-edge and strand line there is wet sand (6); above the strand line the sand is dry (7) and rarely inundated. Here salt-tolerant plants are becoming established, forming a line of fore-dunes. These are (21) prickly saltwort (*Salsola kali*) and (22) sea rocket (*Cakile maritima*). The strand line is composed primarily of dried seaweed, on a sandy shore probably largely channel wrack (*Pelvetia caniculata*), but it has also a scattering of other objects, (17) the egg-cases of a ray or skate (*Raja* sp.), (15) a mass of the egg-cases of the common whelk (*Buccinum undatum*), (14) a 'sea potato', the test of an urchin (*Echinocardium cordatum*), (16) a razor shell (*Solen* sp.) and various residues from human summer holidays, (18) a flip-flop and (13) a polythene bottle. The wrack-line will doubtless be alive with 'sand-hoppers' (*Amphipoda*) and searching for these and other edible animal life are (8) two turnstones (*Arenaria interpres*), one still in breeding plumage, the other in the more sober winter dress, and (19) a ringed plover (*Charadrius hiaticula*) with (20) three newly hatched chicks. On the wet sand (3) a little tern (*Sterna albifrons*) is resting, as are (1) two herring gulls (*Larus argentatus*), one of which has caught (24) a shore crab (*Carcinus maenas*), while an oystercatcher (*Haematopus ostralegus*) probes for lugworms (*Arenicola marina*) of which the casts and dimples (11) in the sand are to be seen. Both oystercatcher (10) and herring gulls (9) have left footprints in the wet sand. A few tubes of (12) the sand mason (*Lanice conchilega*) are to be seen in the same area while feeding along the very edge of the tide are (4) three sanderlings (*Calidris alba*), birds of the year, newly arrived from Arctic Eurasia.

away on any fresh weed growth. They don't travel far, working within a yard or so of their base. And at high water they begin to work their way back home, to the exact spot where they have established a sealed contact with the rock surface, where they can be sure of retaining a spoonful of water inside the safety of the shell.

To fit itself to the rock home, the limpet either grinds the rock surface to suit or it shapes its own shell margin to match the irregularities of the chosen patch. But another mollusc, the piddock, actually bores into the interior of the rock in order to arrange itself a permanent home. Like the limpets and most other seashore creatures, it starts life as a free-floating larva in the plankton, but eventually settles on soft rock, sandstone for instance. Then it bores itself a little cave, rasping its way in with the filing edge of its twin shells. Once inside, it sits tight and grows, entrapped, never to emerge again. It is a most specialized and effective rock borer, working in a whole range of materials from stiff clay to limestone, but preferring soft rocks like sandstone or slate. Piddock holes endure after the death of the inhabitant, then the eroding action of the sea takes advantage of the convenient breach to continue the never-ending work of breaking down the cliffs.

Piddocks lead a sheltered, sedentary life inside their holes. Other molluscs are rather more vulnerable to attack, their armour-plating being

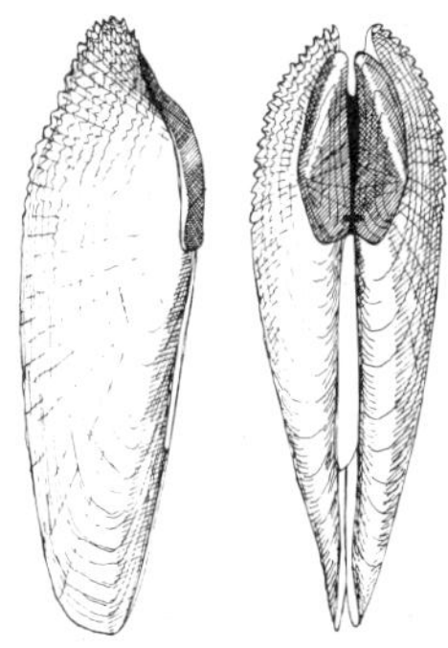

Piddock (*Pholas dactylus*) showing the plates additional to the normal two of the bivalve and the sharply serrated fore-edge of the main valves as an adaptation to boring into the softer rocks.

Lobster (*Homarus vulgaris*).

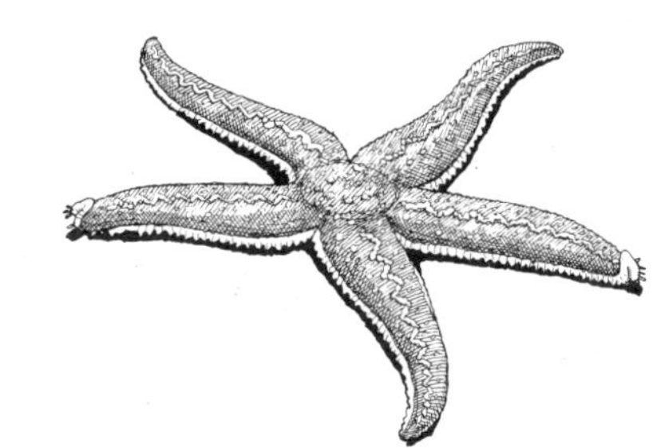

Common starfish (*Asterias rubens*).

breached in any number of ways. Flatfish hunt them actively along the sandy sea-bed swallowing them whole. Lobsters and crabs crush them with their powerful claws. Some molluscs even attack other molluscs, boring neat little holes through the shell to the meat inside. The common starfish first embraces its seashell prey then prises the two valves apart using the powerful suction forces of its myriad tube feet. Then it extrudes its stomach through its mouth and digests the meat directly. (Starfish are not much loved by lobster fishermen, either. They say that if there are starfish in the pot, there's no chance of a lobster.)

Shells are also chiselled open or smashed by oystercatchers, crushed by eider ducks or dropped from a great height by crows and gulls, swallowed whole in vast numbers by a long list of ducks and waders. In fact, a mollusc's life is precarious, to say the least.

Crustaceans are armour-plated, too, but unlike the molluscs they shed their shells

FY518

Fishing boats come in all shapes and sizes, depending on their intended catch. Working out of a semi-natural haven like Polperro, sturdy Fowey-registered day-boats work beam trawls for scallops, stern trawl for flatfish and tend pots and long-lines for crabs, lobsters, dogfish, ling and anything that's about.

periodically, as they grow. Prawns cast their outer skin every two weeks or so in summer, a procedure that is fraught with danger because the animal is clearly unprotected from attack until the new skin has hardened, a process that takes a couple of days, though the old skin is sloughed in only a few seconds. Most of the crabs follow this same path of moulting through periodic shell change as they grow. But the familiar hermit crab has chosen a different way. Having shed the idea of armour-plating, it seeks shelter in a vacant mollusc shell. Its hind quarters are soft and hook-shaped, so that it may back into a suitable snail shell and grasp tight while its legs act as bracing struts. Its larger fore-claw, the fighting arm, folds to form a protective shield across the entrance to the shell when required.

While the hermit crab may start its shell-life in the small home of a periwinkle or topshell, it will move house at intervals, graduating through the increasing sizes of an empty topshell, dog-whelk shell and ending its time, if it lasts long enough, in the former home of a common whelk – the biggest of the freely available shells in British waters. At this stage it will also have retreated lower down the beach slope, and is less likely to be seen by the beachcomber. But if you examine the decks of an inshore potter or crabbing motor fishing vessel you will often see the odd whelk shell home jammed in a corner or in an unhosed length of the scuppers.

Hermit crab (*Eupagurus bernhardus*) in the shell of a common whelk (*Buccinum undatum*) with the parasitic anemone (*Calliactes parasitica*) attached to the outside of the shell.

Although on the face of it the hermit crab is well named, living as it does in a mobile cave, in fact it lives a fairly sociable life. There is a ragworm which creeps in to live inside the shell in close company, and a parasitic anemone which attaches itself to the outside of the shell. While the crab is the active hunter, it provides for both worm and anemone which sweep up the crumbs from the crab's table. But the arrangement is by no means one-sided. Doubtless the scavenging ragworm keeps the interior of the house tidy, and the anemone's stinging tentacles come in handy when the gypsy caravan is under threat.

Crabs are commonly regarded as scavengers, but in fact, given the choice, they much prefer fresh meat. Much the same is true of the omnivorous gulls which have nevertheless made a considerable success of their scavenging propensities.

The bounty of the sea is richest at its very edges, when it comes into contact with the land and enjoys the rich run-off waters. And man has always been quick to take advantage of that bounty, using innumerable ploys with which to sample the fish, shellfish and crustaceans. With line and trap, no edible morsel is safe from our clutches. Even lighthousemen, confined to their remote posts, have used flying kites to deploy their fishing lines with success. But one of the most effective ways of learning about the sea life of a region is to visit the local fish market, and to observe the local fishing vessels.

Fishing boats come in all shapes and sizes, tested by severe conditions and thus adapted to their different functions by much the same forces which have moulded their prey. Open boats up to about thirteen metres in length – crabbers and long-liners, often work from open beaches or natural harbours, taking a daily toll of shellfish, ling, conger, ray and turbot, to say nothing of the holiday trade for learner mackerel fishermen. Larger and more expensive trawlers and purse-seiners work away for days at a time, storing their catch in ice or chilled seawater tanks. In biological terms, the trawler is a voracious predator, highly seaworthy, powerful and with a big load capacity. Something of the sort can be said of our true sea-birds.

Most British sea-birds are carnivorous, feeding directly from the sea and taking an astonishing variety of fish and invertebrates from a wide range of habitats. Some are ocean-going, some inshore hunters, some pirates and some work the shore line itself and also forage inland. Their working methods vary from the near-vertical plunge diving of gannets, the dainty picking of morsels from the surface by terns, the dipping of kittiwakes and fulmars to the underwater pursuit of auks and cormorants.

It has been estimated that a population of well over two million birds may be sustained by the teeming sea life around our coasts. Fishing-boat operations provide one of the ways in which birds benefit. Herring gulls and kittiwakes take the lion's share of this food source, but gannets, great black-backed gulls and fulmars also gain. And great skuas enjoy the bounty at second hand, when they pursue the gulls through the air, forcing them to disgorge their catch. Late in the breeding season, manx shearwaters too have been seen scavenging from fishing boats, and the list of species seen behaving in this way so far totals twenty.

Small whitings are the preferred prize, but dabs and sprats are also sought after, when the 'trash' is hosed from the trawlers' decks. Nowadays most fish are kept in ice and brought ashore for gutting, but when cod or saithe (or coalfish or coley) are gutted at sea the offal is taken enthusiastically by fulmars, which are particularly keen on the livers. When the purse-seiners are active, gannets may take advantage by plunge diving into the filled net when the mackerel are crowded together and helpless.

Gulls, especially herring gulls, are opportunist feeders which have been quick to grasp the possibilities of easy feeding at refuse tips, sewage farms and agricultural bases. But they cast their nets wide, enjoying food from a number of different sources. Carrying shellfish to a height, they let them go in places where the molluscs fall and break upon rock, or a hard road surface, in order to achieve the desired piece of flesh. The same technique is used to persuade hermit crabs out of their shells. A lazier method is to follow curlews or oystercatchers, waiting for the waders to find a choice crab or crack open a cockle, before moving in to bully the rightful owner out of its reward. Gulls also stamp on damp sand or grass fields in order to compact the surface and encourage worms or shellfish to show their faces. Pairs of gulls even work together, standing side by side and achieving better results, more worms. This is an activity which one would expect black-headed gulls to indulge in, incidentally, but they seem not to, at least in Britain.

Breeding gulls, and the not entirely loved sound of their calling, are very much part of the coastal town nowadays. Over the last few decades they have colonized many a chimney and roof, finding that breeding success is even greater in the comparative safety of the rooftops. Many people complain that they don't go to bed at a civilized time, yelling away late at night. But it is in July that the complaints are loudest, like the seagulls, and July is an exciting time for them. Well grown chicks are wandering the rooftops finding their way about and learning to fly. Gulls tend to be most active at dawn and dusk, anyway, but when they're nesting in a town or village they have the benefit of street lighting. So their days are lengthened. At night both parents tend to be at home, with a great deal to say to each other, and when the streets are not thronging with people, the gulls can be searching for fish and chip left-overs and examining the litter bins. It all adds up to a lot of disturbance.

Gulls are to a certain extent the victims of a seaside cliché. The long-running joke about the BBC only having one gramophone record of their cries only serves to strengthen the image. It's true that they are highly vocal during the breeding season, with a great deal of excited screaming,

Black-headed gulls breed on inland marshes and lochsides, and on estuaries in summer.

trumpeting and ha-ha-ha-ing. And they certainly have a piercing 'go-away' call when they are disturbed. A lot depends on what they are doing. Establishing territory and courting produces the well known 'long' call. They squabble noisily over something juicy in a rubbish tip, but at the roost, for instance, they are very quiet, because they do not want to invite disturbance.

The rapidly increasing number of gulls causes some concern, for they are undoubtedly carriers of infectious diseases, and it may be that we shall soon be seeing changes in the law to enable their numbers to be controlled in towns. Certainly many people would like to see gulls back where they think they ought to belong, the sea. But the fact is that most gulls are coastal birds rather than sea-birds.

No one could accuse the shag of being likely to cause annoyance ashore. Shags are birds of the inshore waters, fishing harmlessly, from our point of view, for non-marketable species. Cormorants are not beloved of river anglers, mostly, I suspect, because they are so clearly better at the job than the fishermen.

In fact cormorants do not spend a lot of time in the water, unless they are actively feeding. Swimming low, with very little of their topsides showing, they fish by underwater pursuit. Sometimes, backs awash, they slide underwater gently, but more often they take a purposeful leap and jack-knife down to search for prey, propelling themselves with the broad webbed paddles of their feet. The wings are closed underwater, except for braking or manoeuvring. Mostly they hunt in shoal water, inside the five-fathom mark, often over a bottom that may be less than two or three feet down. They may stay down for a few seconds or half a minute, but sometimes over a minute.

Though they seem to lead idle lives, they work hard while actively feeding, close inshore or over sand or mudflats in estuaries and creeks. Apart from eels, which are common prey, they take mostly flatfish, flounders and dabs. And although they can look surprisingly clumsy when they're swallowing the catch, they are wonderfully well designed for their job. The tongue has a rasping surface in which the rasps point backwards, ensuring a one-way action in which the fish is encouraged towards the throat. The cormorant will arrange the fish so that it slips down head first, shaking it about or even throwing it in the air, so that any inconvenient spines will be laid back in repose. The gullet is a flabby tube, capable of great expansion. While the fish is sliding gently down, the bird may look as if it is swallowing a balloon. Yet while the digestive juices are getting to work, and even before the fish gets to the grinding mill of the gizzard, the bird has no difficulty in breathing. Its windpipe is an elastic tube that is stiffened by rings of cartilage, rather in the manner of a flexible vacuum-cleaner pipe, and these rings protect the windpipe from pinching or collapsing, so an air supply is maintained. The pipe won't kink when the bird's supple neck is twisting and turning, whether it is feeding or preening.

Cormorants enjoying the ritual passing of building material at the nest.

Cormorant chicks are fed twice daily, when the chick puts its head well inside the parent's throat, inducing it to regurgitate a rich mess of half-digested fish. Apart from fishing sessions, cormorants spend most of their time ashore, carefully choosing undisturbed, slightly elevated positions for the time-consuming business of wing drying, oiling and preening. They are gregarious birds, not only at the breeding site, choosing to gather together at well established roost places.

Unlike most water birds their plumage becomes sodden during the dives, and they must dry their wings, standing in the familiar 'open umbrella' position facing into the wind or absorbing the sun.

Diving birds have a blood system which suits their way of life. The primary oxygen-carrying component is myoglobin rather than the haemoglobin which the human system uses. Myoglobin carries more oxygen molecules, and this increased oxygen capacity allows birds to remain submerged longer and dive to greater depths.

Another problem faced, and solved, by sea-birds is that they inevitably absorb more salt than their renal system can comfortably process. Not only divers, but fulmars, terns and gulls ingest seawater both when drinking and fishing. The surplus is carried along the bloodstream to fine tubes connected with the nose glands, to be discharged, so that concentrated sodium chloride drips continuously from the tip of the bird's beak. But in the case of diving birds like auks, gannets and cormorants, whose nostrils are carried inside the mouth (in order to avoid water being forced in during impact with the surface of the sea) the salt solution weeps into the mouth to be flicked away. Anyone who has had the job of nursing guillemots back to health after they have been oiled will know the action very well.

Flight capability is related to the pattern of bird life. Gannets have long narrow wings which give them long-distance endurance, involving a high level of gliding expertise. Shags fly low over the water with rapid wing-beats, neck extended for a certain amount of low-level gliding. Cormorants fly both high and low, a rather goose-like flight, with powerful beating of their relatively short wings.

Terns go in for a rather buoyant flight, and they have the untypical sea-bird facility of being able to hover, in the style of a kestrel, before they plunge for their surface prey. Auks, with their stout bodies and short, narrow wings, have a fast, shirring flight and are quite unable to glide or soar, let alone hover. The fact is that they fly best underwater; in the denser medium they progress in a series of jerks, powered by the flipper-like wings at a much slower rate of beat.

Sea-birds are not agile in the sense of a blue tit or sparrowhawk; there is no requirement for them to jink and turn in order to avoid tree trunks and foliage. But they are supremely skilled at taking advantage of air currents. Whether the up-draught is caused by waves, cliffs or ships, they ride them with consummate ease. Often enough they don't need to indulge in fuel-intensive flapping, but let the wind do the work for them. Gulls are something of a compromise between the high-endurance gliding of a fulmar or gannet and the fast flight of a puffin. They represent the all-rounder, able to use the opportunist approach to take reasonable advantage of whatever food or energy source offers itself.

Sea-birds live both on the breeding cliffs and at sea in tolerable harmony because they are not in broad competition for their food. Gannets specialize in taking fast pelagic fish such as herrings and mackerel. Fulmars and kittiwakes take surface plankton and offal, terns pick small fish from the surface while auks chase them deeper down. Guillemots and the less numerous razorbills feed closer inshore than the more oceanic puffins, taking sprats when they can get them, whereas the puffins specialize more in sand-eels. Incidentally, puffins do not alternate the heads and tails of their sand-eels in a neat symmetry when they carry them back in quantity to the nest. The little fish are held firmly by the head in a groove inside the bird's beak, and it matters not a jot which way the tails protrude.

The auk chicks, whether standing motionless on their perilous ledges or in the dark safety of puffin burrows, must grow fast on the rich fish

Puffins make their nests in underground burrows on cliff slopes; but they enjoy socializing nearby when they are off duty.

diet. Guillemot chicks are fed by both parents on a regurgitated fish mess for three weeks. At this point, half grown but well feathered, they are encouraged by their parents to launch themselves into the air, usually at dusk, and they more or less plummet to the sea below. They are still dependent on their parents for food, but learn their trade in the company first of both parents, then of one only. Since the colony acts almost as a single organism, the eggs laid on the same day and hatched synchronously, the young all achieve the three-week departure day together. But the family parties disperse once afloat, and paddle about the coast for a few months, although after a short time only one parent remains with the juvenile.

Pair of adult gannets at the nest with a young chick, or guga, in its first downy plumage.

Puffin returning to feed the chick in its underground burrow-nest. The beakful of sand eels is gripped firmly by grooves in the specially adapted mandibles.

Puffin chicks remain in their burrows for about six weeks, fed by both parents on whole sand-eels. Then they are abandoned, to fast a few days till hunger forces them to run the gauntlet of the gulls and find their way to the sea where, fully feathered and fat, they must teach themselves to fish. By August, the colonies are deserted by all of the auks. Only the fat fulmar chicks remain in the clifftop ledges, to fly in mid September after being fed by both parents for eight weeks.

Puffin numbers are often quoted as examples of the dire consequences of marine pollution. And it is certainly true that their populations have taken a heavy knock in the southern part of Britain. On Lundy, in the Bristol Channel, this 'Isle of Puffins' has sadly all but lost its teeming hordes, and the story is much the same in other parts of Devon and Cornwall. There has been a general retreat at the southern end of the species' range since the beginning of the twentieth century. But the overall picture is far less gloomy, in fact it is one of stability and even increase, marred by some disturbing events of the past few years.

The world population of puffins is something like fifteen million, and this number seems to be holding its own with two notable exceptions. In Newfoundland the birds are suffering because of over-fishing of the capelin, their preferred fish prey, and in the Lofoten Islands of central Norway they have had disastrous breeding seasons since 1969. In 1981, the reproductive effort of three-quarters of a million breeding pairs was a total failure. Half a million chicks were born but all of them died before they fledged. It seems that there are no supplies of suitably sized fish for the adults to catch for their young. If the fish are too big then the chick can't swallow them, too small and there isn't enough fat on them to fuel the chicks' growth. So they die of starvation. Norwegian ornithologists have collected, weighed and measured large numbers of dead chicks. Their results show that there is no question of pollution, predation or exploitation being the cause of the disaster. It seems that after the herring stocks had been fished out by the Norwegians they turned their attention to sand-eels and sprats. These are now fished commercially, but taken in such quantities, to feed pigs to make bacon, that there is no surplus to feed the puffin chicks. Unfortunately, this could soon be the state of affairs in the Shetlands, where there is a British population of some half a million puffins.

Fishermen tend to over-exploit fish stocks in a way which reduces their eventual harvest. When herrings are fished out they turn their attentions to mackerel. Using catching methods of awesome efficiency they have the capacity to bring populations near extinction. If there are no herrings and no mackerel they look elsewhere. And in Shetland at the moment they are rapidly expanding their capacity to process the vast stocks of sand-eels. At the beginning of the 1970s they landed none at all, by 1981 they were landing fifty thousand tonnes. The processing plants are growing like mushrooms and will soon be capable of dealing with a vastly increased tonnage. And it's those very sand-eels which ought to be providing for the fattening of young puffins. It seems highly likely that the current expansion of puffin numbers is due for a reversal. It would be easy to cast the fishermen as villains, but the problem is that fishermen are themselves in some danger of extinction – fighting for survival in a world where their own indiscriminate harvesting has reduced their potential catch while ever-increasing sophistication gives them the capacity to drain the ocean of fish.

Violent fluctuations in populations are part and parcel of the lives of sea-going birds, but if their food is denied them they inevitably starve. We need to find a way of providing for our own fish requirements which leaves enough in the sea for creatures like puffins. Puffins can cope with storms at sea and predators on land, but not with starvation.

Gannets, too, have a long incubation and fledging period. Laying the single egg in April or May, it will be late August before the chicks go to sea. Like the puffins the fat brown/black gugas must run the gauntlet, this time of other gannets as well as gulls, before they can leap into the sea. Too fat to fly, the young gannet swims about for a period till it has slimmed down. Then it takes off to migrate to the waters of equatorial West Africa, a distance of some four thousand miles. It will find its way back home again in four or five years' time, to court and breed first at five or six years of age, establishing a nest site to which it will remain faithful, as it does to its partner, until it is perhaps twenty years old.

It is typical of sea-birds that they are slow to mature. They need time to get to grips with the hard sea-going life before they attempt to breed. But that life is fairly safe, and sea-birds tend to be long lived, in striking contrast to woodland or back-garden species. And because their survival chances are high, they can afford to raise small families. Some species, albatrosses for instance, don't even breed every year. The sea-going life may be hard, but if the animal is well adapted to it, it is remarkably safe.

Autumn

View along the rock-strewn foreshore
at Gunwalloe, West Cornwall.

As summer visitors, here only for the breeding season, most of our sea-birds disperse before the autumn, though some, like fulmars, will still be on the nest ledges well into September. After the rigours and demands of rearing families, most will be off to the open sea. At observatories all round the coast, places like Dungeness, Skokholm and Cape Clear, and from other famous sea-watching points, birdwatchers will see a seemingly continuous procession of birds moving south, some on passage to the rich winter waters off the Iberian coast and West Africa, some even farther afield. At peak times, observers at Cape Clear have clocked up 40,000 sea-birds an hour.

Land-birds, too, will be sweeping down to the coast, gathering themselves for the traumatic passage across the Channel, en route to the wintering grounds of the continent and Africa. Red admiral butterflies will flutter low over the coastal water to astonish yachtsmen who find it difficult to believe that these tiny scraps are seriously undertaking Channel crossings.

The terns which bred along our coastline are now moving west and south towards their winter quarters. And in autumn comes our best chance of seeing the black terns which, while being extremely rare as breeding birds in Britain, do well in eastern Europe and are passing by on their way to tropical Africa. In the West Country, where terns find it difficult to breed because, although there are plenty of suitable places, the rate of disturbance is too high, we do at least see a good deal of tern activity in autumn, when passage, sandwich and common or arctic terns stop by to feed along the shores and in the mouths of the estuaries. In August it is a common sight to see a tern perched on almost any mooring buoy, or gracing the masthead truck of a yacht. Along the coast any exposed isolated rock is likely to have a sandwich tern or two decorating it. The arctic terns cover the most remarkable distances, commonly flying some 10,000 miles from their Arctic breeding places to 'winter' in Antarctica, thus living a life of perpetual summer. One record showed that an arctic tern which bred on the Arctic coast of Russia flew all the way to Australia, 14,000 miles. A nestling ringed by the British Trust for Ornithology in Britain, where perhaps 40,000 arctic terns breed, was recovered 11,000 miles later in Melbourne, having covered that distance at an average speed of 94 miles per day.

Of the gulls, the only truly sea-going species is the kittiwake, which works the open Atlantic picking plankton and small fish from the surface waters and making a particular feature of following fishing boats for offal or 'trash'. One of the pleasant sights of summer is the bathing parties of kittiwakes enjoying a freshwater pool or stream near the breeding cliffs, but in mid August the birds leave the nesting place, first gathering at a safe place like an island, before setting off to sea. At this stage the juvenile birds of the year are conspicuously marked with a black zigzag pattern across the wings.

Other gulls abandon the breeding cliffs and slopes to spend their days visiting their several feeding grounds. The daily pattern may involve carefully timed appearances at rubbish tips and fish quays, timed so that they take maximum advantage of feeding opportunities. Large numbers of black-headed gulls will migrate from the continent to spend the best part of the winter in the British Isles.

Vast numbers of waders, ducks, geese and swans will begin to fly in to our coast as the Arctic and eastern European summer ends and the short season of plenty tails off. Some purple sandpipers and black-tailed godwits will arrive as early as mid July, still in their breeding plumage but perhaps having failed for one reason or another to breed successfully. But the rush of immigrants is more typical of autumn.

The first barnacle geese arrive in early October, escaping the extremes of the Arctic winter. Many fly in to the island of Islay, the southernmost of the Inner Hebrides. Islay is their main wintering stronghold, enjoying the largest wintering population in Britain. The barnacle is an exceedingly rare bird; the total population may only be in the region of thirty to

Barnacle geese bathing in a rain-water pond. In winter the British Isles play host to a major part of the world population of these rare birds.

Sanderlings chase morsels at the water's edge, snatching them and dashing back from the swash.

forty thousand birds. But thirty per cent of this population winters on the relatively small island of Islay, and this creates something of a problem since the island farmers are in competition with the geese for the grass. And while the geese have a long tradition of 'ownership' firmly on their side, the farmers, who equally firmly claim rights, have steadily 'improved' the coastal grazing. The geese, naturally enough, prefer the protein-rich new growth of grass encouraged by the farmers, and conflict is joined. The geese are sociable birds, concentrating in large flocks and carefully choosing the choicest grass. It's easy to sympathize with the farmer's objections when the birds take his grass (five geese have the grazing capability of one sheep) but unfortunately the rare barnacle is in danger of becoming rarer. Several poor breeding seasons have reduced the proportion of juvenile birds in the winter flocks, a state of affairs which is not encouraging for the long-term breeding performance of the population.

From a birdwatcher's point of view, all geese are magic, and Islay draws him as to a honey-pot to see the barnacles flight into the feeding grounds, yapping like a pack of terriers, flying in close company, endless skeins of birds tumbling out of the sky. The farmers are naturally incensed when the geese home in on the lushest grass, and the local newspapers are full of shock-horror stories about the winged menace swarming in for a seasonal orgy of destruction. The law requires farmers to persuade the geese to move elsewhere, using any number of scare tactics. But as a last resort, for the purpose of preventing serious damage to crops, the geese may be shot, under licence. Curiously, though, it is not the farmers who work the land who get the licence, it is the landowners, who have a vested interest in sport shooting, an interest which is legally denied in the case of barnacles which are exceedingly rare in world terms but exceedingly common on the small island of Islay.

The landowners delegate the responsibility for the shooting, as they are legally permitted to do. But not unnaturally they tend to offer the job to sportsmen, who pay for the privilege. So the job of pest control is being performed for farmers who simply want to see the backs of the geese, by sportsmen whose principal interest is to keep the geese coming towards them to be shot. It's a crazy situation, and not surprisingly there have been many reports that the law has not been strictly observed. Clearly there is a need for a sanctuary area to be established, with the prime aim of attracting geese by grassland management carried out in their interest. Over the years agricultural interests have drained and reclaimed the estuarine marshes which traditionally provide a winter home for the geese. Fortunately the RSPB has been able to buy a substantial reserve area; their aim is to provide roosting and feeding refuges which will safeguard the goose population and relieve farmers of a burden.

Autumn also brings the influx of shore-birds which have taken advantage of the short but plentiful Arctic summer in which to raise families. They, too, suffer from the increased taming of the wild estuaries and coastal grazing, but there are encouraging signs that more people realize the importance of their chosen habitat.

After the breeding season, waders form sociable flocks, feeding and roosting in close company. Their movements are closely matched to tidal movements, and although the great expanse of mud may look uniformly barren to the casual eye, the birds know better, choosing the most productive patches as the falling tide reveals them, and staying till the last moment when the flooding tide covers them. At neap tides, when at high water there may still be a fair expanse of mud, the birds remain spread out in their customary manner. At high water of medium tides they begin to congregate in roosting groups around the areas of mud last to be covered. On big tides they gather in tightly knit groups at places which offer them the all-important safety factor of lack of disturbance, places where the salt-marsh vegetation is hammered flat by the pounding feet, and where there is always a scattering of feathers and pellets to delight the wandering naturalist. And at the equinoctial tides which inundate even the tips of the salt-marsh plants, the waders and ducks go up into the waterside fields to sit it out. Though it has to be said that shelducks and curlews, for instance, spend a good deal of time on ploughed or grass fields in the ordinary course of events, generally speaking, it is the larger birds which come into the roost place earliest. The dunlin, redshanks and other small waders need the extra feeding time, while the curlews, godwits, oystercatchers and plovers, feeding on larger prey items, tend to fill their stomachs first.

Ospreys are regular visitors to the estuaries as spring and autumn passage birds, especially on the east coast but often enough along the south and west. I well remember being told by an incredulous pleasure-boat skipper that he had seen a 'buzzard splashing into the water and coming up with a fish' on the Dart estuary years ago. We promptly set off after it and had good

ABOVE: a few ospreys breed in Scotland, but fair numbers visit English and Welsh estuaries on passage at migration time, when they stay a week or two to enjoy the fishing.

BELOW: whimbrels also breed in northern Scotland, but visit the coast further south on migration.

ABOVE: salt-marsh plants flower late in the summer. Marsh samphire, sea purslane and cord grass.

RIGHT: grey seals on the Farne Islands.

views of a bird which has been a regular September visitor to the Dart for many years now. Visitors to the Devon coast are often reluctant to believe that ospreys are seen here, believing that these birds are rare as breeders and confined to Scotland. In fact, as recently as the early part of the last century they did breed in Devon. But of course there are fair numbers of Scandinavian birds which winter off the west coast of Africa; these use British waters as refuelling stops on their twice-yearly journey. They commonly take mullet and on fresh waters they take trout, especially from the fish farms which provide such convenient bird-tables for cormorants as well! One might well wonder how it is that ospreys can manage to grip and lift such slippery prey as a fish, but of course they are specially designed for the job, with a spiny under-surface to their toes, and, as is the case with owls, their fourth toe can operate either backwards or forwards, whichever is most convenient for the job.

Ospreys are long-distance travellers, but much smaller birds undertake similar journeys. Ringed plovers may breed in Greenland yet prove to winter as far south as Ghana. One particular record-breaker was a plover which was caught and ringed on the Wash in the first half of September. From its size it was known to be from the Greenland population on its autumn

migration south. On 12 December this bird was caught again in Ghana – the furthest south ever recorded for a ringed plover—having flown 3196 miles. A few days later a second plover, also from Greenland, was found in Ghana – slightly further south.

Waders are able to make these astonishing journeys by virtue of the fact that there are conveniently spaced fuelling stations – tidal mud places with an abundance of worms and molluscs – along their route. And it is of the utmost importance to them that we maintain these wild places in their interest, as well as our own.

Many waders use our estuaries and coast on their passage journeys, but enormous numbers call the British coast home for the winter. Sanderling, for instance, breed on the barren Arctic tundra, well away from the sound of the sea, but then they come south to spend the greater part of the year on the European coast. Often enough on the mud, they prefer sandy shores and sandflats. Indeed non-breeders may stay on our shores throughout the year. They are little, plump birds, with short straight bills, best characterized by their industry. Always seemingly in a panic, dashing along the edge of the breaking wavelets like clockwork toys, they hardly seem to stop to eat, taking sandhoppers and small stuff in the backwash, then dashing out of the way of the swash. Small parties of them haunt the sea-shore, pale birds with head and underparts white, and with prominent white wing-bars. Often enough they are on the same beach as large numbers of turnstones. But the turnstones are masters of camouflage, busily turning weed and pebbles at your very feet without your noticing them.

Another tame, confiding little wader which is often in company with turnstones is the purple sandpiper. Very much a coastal bird it too breeds in the Arctic, but comes to us in the autumn, choosing rocky places, weedy shores around piers and groynes, searching among the weed fronds for titbits, dodging the sea.

The divers, red-throated, black-throated and great northern, move south in September, sometimes in large numbers, to winter along the coast. Many birds have learnt the value of diving as a way of reaching rich food stocks. But it is the mammals which have carried the technique to a high degree of perfection.

Seals actually exhale before diving, so that their lungs do not act as buoyancy chambers underwater. Their pumping action and rate of heart-beat is reduced, and oxygen is stored to high capacity in the myoglobin bloodstream. Using these methods of oxygen husbandry the seal can indulge in high-energy underwater chases for short periods or it can sleep on the sea-bed for as much as twenty minutes, surfacing only to restore the oxygen balance by deep breathing.

There are three separate populations of grey seals; those breeding in the Baltic and the western North Atlantic pup in early spring, on the ice, while our eastern North Atlantic animals come ashore in autumn to breed. This British stock now constitutes something like half the world population, so clearly it represents an asset to be greatly valued, and it is something of a pity that the controversial subject of seal management should arouse such emotion.

While the smaller common seal is more associated with sheltered sandbanks and loch islands on the east coast linked by the North Sea, the grey seal is an animal of the wild Atlantic coast. Its breeding beaches are isolated either on islands or at the remotest mainland beaches, exposed and subject to storm conditions. Before and after the breeding season they tend to spend a lot of time in sociable gatherings, choosing undisturbed beaches where they may lounge about and sleep away a great deal of the day, interspersing the inactivity with bouts of play and fishing expeditions. It is at one of these assemblies that one is able to enjoy the best lesson in distinguishing the sexes. Although it may be fashionable to say that bull seals may be sexed simply by their larger heads and generous Roman noses, in real life it is not so easy.

The bulls are generally more heavily built

Knots are masters of aerobatics, flying in close formation and flashing first white and then dark as they turn in synchrony. They are passage migrants and winter visitors to estuary and coast.

N.W.CUSA.

ESTUARY AND MUDFLATS

Early autumn on an estuary. The tide is out and (9) wet mud stretches ahead to the river (10) now running fresh to the sea until the next tide brings a new surge of salt water. At our feet the salt-marsh turf (4), principally composed of red fescue (*Festuca rubra*), has also (2) sea-lavender (*Limonium vulgare*), (1) sea aster (*Aster tripolium*) and (3) sea purslane (*Halimione portulacoides*) which, elsewhere on the marsh, is dominant. At the edge of the mud certain plants are becoming established: (8) cord grass (*Spartina townsendii*) and (5) glasswort (*Salicornia portulacoides*), the poor man's asparagus. These plants are the means of extension of the marsh. Among them are to be seen (6) a wood sandpiper (*Tringa glareola*) and (7) a snipe (*Gallinago gallinago*). Out on the wet mud, newly exposed by the tide, numerous wading birds rest or feed. These are (12) avocets (*Recurvirostra avosetta*) which have bred nearby and have not yet moved south and west, (13) redshanks (*Tringa totanus*), (14) a curlew (*Numenius arquata*), (15) a black-tailed godwit (*Limosa limosa*), still in its breeding red, (16) three dunlin (*Calidris alpina*) still with the black belly of summer, and (17) another dunlin, this one a juvenile bird. A heron (22) (*Ardea cinerea*) fishes, wading, at the river edge and (19) a cormorant (*Phalocrocorax carbo*) has just come to the surface from a fruitful dive with a flatfish (20) probably a flounder or dab (*Pleuronectes* sp.). On a mudbank in the river are (23) three brent geese (*Branta bernicla*), very early forerunners of the big flocks to come. A small flock (21) of knot (*Calidris canutus*) flies past. Finally, on the mud, a stippled, unreflecting area (11) probably indicates the presence of a host of the tiny snail (*Hydrobia ulvae*) and (18) shells of the common cockle (*Cardium edule*) are significant of the multitudes beneath the surface.

than the cows, they have a greater breadth of muzzle and thicker necks, and they do indeed have a convex head, while the cows have a straight profile. But young bulls have more of the characteristics of cows, and old cows may look decidedly bullish.

The most conclusive way of sexing the grey seals is by studying the tonal contrast in their coats. Ignore the general colour, which may be anything from pale grey through reddish-grey to dark grey and almost black. Concentrate on the patches which mark the pelage (or fur). In the male there are lighter patches on a dark background, in a female dark patches on a light background. Taken in conjunction with the general shape of the head and neck, this should do the trick.

Grey seals begin to pup in the Isles of Scilly as early as late August, but the dates get later as you travel up the west coast, till Orkney and Shetland animals pup in November. On the Welsh islands, the peak period is in the beginning of October, when there are pups of every age from new-born to a month old on the beaches.

At birth, when they are less than a yard long and weigh just over thirty pounds, they have a creamy yellow-white coat of long hairs. Although they don't grow much in length they soon become fat on the mother's milk which has a very high fat content. In the third week they begin to moult to greyer hair as the white drops off, sometimes to lie in a fringe around the juvenile in situations which are so undisturbed that the animal doesn't move. By this time it will weigh nearer 100 pounds, and is bloated with blubber. The cow will have stayed close by all this time, only going into the water when disturbed, but now she goes back to the sea and the bull which is waiting to mate. The pup starves for a week or so before hunger forces it to sea and the first tentative efforts to find food.

The first-year pup seals will travel fair distances, the Welsh animals perhaps turning up in France and the Scottish-bred visiting Norway, and they face hard times and hard weather at first. Many succumb to storms, many find themselves ashore on unsuitable beaches where they are subject to well-meaning but misplaced attempts at rescue. In most cases they simply need a few hours' rest and sleep; quite the last thing they want is to be slung back into the sea!

On the other hand, when whales are found ashore, they are certainly in considerable trouble. Often enough they are the victims of a falling tide which leaves them stranded on a shelving beach. And while porpoises or dolphins may survive a long time ashore, the larger beasts are unable to breathe because their sheer unsupported weight crushes their lungs.

Records of whale strandings have been kept by the British Museum (Natural History) since they were started in 1913, with a great deal of co-operation from the Coastguard and Receivers of Wreck. Over recent years the number of strandings has been increasing, for reasons which are not at all clear. Single whales may simply come ashore because they are sick and crave a superabundance of air, where they may be followed by others of their school in a state of distress. Other possible reasons for mass strandings have been suggested. For instance, the school may have chased a shoal of fish into the shallows, or their sonar systems may have become confused by navigational problems of narrow channels, shoals and beaches.

Whales, though everyone knows they are mammals, by law are Royal Fish. As such the stranded specimens are dealt with under the Wreck Regulations. Fishes Royal, which include sturgeon, belong to the Crown and are the prerogative of the monarch by ancient usage as a tithe rendered in exchange for guarding the seas and protecting the coast from pirates and robbers.

They belong to the Crown not only when stranded but also when caught in territorial waters. Although the practice dates back to Plantagenet times the first recorded example in the English language is of an Elizabethan lawyer who wrote in 1570 of 'greate or roialle fishe, as whales or such other, which by the Law of

Coastal plants benefit from the mineral-rich droppings of birds, but need to be hardy to survive in the salty and wind-blown conditions.
TOP: sea-campion.
CENTRE ABOVE: sea cabbage.
ABOVE: rock samphire.
RIGHT: thrift at Land's End.

A whale stranded in the Firth of Forth, 1850.

Prerogative pertain to the King himselfe'. Edward I declared that the whole sturgeon was reserved for the King, but that in the case of a whale the King should have the head, the Queen the tail and the captors the carcass. But Edward II made a clean sweep and proclaimed: 'The King shall have wreck of the sea throughout the Realm.'

Sadly the larger royal fish have little economic value, but they are of great interest to marine biologists, who examine and record the remains, an activity co-ordinated by the British Museum (Natural History) with the warmly appreciated help of HM Coastguard Service.

The putrefying remains of stranded cetaceans often pose local authorities considerable disposal problems, and it is as well for all of us that the Crown recognizes responsibility for tidying them away. Mostly they are towed to sea and sunk.

Both stranded whales and pupping seals are best seen from a vantage point on the cliffs. And if there are no great mammals to be seen, then you may allow your gaze to rest on the character of the slopes themselves, a study well rewarding. The trampling of seals and birds has a profound effect on cliff vegetation. Not only do the animals stamp and roll about on the surface, but they produce mineral-rich droppings which provide nourishment, sometimes too much of it, for the plants.

The plants which colonize this roosting and breeding ground between land and sea cannot move to warmer climes when breeding is done, but must complete their life cycles in the teeth of gale-blown spray, the scorching heat of summer, come rain, snow, frost or landslide. The land plants which creep closest to the sea itself are lichens of the splash zone, themselves often colourful splashes of brilliant colour. Lichens sometimes pave the way for more demanding plants, by holding some moisture, but most of the cliff colonists rely on a crack or crevice to provide a first foothold or, if the crevice is big enough, a relatively sheltered micro-climate. As the structure of cliffs and the local environment are so variable no clearly defined plant communities occur, but certain species are characteristic. Rock samphire, for example, is a typical plant of rocky cliffs at all heights, often springing from a tight crack with no apparent soil – its long tough root tapping deep moisture and tolerating a high degree of salinity. The dainty thrift and sea-campion share these probing roots, a necessity in a free-draining environment where there may be little or no soil let alone soil humus to hold the moisture. When fresh water is available, it is often in excess, washing downwards in rivulets which sweep seeds, soil and whole plants to the inhospitable sea below.

This unstable environment is something which cliff plants must live with, and many species – like the sea-cabbage with its huge blue-green leaves and pale yellow flowers – grow tough and strong in a very short space of time. The instability favours some, like sea-beet, which, with its spreading form, is quick to colonize the broken ground of new cliff falls and slumps.

Other plants favour particular micro-climates which are often formed by the activity of birds. Severe trampling and guano production around the breeding sites will kill all plant life, but moderate manuring will benefit greatly the sea-campion, and tree mallow for example grows lushly amidst the jumble of herring gull and cormorant nests. The trampling of puffins around their clifftop nest burrows lays the land bare, but as soon as the breeding season is over annuals, like the chickweeds, will take root for their short span.

On the open cliff face plants survive by developing water-conserving habits like fleshy leaves and stems, waxy cuticles, and small ground-hugging forms. On the cliff tops other battles must be fought with plant competitors, and the winners and losers are often influenced by the preferences of grazing rabbits. The plump pink cushions of thrift, for example, would often be suppressed by the vigorous grass *Festuca rubra* without the grazing and burrowing of rabbits. The burrows effectively deprive the overlying soil of moisture, but with a long root, reaching down as far as a yard, thrift competes favourably with the grass when rabbits are abundant.

As rabbits affect the community they live in, so all the plants and animals of the cliffs help to build their own landscape, feeding on each other, manuring the land and spreading seed. For creatures which are resident on the cliffs, unlike the visiting sea-birds which return year after year for one function only, a healthy cliff community is vital and many roles are played out here.

Many species of birds visit cliffs as opportunist feeders where, because of the great variety of micro-habitats, a full range of terrestrial insects and crustaceans may be found: grasshoppers, spiders, woodlice, ants, snails are all there, and birds of the neighbouring countryside will venture over the cliffs to seek them. But cliffs are unpredictable hunting grounds. Wind is a very important limiting factor and insect activity, for instance, is often at a standstill for days during severe weather. The cliffs are fine places on fine days – for pigeons to sun themselves on sheltered ledges, lizards to bask on sandy slopes, sand martins (which excavate their nest tunnels in soft cliffs) to scoop flying insects from rising thermals. But they are more often harsh and forbidding places where the true colonists are hardy and well adapted. For us, cliff tops make superb vantage points from which to watch perhaps the soaring and wheeling of fulmars, auks whirring on their short stiff wings, or seals bobbing. We may look up at the cliffs from the beach below or gaze seaward from the heights but cliffs themselves are wonderfully inaccessible and secret places.

Winter

Treyarnon, Cornwall (not NT).

A winter walk on the beach is almost as much a part of the British institution as the seaside summer holiday. We like to walk on the edge, whether dizzying cliff top or foot-splashing waterline, and are fortunate that so much of the coastline is accessible to us, particularly in recent years through the National Trust's 'Enterprise Neptune', the successful campaign to buy for the nation the most interesting and scenically attractive stretches of Britain's coastline.

This desire to walk the coast, for pleasure, is very much a twentieth-century phenomenon but many of the paths which we use today were first beaten out in the course of duty by the coastal patrol officers of the Revenue service during the heyday of smuggling in the last century. Nowadays one of the many benefits of 'Enterprise Neptune' is that under Trust ownership the cliff paths are expertly maintained and improved. These paths ride up hill and down dale, sticking close to the edge for the best views, but that edge has not remained constant. It changes – cutting back here, jutting out there – as the elemental forces of land and sea take their toll on the fabric of the land.

Winter is usually the best time to see these forces at work. Although coastal change goes on throughout the seasons the weather of winter usually conspires to give us the most dramatic episodes, many of which are chronicled by our social and economic historians as well as coastal physiographers. Cottages falling into the sea, whole villages washed away, farmland foundering. Such changes have colossal impact on the coast where they occur, and in some parts of the country land loss is an accepted fact of life.

Take the East Yorkshire coast of Holderness, for example, probably the best known case of coastal erosion in the country. It has been estimated that about eighty-three square miles have been lost since the time of the Romans. The sea cannot always reach up to a cliff to make its attack but here the low cliffs of easily eroded boulder clay are unprotected by a fronting beach because the southward drifting beach material is held back by Flamborough Head to the north, and so the erosive power of the waves is unchecked. As the friable glacial cliffs are cut back a lot of debris is produced but is soon swept away southwards by the predominantly northerly waves, so denying its parent cliff any protection in the form of a beach on which the sea might dissipate its energy. A small proportion of the material travels south to help build the sandy spit of Spurn Head, the rest is lost to sea, building banks and shoals we cannot see.

Whether or not a particular stretch of coast suffers erosion is probably determined by the nature of the rock more than any other factor. Holderness has a long history of erosion: in North Yorkshire Robin Hood's Bay is notorious for its crumbling cliffs and falling houses and here again the weak glacial material is the culprit. There are similar stories in East Anglia and Suffolk where former settlements of famous villages like Dunwich have disappeared to leave behind them the haunting stories of church bells tolling beneath the waves.

But however weak the cliffs may be they cannot be cut back and moved away wholesale unless the sea can get at them. Sea level is not constant. On the long-term scale of geological time the level of the sea has changed by more than 100 feet in places influenced, for example, by the melting of glacial ice which poured more water into the oceans. Such changes have created whole new coastlines and drowned others, leaving submerged forests as evidence. But on the day-to-day scale of our lives the actual level reached by the sea has a significance best appreciated when it reaches extremes as a result of the combined forces of tidal height and weather. A storm which reaches its peak at the time of high water of spring tides has far greater opportunity to wreak havoc than a storm of the same meteorological order acting at low water. Such combinations of tide and weather created the storm surges of 1953 and 1970 in the North Sea which did such tragic damage to the low-lying coasts of East Anglia for example. Similarly, the steep destructive waves generated

The ceaseless battle between land and sea.

by an easterly storm over-ran the shingle barrier beach at Torcross in South Devon at high water in 1979, plundering ill-sited houses and forcing the decision that a sea wall should be built.

To watch the sea in all its fury is an awe-inspiring experience. When you have witnessed crashing waves dragging a shingle beach away before your eyes or felt the sting of wave-flung pebbles it is easier to appreciate that, albeit on a gentler scale, the sea is carrying on its work all the time. The coastline is in a constant state of flux, never completely stable. Coastal changes are complex, depending in any one place on the weather conditions which in their turn affect the state of the sea and its conspiring land-based forces. But broadly speaking the elemental forces are either constructive or destructive, creating in the long term a particular type of maritime habitat and refining it, often with rhythmic changes according to season, in the short term.

The same force may be destructive in one situation, constructive in another. The summer wind which lifts and carries sand to lodge against an obstacle and found a sand dune is more likely to create a damaging 'blow-out' in duneland in winter. In summer the thrusting marram grass which thrives on sand inundation – growing upwards rapidly to reach the light – quickly binds the sand with its underground network of rhizomes and tough surface tussocks. In winter when plant growth is at a standstill, the wind can soon exploit a chink in the vegetation cover and lead to large-scale damage.

Fresh water, life-giver to the clifftop turf in summer, can destroy chunks of the habitat when heavy rainfall channels itself into erosion gullies, carrying away soil and stones as it plunges seaward over the cliff edge. Or too much may soak in, creating slumps and falls as chunks of the cliff become mobile. These slumps may be small bites out of the cliff top or huge, dramatic slips which create an entirely new habitat like the famous zone of landslips on the borders of Devon and Dorset, or the Warren at Folkestone. The rain water which creates erosion by slumping does, in moderation, encourage the flourishing of the plants which will bind the new unstable land. A fresh fall, bare in winter, will burgeon in spring and summer. Sea-beet, for example, is particularly associated with this kind of disturbed ground.

The work of drainage water, wind, sun and

ABOVE: Chesil Beach, Dorset. The shingle bank separates the sea from the Fleet—the brackish lagoon.

LEFT: chalk cliffs at Thornwick Bay, Flamborough, near Bridlington, Humberside.

frost which act on the cliffs is sometimes quite divorced from the work of the sea on account of a protective beach which denies it access. But if the sea can get to work on a cliff face it acts in several ways, all destructive, the rate of destruction varying according to rock type, degree of exposure, and depth of water. Waves which arrive at a cliff base in deep water exert an enormous hydraulic pressure on any air trapped in joints and crevices. The air is compressed by the oncoming wave and the sudden expansion when the wave withdraws creates an explosive force which can widen cracks and detach rocks.

When waves reach their target in shallow waters the debris which accumulates at the cliff foot is rolled and scoured across the sea-bed,

The striped cliffs at Hunstanton, Norfolk. A top layer of white chalk, a base layer of brown carstone and a thin band of red chalk between.

developing as it goes a relatively level rocky foreshore known as a wave-cut platform. When the abrasive action is going on, on an exposed shore, there's not much opportunity of seaweed growth, but an old wave-cut platform, no longer being eroded because conditions have changed, offers ideal conditions of gently shelving shore for the study of life on the rocky shore.

The material which falls does not remain long at the base of a cliff if the sea can get at it. Transport is a major role. Material is moved, according to its size, great distances away from its place of origin. The big boulders may not move far (until they are battered to a more manageable size) but by the time the rock has reached the size of shingle or sand grains it can be rolled along, lifted and carried by the waves. The process by which this movement is accomplished is known as longshore drift and on any stretch of coast the movement is in a particular direction according to the dominant waves. Any obstacle, natural or artificial, will arrest the movement, which is why we erect groynes when we don't want the golden sands to desert us. The sand piles high on the up-wind side of the groyne, leaving a convenient jump down to the lower side. Gradually, as the barriers do their work, the groynes are buried by sand on both sides and the beach is increased, built higher out of the sea.

It may be normal for a beach to enjoy constructive waves which build beaches, but a winter storm can be a rude interruption, changing the beach profile overnight. Destructive waves, steep seas with downward plunge and powerful backwash generated by strong onshore winds, often drag shingle and sand from beaches in winter. The material lies offshore, usually to be returned when more normal conditions prevail. Such onshore storms can also produce permanent features, ridges of shingle thrown high above the usual reach of wave action. The high storm ridges on Chesil Beach, for example, are a legacy of such conditions.

Storms can do enormous damage to land and property and change the character of the coast in low-lying areas. The North Sea floods of 1953, for example, removed completely some coastal dune systems which have since re-established themselves – showing the positive face of coastal change. On high-cliffed coasts the combination of tide and storm means that salt spray and wave-flung boulders can reach higher to destroy vegetation and ease loose rocks from their footings. It is fortunate for nesting sea-birds that most of these dramatic storms do occur in the winter when they are away from the cliff faces. In fact the birds are done a good turn as the coast is chipped and battered to provide new ledges, cracks and crannies to be exploited as nest sites in the spring.

Birds are quick to explore the new opportunities created by falling blocks or gentle weathering, and sometimes they, too, contribute to the process of erosion. Puffin burrows, like those of the neighbouring rabbits on the grassy clifftop slopes, weaken the skin of vegetation, lay ground bare and generally invite erosion by wind and rain. The same kind of damage is done, on a grander scale, by the trampling of human feet on grassy cliff tops. The plants which grow on exposed cliff tops are small-scale by nature, beaten into ground-hugging rosette forms to avoid excesses of wind, spray and desiccation, and are easily worn away in the shallow soil with its deficit of water. The familiar thrift, plantains, and stonecrops as well as the grasses hardly show their faces above ground level and are easily destroyed. Break-up of the plant cover has a very poor effect on the stability of the cliff top. Eroded gullies formed by rainwater run-off, and wind-blown hollows are commonplace. For these reasons the careful management of coastal footpaths is of crucial importance for the enjoyment and safety of people and the well-being of the wild inhabitants of the region.

In fact man's impact, deliberate or unintentional, is strongly felt on the coast. Because we don't like to see beach sand drifting away we build groynes, artificial 'beaches' in the form of concrete promenades and sea defences,

N.W.CUSA.

ROCKY COAST WITH ROCK POOL

A rocky shore on the west coast of Britain. It is a calm day in early winter but a heavy swell from storms in the far Atlantic occasionally breaks on the rocks. A spring tide is at low water and at our feet two kinds of kelp or oarweed are exposed, *Laminaria digitata* (1) and *Laminaria sacchariza* (2). On the fronds of the former are to be seen (3) a few blue-rayed limpets (*Patina pellucida*) and on the stem, or 'stipe', of the same plant there are (4) the egg-sacks of the lesser spotted dogfish (*Scyliorhinus caniculus*). The rock in the foreground is festooned with (5) serrated wrack (*Fucus serratus*) and there is also a little (6) bladder wrack (*Fucus vesiculosus*) which normally grows at a rather higher level. At the top (8) is a group of acorn barnacles (*Balanus balanoides*), which also encrust the more distant rocks, and lower down are four of (7) the common limpet (*Patella vulgata*) while near the edge of the tide (28) a painted top shell (*Calliostoma zizyphinum*) is active. On the rock beyond, besides an incrustation of barnacles, there are a few periwinkles (9) (*Littorina littorea*). To our right there is a rock pool. It is lined with (20) an encrusting red seaweed (*Lithophyllum* sp.) on which also grows (21) near the water surface another red weed (*Corallina officinalis*) and a single tuft of (18) a green weed (*Enteromorpha* sp.). Also in the pool, dimly visible in an oblique view of the water, there are a number of animals: (19) a prawn (*Leander serratus*), (17) a common sea urchin (*Echinus esculentus*), (16) a hermit crab (*Eupargus bernhardus*) in its portable home, the shell of a common whelk (*Buccinum undatum*), (15) a dog whelk (*Nucella lapillus*) and (11) a beadlet anemone (*Actinia equina*). On the rock beyond is another beadlet anemone, the tentacles withdrawn, and beside it (14) a snakelocks anemone (*Anemonia sulcata*) which is unable to withdraw its locks. There is also (13) a chiton (*Lepidochitona cinereus*) and, beyond, a small bed (10) of the common mussel (*Mytilus edulis*) on which (23) an oystercatcher (*Haematopus ostralegus*), with the white half collar of winter plumage, feeds. Nearby is (22) a purple sandpiper (*Calidris maritima*) and (24) a rock pipit (*Anthus spinoletta*). Offshore, in the sheltered water, there are two (26) eider drakes (*Somateria mollissima*) and (25) a grey seal (*Halichoerus grypus*) surveys the human intruder while others of the same species are hauled out on the reef on which also there rests (27) a great black-backed gull (*Larus marinus*).

piers to protect harbours and make safe landing for boats. Every action we take has an effect on the dynamics of the sea coast and its inhabitants.

The groynes which accumulate sand on their windward side also accumulate a jungle growth of weed, just as if they were naturally occurring rocks. Here, plants and creatures of the rocky shore can be found in the zone of a sandy bay, open to inspection when the tide goes down. But the concrete aprons and sea walls do not offer the same possibilities for colonization as do their natural counterparts. A protective shingle beach – often highly mobile during winter gales – can surprise you with its blooms in summer as well as its new-found positions in winter. By contrast to this kind of defence which allows breeding grounds for birds in spring and summer, the concrete versions are almost devoid of life. Cracks and crannies are definitely not permitted.

Man's work on the coast is, naturally enough, mainly to do with defence – guarding the land from assault. Sometimes we attack the coast too – quarrying and dredging, for example. Like the water in the oceans which is constantly in motion, the shingle and sand deposits of the beach and those offshore are always on the move. Material dredged from one place will be replaced, naturally, from an outside source. We undertake these arduous tasks for economic reasons, deep-water channels, building materials and so on, whereas the sea shifts its load around in response to physical conditions. From our point of view, the varying physical conditions provide a riot of changing coastal scenery, and from the point of view of plants and animals a potential new home is created every time a rock is shifted or a new sand dune begins to grow.

Man's influence at the coast naturally extends to the inshore islands which are one of the results of the sea's work of erosion. With the exception of seals and, in the far north, otters, for instance, most mammals have found their way to Britain's off-islands as a consequence of human activity.

In prehistoric times, men brought sheep and cattle to islands in order to take advantage of the summer grazing – at the same time helping themselves to the abundant supplies of birds and eggs. In mediaeval times they introduced rabbits in order to harvest their young in the winter. More recently, the export of island-fattened livestock has flourished because of the prime quality of the animals. The problems have always been those of transport and wintering.

In the St Kilda group, there have been Soay sheep for at least a thousand years, their ancestry directly relating to the Neolithic root-stock of domestication. Small, goat-like and dark chocolate brown, they are the most primitive of breeds, but they are able to endure the harsh winter without assistance. They owe their survival in such unchanged form to the benefits of island isolation – no fresh blood disturbing their genetic flow. Soays may also be seen in Ailsa Craig and Lundy, and there is a thriving flock on Cardigan Island, though the animals which were introduced to the Pembrokeshire islands of Skokholm and Skomer no longer exist. I remember the wild frustration of trying to capture these sheep on Skokholm, when Ronald Lockley wanted to establish a flock at his embryo field station at Orielton. However we tried, there was no way of herding them; they dashed in all directions and then found sanctuary on impossible cliff ledges. Unlike the currently fashionable domestic breeds, these Soays are very much at home on fearsome cliff slopes.

On North Ronaldshay, the most northerly of the Orkneys, there is a breed of small short-tailed sheep that lives largely on seaweed, their meat being dark and rich with iodine. Under the auspices of the Rare Breeds Survival Trust, a flock nucleus was shipped to the tidal island of Lihou, off Guernsey, some years ago. They flourished on a diet which consisted of one-third grass and two-thirds seaweed, and now there are about a hundred of them. Every day, as the tide drops back, the sheep pick their way over slippery boulders to graze the rich meadows of wrack and kelp.

Goats have wrought more havoc to the islands

ABOVE: Lundy; view towards the South Light.

LEFT: the lighthouse keepers reintroduced goats in order to enjoy their milk.

of the world than it is possible to imagine. Released by generations of island colonizers or passing mariners to multiply and provide milk and flesh on demand, they have taken to the feral life with gusto, reducing many a paradise to a barren slum. It might have been better for us all if these creatures, first domesticated thousands of years ago, had been left undisturbed in their rocky fastnesses in the far corners of Europe and Asia. But apart from their usefulness as a provider of milk, they have served sheep farmers in a curious manner. By eating the choicer grass, which is to be found on the most awkward cliff ledges, they reduce the incentive for the less agile sheep to try to emulate them – thus reducing the shepherd's losses.

Red deer on the island of Rhum, where they are studied by Nature Conservancy scientists.

On Lundy, in the Bristol Channel, feral goats were abundant, but the last survivors of a large herd of white goats were killed in the late nineteenth century. The Trinity House lighthouse keepers reintroduced them, for milk, in the late 1920s. At one time there was a wild population of some 200, though there are fewer today.

Broadly speaking, the same is true of red deer. Once ranging the greater part of Europe, they have been progressively exterminated by destruction of their forest habitat and, on islands, by persecution. In the nineteenth century they were reintroduced to the Scottish islands in the name of sport. As the years go by, the scramble for prize 'heads' has been overtaken by the more logical and ecologically acceptable concept of management, where the annual cull, though it may well be exercised by sportsmen paying large fees for the privilege, is nevertheless aimed at maintaining a healthy population. The victims are selected not for the excellence of their antlers but in order to leave behind a balance of age groups representing the healthiest stock. On the island of Rhum, in the Inner Hebrides, the reintroduced red deer are farmed by the scientists of the Nature Conservancy, whose object is to study the biology and management of the species. Though the native stock was exterminated in the eighteenth century, there are some 1500 of these magnificent beasts on the island today.

As part of the management programme the island also supports a couple of dozen Rhum ponies which serve as pack animals bringing in the deer carcasses from the hills. These small horses, never higher than fourteen hands, are the product of Arab sires and West Highland mares. Kept free of Clydesdale or other similar heavy-horse blood, they are typical of the saddle and pack animals which serve remote island communities. Big enough to do the required work, they have small appetites, fending for themselves throughout the year; though mares in foal and foals and yearlings get some extra feed. The Shetland pony is a triumph of selective breeding, less than eleven hands high, by comparison with the shire horse's seventeen. But the Icelandic pony is the typical form of light Celtic horse, one of several sub-species deriving from the original prehistoric European stock. Good load carriers but frugal eaters; some of them can subsist to a certain extent on a seaweed diet.

Like the sheep and goats, rabbits were brought to islands by farmers in search of an honest profit. While rabbit warrens were first established on the mainland, in the Middle Ages, the species could have been designed for islands, with their lack of ground predators. Rabbit meat and rabbit skins were long regarded as luxuries, fetching a high price.

In 1324 the Earl of Pembroke held the rights to Skomer Island, and at that time the pasturage was valued at £2.75, the annual return from rabbits £14.25. So a pattern of farming was established. Through the winter ferreters worked the warrens. In spring the sea-bird eggs and later the fat chicks were collected. Then the grazing was enjoyed by summering cattle and sheep. Arable farmers arrived in around 1700, building a farmhouse and exporting high-quality seed corn. The Skomer farm flourished till the mid twentieth century when labour and transport problems brought it to an end.

Through the centuries the warreners' rabbits have escaped, times without number, to set up feral populations and increase mightily. It seems incredible today to consider that at the turn of the twelfth century the tenant of Lundy was permitted, by privilege, to take fifty rabbits only in one year.

In 1955 myxomatosis wiped out the major part of all rabbit populations on the islands, as on the mainland, but the inevitable recovery took place and while the disease is well established, rabbits have come to terms with it. On some remote islands black rabbits, selectively bred for their fur value in ornamental trimming, can still be seen.

The influence of the rabbit on island pasture is clear – continuous nibbling produces a close-cropped turf which is springy and pleasant to walk over. The constant cropping encourages the spread of ground-hugging plant forms. Because the rabbits enjoy grasses, sea-pinks have room to flourish and decorate the cliff slopes; in fact the cliffside vegetation is held in equilibrium by their activities. However, it is true to say that where there are no rabbits there is a more luxuriant growth of more species of plants.

While the sheep, goats, cattle and rabbits were brought intentionally by island-colonizing man, other less welcome mammals arrived unintentionally. The mainland wood mouse, shrews and brown rat were transported along with the fodder for the domestic animals. Some of these creatures have undergone an island-change through the thousands of years in which they have been isolated from their original island stock. As living proof of the effects of ecological isolation we have the Rhum mouse, the St Kilda mouse, the Orkney vole and so on. Skomer is famous for its vole, an island race of the familiar bank vole, and it also has a field mouse of distinction. Although neither of these animals is a separate species in the strict scientific sense, since each can breed with its mainland cousins to produce fertile young, they nevertheless have distinctive features resulting from their adaptation to island life.

The Scilly shrew represents a creature with a counterpart on the mainland. One of two species on the British List, it has white teeth, unlike all mainland shrews whose teeth contain a red pigment. The white-toothed shrews, Crocidurinae, live only on Scilly and the Channel Islands; possibly descendants of a mainland population which was wiped out after the last glaciation or more probably the result of introduction by man, since they are common elsewhere in Europe. On Scilly, the animal has foxy ears and long silky bristles on its tail. Its hunting ground is the tide-tossed kelp on the strand line of exposed beaches. Indeed the strand line is a happy hunting ground for other mammals, as well as insects and birds. Apart from treasure-hunting beachcombers, rats and mice tunnel into the weedy piles searching for sandhoppers and carrion.

In the Scottish islands, and round the coast of Orkney and Shetland, otters are relatively common, leaving their webbed footprints in the sand. While they are retreating and sadly decreasing in England, their numbers are much healthier in the north, where they are more marine in character, fishing for sea fish and crustaceans close inshore. In areas where they are undisturbed they are to be seen during daylight hours, but otters are masters at concealment, and you need to cultivate your local contacts if you are going to see one.

While islands and, particularly, otters are hardly everyday experiences for most of us in the winter, there may often be opportunities for beach-walking along mainland coasts. And winter, time of the greatest gales and strongest winds, is the best time for the time-honoured pastime of wrecking. Far removed from the romantic fiction of the wild figure with his lantern enticing ships to destruction on dark winter nights, the true picture of a wrecker is a man patrolling the shore in the hope of finding a choice piece of timber or a crate of oranges – 'wreck'. But quite apart from valuable timber and odds and ends of all sorts, there are many natural objects of great beauty and interest thrown ashore by wind and current to find a place at the top of the beach.

On a calm day, the flat blue sea may look barren. The plunge of a hunting gannet may disturb the surface and hint at a great wealth of life – plants and animals attached to the sea-bed, floating or swimming at all depths, drifting on the surface, or just splashing in occasionally. Representatives of this storehouse of life, from the most primitive hydroid to an enormous whale, are quite likely to turn up on the beach; no longer hidden below the surface but open to our inspection. They will be found in a random straggle of material known as the strand line.

The water of the sea is in constant motion. This is obvious enough on a rough day when the wind has whipped up waves which pound and roar on the beach; but even during calm periods when hardly a ripple disturbs the surface, great masses of water are being shifted round the coast by tidal currents which are governed by the phases of the moon. As the water moves, so it transports any material which finds itself floating or in suspension without any independent means of propulsion. A fish may swim against the current, but a dead bird or a cuttlefish bone will bob along at the whim of tide and waves. Eventually, a proportion of the sea's cargo will reach the shore where, if an onshore wind is blowing, the waves will carry it to high-water mark on the beach, dump it, then leave it high and dry as the tide falls back. This abandoned material forms the strand line, stretching the length of a beach (until interrupted by rocky headlands, for example). If the next high tide, twelve hours or so later, rises even higher, this jumble of weed and assorted life will be pushed even higher up the shore, augumented by the latest arrivals. If, on the other hand, the tides are decreasing their range as they move from springs to neaps, a new strand line will form lower down the beach; then another below that at the level reached by the subsequent high tide. A whole series of strand lines may mark the progress of the tides from high-range to low-range, unless of course the weather changes and an onshore gale drives the whole lot up to the very top of the beach or an offshore breeze sends it all to sea again.

The most dramatic quantities and varieties of strand-line debris are usually found after a winter gale when the prodigious energy of the waves not only transports the existing cargoes but also tears up forests of seaweed, churns living shells from their sandy-bottom havens and batters others from their rocks. So strand-line hunting is a good winter pursuit, when the sea itself offers a less inviting playground.

At first glance the strand line appears to be nothing more than seaweed, mixed with a variety of man-made junk which always seems to include a smattering of odd shoes, light bulbs and plastic containers of every conceivable shape and size. Closer inspection confirms that seaweed forms the main bulk of the strand line, but prodding and searching will reveal many creatures which, in company with the weed, have been cast ashore to die.

If the weed is freshly cast ashore it may be damp and glistening (in contrast to that of an old strand line which is dry and cracked on the surface, slimy and rotting in the lower layers), but still a poor substitute for a view of the growing weeds which float and sway in the water. Dead though it must be, torn and tattered and hopelessly out of context, it is still possible to learn something about the life styles of the different species. Seaweeds have no roots through which to draw nourishment as this is gained from the water itself, but they do have root-like structures known as 'holdfasts' which effectively anchor them. Heavy seas will rip the holdfasts away from the rock and a careful look at the different kinds of weed on the strand line will distinguish the tenacious disc-like base of the wracks and the huge claw-like holdfasts of the *Laminaria*, for example. The differently shaped fronds, green, brown and red, some like the wracks with air bladders to float them upwards towards the light when the tide is in; some of enormous length like the 'bootlace' weed *Chorda filum* which may stretch for twenty feet, are heaped together irrespective of the position they occupied in the living community.

The growing plants form a forest of life with some creatures feeding on the weed, some seeking protection or attachment on it, or using it to shelter and retain eggs. But when the weed reaches the strand line these different creatures, with different life styles, lie cheek by jowl amid the weed, sharing only the certainty of death.

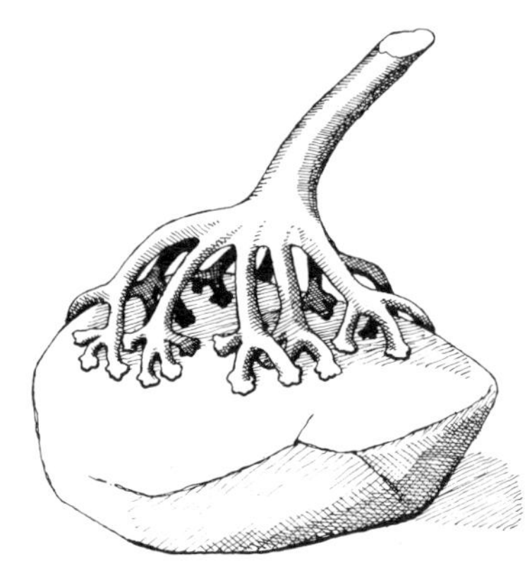

Holdfast of oarweed (*Laminaria digitata*).

The fresh strand line is most rewarding. The fronds of weed will bear rasp marks where common limpets have grazed. A beautiful blue-rayed limpet with its translucent shell and rows of bright blue spots may still nestle in a shallow depression eaten in the stipe (stem) of an oarweed, or may be searched out from the giant holdfast to which it migrates in late autumn to avoid being carried away when the fronds break off after fruiting. Many creatures which feed on the passing plankton fix themselves to the seaweed; others find temporary shelter. The weed of the strand line displays the limy tunnels of polychaete worms, the flabby remains of sea-squirts and the communities of sea-mats which carpet the fronds with minute compartments, each occupied by one member of the community. The holdfasts may shelter tiny porcelain crabs.

Dog whelks (*Nucella lapillus*) with egg capsules and with their principal food, acorn barnacles (*Balanus balanoides*).

Some creatures die on the strand line before ever reaching maturity. The most frequently found are the egg masses of the common whelk (a spongy group of off-white egg capsules which together form a mass about the size of a tennis ball), and the 'mermaids' purses'. The pale-coloured purse is the case of a dog-fish which, with embryo inside, is lashed to the kelp by twisting horny threads. The darker purses, easier to find, belong to the skates and rays. The developing fish may still be in the case when you find it, or a definite slit in the egg-case will show where it emerged into the sea after about six months inside.

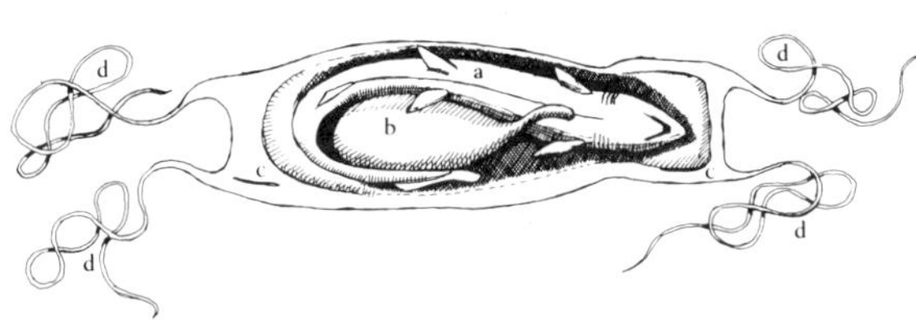

Egg-case of the lesser spotted dogfish (*Scyliorhinus caniculus*), dissected to show (a) the embryo with (b) the attached yolk-sac on which the embryo lives for some time after hatching. The slits (c) permit circulation of water to the developing embryo while the egg-case is attached by tendrils (d) to the deeper seaweeds.

On the strand line it is possible to find absolutely anything which has lived in the sea: sometimes common creatures which we can see easily enough at low water – mussels, winkles, cockles, whelks – empty shells destined to form a part of the beach sand, or meat-filled to form a ready meal for a scavenger. Others are rarely seen except dead on the strand line – razorshells which inhabit the sand at extreme low-water mark and below, sea-potatoes, sea-urchins, sea-mice, sand-masons, cuttlefish bones – curious creatures with curious names which can be identified from the pages of a good Field Guide. These creatures, or their remains, are merely interesting to discover and observe. The flexible tube of the sand-mason, for example, which is often dragged from the sandy shore by rough seas, leaving the long worm behind, is a wonderful piece of architecture. The tube-worm constructs the tube from tiny sand grains which are cemented with sticky mucus. When the tide is in the creature feeds on debris by protruding its tentacles through the top of the tube which the worm can reconstruct with more sand grains and prepare to weather another storm.

Other creatures are collected, not just admired. One of these is the 'bone' of the cuttlefish. The cuttlefish is in fact a mollusc but has its shell inside rather than outside like most snails, and this shell forms the bone which floats to the surface when the animal dies. Gleaming white, it is easily picked out on the strand line and if boiled for cleanliness proves a welcome gift for the pet budgerigar.

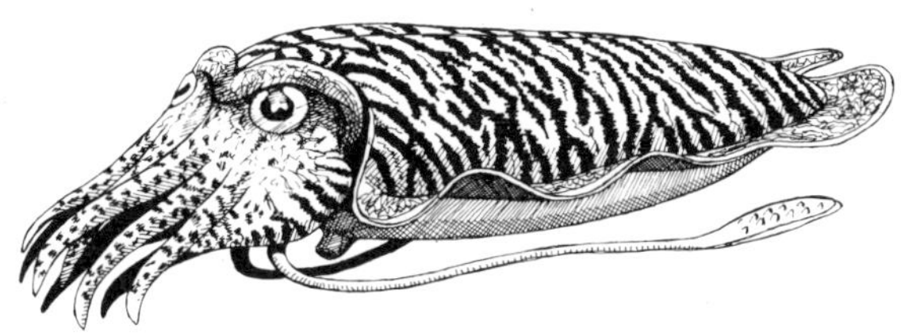

A cuttlefish (*Sepia officinalis*).

Some creatures stand out by virtue of their sheer size. Dead birds are quite easy to spot, and sadly they are often found to have died as a result of oil pollution or entanglement with a fishing line. Surface oil takes a particular toll of auks – razorbills, guillemots and puffins – as they spend so much of their year swimming on the surface. Shags and cormorants too are ready victims. Some oiled birds which are still alive can be treated at specialist cleansing units, reached by way of the RSPCA. If you find a dead bird it is always worth looking for a ring on the leg which, if sent to the British Trust for Ornithology at Tring, will reveal something of the bird's history.

Most of the organic debris soon disappears by natural processes for the strand line – an ephemeral habitat – supports a full community of scavengers and decomposers. As soon as the material is deposited it is visited by armies of creatures intent upon its destruction. Scavenging sandhoppers (*Talitrus*) feed on the rotting weed along with many land-living beetles, worms and flies. Kelp flies lay their eggs where the subsequent larvae emerge to a rich feast. More obvious are the birds which patrol the strand line to feed on the debris as well as the flies and sandhoppers which swarm to it. Herring gulls search out crabs, molluscs, old sandwiches and corpses of birds and fish. Here they find the marine equivalent of the rubbish tips on which they flourish inland. Crows are on the same job. Shore-birds, like the wonderfully camouflaged turnstone, work in busy parties turning the weed in search of small invertebrates. A surprising number of land-birds also visit the strand line to take advantage of the temporary bounty. Pied wagtails, robins and starlings are all part of the scene.

Quite often the human scavengers play a large part in the removal of strand-line material. On holiday beaches the authorities fear that the rotting material will prove offensive to the visitors and bulldoze it away. On a more positive note farmers and gardeners collect it as a rich source of humus and fertilizer. Whether a sackful for the cabbage patch or a trailer load for the market garden, these sea-borne nutrients have long been collected in the remoter coastal communities like the Isles of Scilly and the Scottish islands.

The humus and nutrients from the strand line which are carried away to fertilize the land can perform that same function for land plants at the top of the beach if the strand line is cast high enough. The humus, with its accompanying moisture, may make it possible for sea-beet seeds to germinate and flourish amid the otherwise sterile shingle; also sea-holly and common sea-blite often grow from the shingle in a line which marks an earlier strand line. A strand line of weed deposited to rot on a sandy beach may form the basis of a completely new habitat – sand dunes. Blown sand transported by the wind will fall when it meets an obstacle such as a ridge of weed, and provided it is high on the beach, above the reach of ordinary high tides, the pioneer plants like sand couch grass and lyme grass (which both grow rapidly with spreading rhizomes) soon begin to stabilize the sand. The succession which, if conditions are favourable, leads to mature dunes may have been triggered by the presence of a particular strand line.

These strand lines of the open coast can provide humus for the growth of land plants, but on the estuary beaches where strand lines are just as much in evidence they often play a more significant role. The high spring tides of autumn will bring in many seeds and concentrate these in lines at the very top of the beaches where such plants as sea-beet and oraches will sprout in the spring. Seeds and debris will form strand lines across the salt-marshes, too, and if not destined to grow they provide food for ducks and land-birds in winter.

A strand line can form anywhere where tidal water reaches, but those of the open coast are the most exciting for, in addition to all that weed and the common or garden shells, there is an element of surprise and the lust for treasure. Because of the system of surface ocean currents in the North Atlantic which results in water of tropical origin washing the western coasts of Britain, there is always the chance of finding an exotic creature, far from home, washed ashore by the prevailing wind. There may be Portuguese men o' war, turtles from the Caribbean, timber bearing goose barnacles, or tropical beans from a sun-drenched shore. And in addition to all this natural treasure there is always the chance of finding the other sort, a light bulb that works, a diamond ring or whisky galore!

Winter walking on estuary beaches may at first sight seem a tame offering by contrast with the storm-tossed bounty found on open Atlantic shores, but estuaries blossom late in the year and are at their best around Christmas, when the wintering birds are at their most numerous.

ABOVE: trampling feet and winter storms play havoc with dune systems. The fence-lines provide a welcome shelter for the Plants which struggle to bind and stabilize.

FAR RIGHT: Portuguese man o'war (*Physalia physalia*).

RIGHT ABOVE: loggerhead turtle (*Caretta caretta*). Turtles are tropical animals but several species, this being the most common, are occasionally reported in British waters.

RIGHT BELOW: a floating log of wood riddled with the borings of the shipworm (*Teredo norvegica*) and with a pendant group of goose barnacles (*Lepas anatifera*).

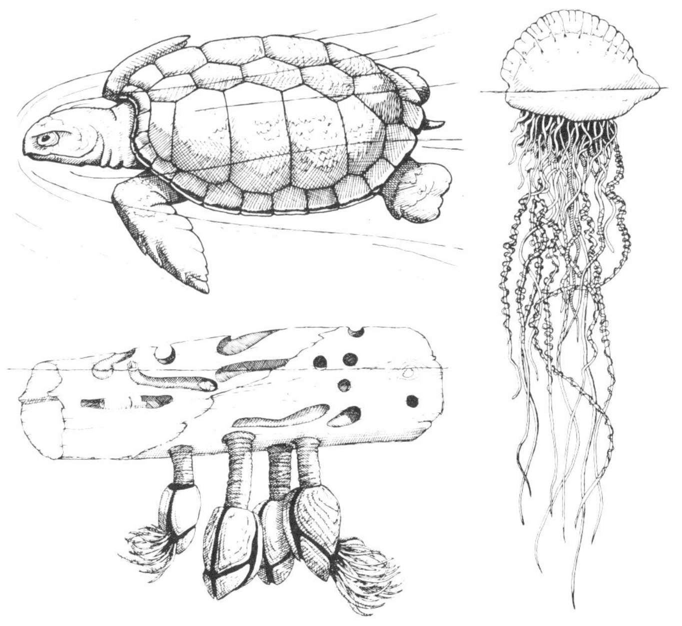

The Beaulieu river estuary at low water in summer (top). In the harsher days of winter, shore-birds like the turnstone (above left) will forage over the mud when the tide is out, while vast numbers of cockles (above right) will filter-feed when the tide is in.

They flock to these open desolate places because of the cornucopian riches supported by the open mudflats.

Mudflats – from the human point of view – are a transient habitat, visible only when the tide is out. And unless we have business on the mud, as bait-diggers or cocklers for instance, we rarely trespass on to this difficult terrain to witness at close quarters the teeming life which inhabits it. But they repay attention, and in Britain we are fortunate in having fine examples of tidal estuaries all round our coast.

Our tidal mudscapes represent some of the most fertile land, biologically, that we possess. They are more productive than the glowing corn fields or rich cattle pastures which may have contributed to their soil. These mudflats are formed in estuaries where, lacking the energy to transport a cargo of silt any further, the river has dumped it. Silt is collected by the river throughout its ever-downward journey towards the sea. In the upper reaches a fast flowing stream can erode and transport boulders and big stones, deriving the energy for this work from the steep gradient of its course. But as it flows nearer to the sea the heavier burden of stones and gravels can no longer be carried along; and by the time a river has reached the near sea-level region of its estuary it is bearing only the fine muds and silts which travel in suspension. The relatively sluggish flow of an estuary causes much of the mud to be dropped, and this deposition is increased when the fresh river water mingles with tidal salt water of the sea: by a process known as 'flocculation' the suspended sediments are attracted to each other and, clumping together, they grow bigger and heavier until they fall. As this process continues with every tide mudbanks grow.

Once a mudbank has started to accrete, the process is self-perpetuating. The dumped material causes the water to be more shallow, water flows less swiftly in shallow areas and is therefore less capable of carrying a load. More mud is dropped. This deposition continues over hundreds of years until a mudbank reaches high enough to support vegetation, at which point salt-marsh succession takes over in a bid to create solid land.

These changes from bare mud to salt-marsh community take hundreds of years; sometimes, in the over-deepened valleys of the West Country for example, which have been striving to fill their estuaries with mud since the end of the last glaciation, the mud deposits may be as much as a hundred feet deep. But whatever the depth of mud, it is always the shimmering surface layer – in contact with the life-giving light, water and air – which supports the chain of life from algae and bacteria through worms and shellfish to fishes and birds.

The material from which mudbanks are built varies from estuary to estuary, some being quite sandy with relatively large particles, others of very fine silt. But whatever the quality of the mud, the mudflats all share the experience of tidal inundation twice every twenty-four hours, and it is this tidal rhythm which governs the lives of all the creatures which live in, on and over the mud.

These tidal rhythms bring violent changes of environment – from dried-out mudbank baked by sun or lashed by rain or snow, to a habitat bathed by salty estuary water – which call for adaptation on the part of the inhabitants. They must sit out the unfavourable periods, in as much safety as they can devise, until the good times return. Such problems are shared with creatures of the open sea-shore, but on the mudbanks there are other problems which effectively limit the number of species which can live there. Varying salinity is the major problem: sometimes almost full-strength seawater washing in, sometimes – after heavy rain for example – a much higher proportion of fresh water. So the creatures which inhabit the mudflats as permanent residents are highly specialized to cope with this changeable medium. There are relatively few species, but they more than make up for this by occurring in vast populations, hidden from our view within the mud or in the murky water.

Soft mud is easy stuff to burrow into, and with its structure of fine particles (unlike the coarser grain of many sandbanks) is suitable for permanent burrows. Many of the worms and shells of the mudflats conceal themselves in the mud itself, probing above the surface into the tidal water to feed. The Baltic tellin (*Macoma baltica*), for example, one of the most widespread creatures of estuary mud, is a mollusc which lies hidden below the surface at all times, but is equipped with siphons which filter organic material from the water. This particular bivalve mollusc can also feed directly from the mud surface, using a siphon as a kind of vacuum cleaner to suck up minute particles of organic debris and living algae. This is also the method used by the peppery furrow shell (*Scrobicularia plana*) to achieve a meal. This mollusc, 1–1½ inches long and with markedly flattened shell, has a large foot muscle which allows it to burrow more deeply than the Baltic tellin. Another mollusc, the common cockle (*Cardium edule*), hardly burrows at all, the upper edges of the two shells often standing clear above the mud surface.

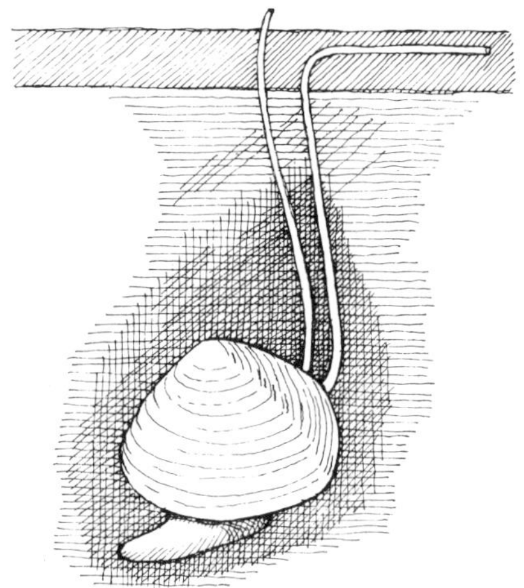

Peppery furrow shell (*Scrobicularia plana*), drawn diagramatically to show the extraordinarily long siphons with which this tellin feeds in the surface layers from its burrow deep in the mud.

Another abundant burrow-dweller is *Corophium volutator*, a crustacean, one of the sandhoppers. The usually U-shaped burrow conceals the creature when the tide is out (leaving the mud surface pock-marked with tiny holes) but when the tide is in and feeding is possible *Corophium* crawls over the surface picking up tiny fragments of organic debris with a pair of legs. It can feed within the burrow, also, sucking material into the mouth from the water current (required for respiration) passing through the burrow.

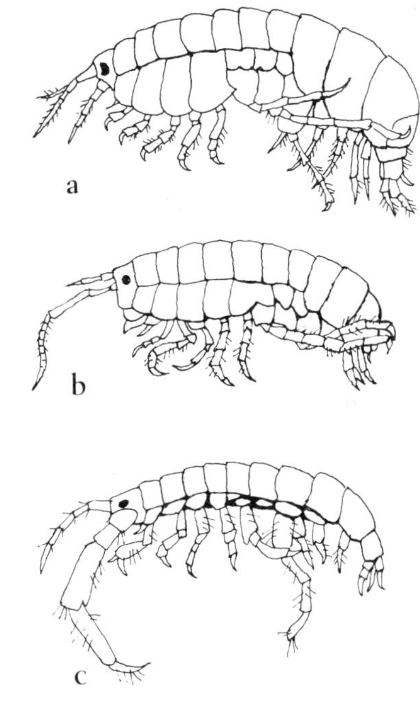

Three kinds of sandhopper. From above (a) *Gammarus locusta* (b) *Talitrus saltator* and (c) *Corophium volutator*. The first two are common animals of the shore, especially among rotting seaweed. The third is not strictly a 'sand' hopper. It lives in mud burrows.

Most of the estuarine worms also spend their lives buried in the mud. The lugworm and ragworm are probably best known, if for no other reason than their association with anglers. But they have very different life styles. The sedentary lugworm is a detritus feeder which spends most of its life at the bottom of the 'U' of its U-shaped burrow; swallowing the very mud in which it lives, the worm extracts and digests the organic component and then backs up the

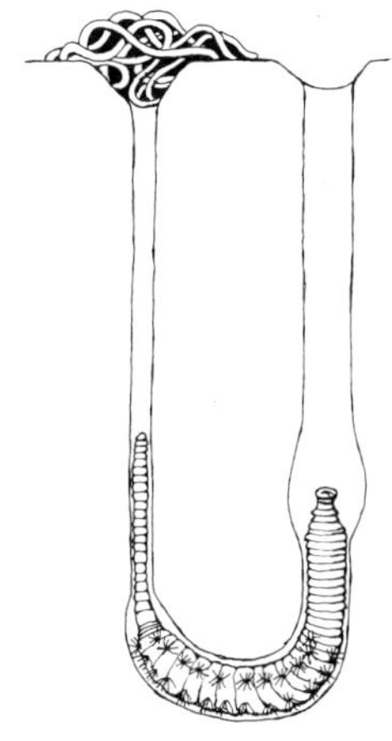

Lugworm (*Arenicola marina*) in its burrow, shown in section.

tail shaft of the burrow to reject the inedible portion as the familiar 'worm cast'. As the lugworm eats mud from the head shaft more subsides into the burrow to take its place, leaving the characteristic small depression found a few inches away from the cast. The ragworm, by contrast, is an active predator, although it does have a more or less permanent slime-lined burrow. This worm, with its characteristic red line of blood vessels running down the length of the back, reaches out of the burrow to scavenge on the mud and to catch creatures like the abundant opossum shrimps which pass by. These are seized with powerful chitinous jaws.

One tiny gastropod snail, *Hydrobia*, seems to have the best of both worlds, engaging in some feeding when the tide is out as well as in. These tiny snails, each no longer than a grain of wheat, occur at very high densities on fine mud. When the tide has just ebbed from the mudflats they crawl over the surface feeding on detritus. After an hour or so they burrow and continue to feed on organic material on the mud particles. When water covers the mud on the next tide they emerge from their burrows and manage to float, hanging upside down on the surface, trapping yet more feed from the water. When the tide drops they sink on to the mud and the cycle begins once more.

This tidal cycle is crucial to the lives of the mud-dwellers, and although life is easier when the tide is in – food is available and the worst excesses of the weather can make no impact – they are beset by predators which are also active during the high-water period. The ubiquitous shore crabs scurry across the mud, hunting and scavenging. Fish swim in to take advantage of the exposed invertebrate life. Grey mullet, for example, will suck up the mud, straining out living organisms and organic debris and also grazing on the surface algae. The flounder, most typical fish of the estuary, is a carnivore feeding on worms, crustaceans, or always ready to snatch the siphon of a feeding mollusc.

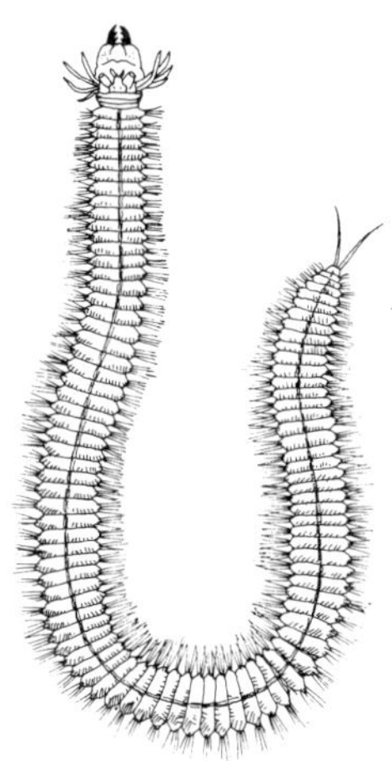

Ragworm (*Nereis diversicolor*).

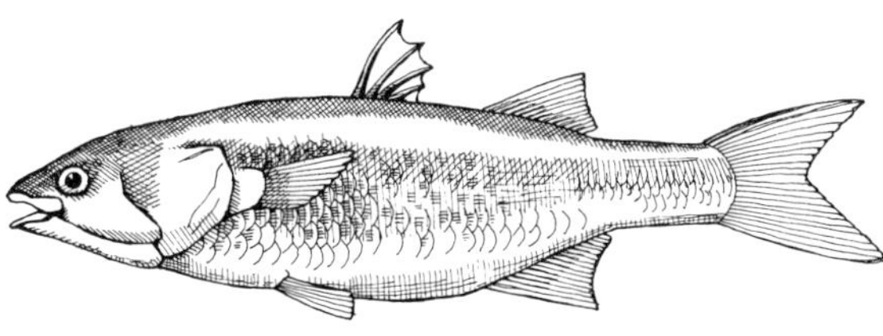

Grey mullet (*Liza auratus*).

When the tide covers the mudflats, their life seems as remote as the far-off jungle. But when the tide ebbs the flats become part of our world once more with the very obvious coming and going of birds and the tell-tale signs of many other forms of life.

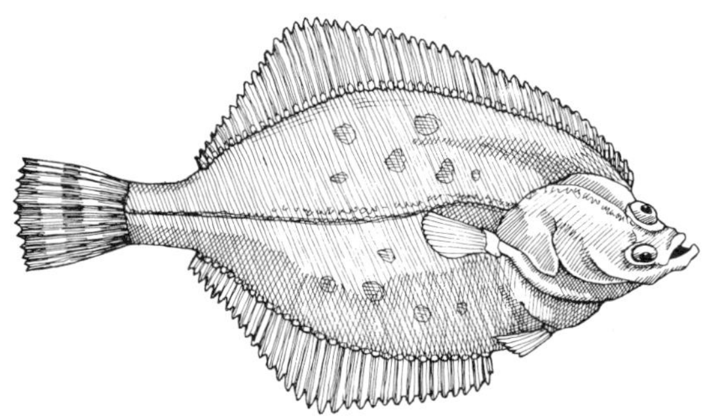

Flounder (*Pleuronectes flesus*).

The mud surface itself may be thick with tiny shells of *Hydrobia*, seen before they burrow. Worm casts point to the presence of lugworms, sheltering, hoping to avoid the bait-diggers, in their underground galleries. Shallow grooves in the mud point to a place where mullet sucked the surface a few hours earlier. Star-shaped markings will reveal the underground position of a peppery furrow shell which marked the mud with its probing siphon, reaching out in all directions in search of food when the tide was last in.

The surface of the mud is not uniform, but is often crossed by drainage gullies. Quantities of empty shells accumulate in these gullies – each different shell pointing to the presence of its species as a member of the living community. There may also be stony patches, sufficient to support a mussel bed where these molluscs, tight-closed against the air, may be inspected or collected for the pot at low water. The mussels (along with oysters) represent the true filter feeders of muddy water. Filtering food from the water is easier at sea, where more creatures employ this method of feeding, than in the silty waters of the mudflats where filter and respiration mechanisms can easily become blocked by fine particles. Cockles, too, are usually more abundant on clean sandy beaches, but they're well worth seeking on the grittier parts of mudflats for their delicious meat. They often lie partly exposed at the surface, to be hand picked, although it is more usual for cocklers to rake in search of them.

We may collect cockles for the pot, dig ragworms as bait for fish, or sieve a spadeful of mud to reveal the many different creatures which inhabit such a sample, but probably the best way to appreciate the vast quantities of life hidden in the mud is to watch the birds which also descend on the mudflats to hunt and feed.

Birds are only visitors to the mudflats. The curlews, redshanks, dunlin, plovers, godwits, ducks of all kinds, do not live there, but fly in to feed or to roost when the tide allows. Because they are relatively large and easily seen, to us they characterize the mudscape far more than the shells and worms whose domain it is. Autumn and winter are the times to catch this true flavour of the mudflats, when the resident herons, cormorants and shelducks are joined by vast numbers of waders stocking up for the winter on the rich invertebrate life. These waders arrive in their thousands – trickling in from the breeding grounds from July onwards to reach a peak around the turn of the year – and the different species are able to feed amicably together on the same mudflats because each chooses a different victim or a subtly different time to exploit it.

The waders find food by touch, taste and movement, watching for tell-tale signs of a retreating worm, searching with sensitive beaks. Creatures which may lie exposed at the surface like the tiny *Hydrobia* or the armour-plated mussels are no more vulnerable than the crustaceans, molluscs and worms concealed within the mud, for the birds are equipped to winkle them out. Long-billed curlews search and feel for the deep-burrowing lugworms and ragworms; short-billed dunlin catch the slightly hidden *Corophium*, for example. Beak length is obviously important, making it physically possible for different birds to reach different prey at varying depths, but birds also employ different methods to hunt the same prey in various parts of the mudflats and at different stages of the tide. The redshanks and shelducks, for instance, tend to hunt at the water's edge, following the ebbing tide, to prey on *Macoma*

Avocet, aggressively displaying in defence of its eggs. In winter, these elegant birds congregate on the Exe and Tamar estuaries in Devon.

and *Hydrobia* before they burrow. The grey plover concentrates on ragworms, hunting by sight like all the plovers, watching for movements at the mud surface. The plover, with its relatively short beak, must catch this worm at the surface, whereas the curlew with its long down-curved beak can probe down and extract them from their slimy burrows. Oystercatchers, with their strong red bills, can probe delicately in the mud for worms or shells like peppery furrow or shallow-buried cockle, but their dual-purpose beaks are equally happy to smash mussels, hammering away at one valve until it breaks or inserting the beak between the shells to cut the adductor muscle which holds the two shells together. In this way the oystercatchers will work diligently at the mussel beds until finally forced off, reluctantly, by the rising tide.

Avocets, while superficially as black and white as the oystercatchers, have long turquoise legs and delicately upturned bills, the mirror image of the curlew's probing tool. Scything the surface of the mud or the shallowest edge of the tide, they sieve *mycid* shrimps. They breed in large numbers on the north-east coast of continental Europe and in small numbers on the coastal lagoons of Suffolk, particularly at the Royal Society for the Protection of Birds reserve at Minsmere, a birdwatchers' paradise between Southwold and Aldeburgh. They winter in the milder south-western estuaries of England, as well as on the Mediterranean coast, and one of

A sea-bed of eel grass exposed by the falling tide. Choice feeding ground for brent geese. Also in the picture are clumps of japweed, the invading *Sargassum muticum*.

the annual pleasures for National Trust Centres in the West Country is the exploration of the Tamar estuary in December, when we brave the worst of the weather in order to see the elegant parades of avocets as they feed through the flooding tide.

Brent geese spend the winter on our coastal mudflats, places like Foulness in Essex, Chichester harbour and Exmouth, after a breeding season spent along the coastal strip of the Netherlands, West Germany and Denmark. Typically close packed, and growling away at each other, these 'sea-geese' roost on the open water waiting for the falling tide to reveal the beds of eel-grass which they graze. Up-ending at first, then walking as the water recedes, they feed on the ribbon-like leaves and juicy rhizomes. When the eel-grass has been worked out, they turn to other green vegetation in sequence, till in spring they take the succulent glasswort and, more often nowadays, the protein-rich new grass grown by coastal farmers who do not much appreciate the visitors. From the brent's point of view, they are simply taking each food item in turn, as it is at its most active growth period, when the maximum amount of protein and nitrogen is in the growing tips. But the preferred food is the lush eel-grass, and they seem most content working the open mudflats while the tide allows.

When the incoming flood-tide covers the mud the scattered waders begin to crowd together on the steadily diminishing feeding grounds. While some of the larger species, like curlews, godwits and plovers, may have achieved full bellies and moved off to roost earlier, the smaller ones will feed hard until the last possible minute, sometimes changing their feeding techniques as

Sea-aster (*Aster tripolium*).

Herons jealously guard their fishing rights. A young bird like this must work the least rewarding shores.

dry mudbank is overtaken by rising water. The shelduck, for example, digs in the surface for *Hydrobia* (its principal food) when the mud is dry, scythes its beak across soft wet mud for the same tiny snail, and dips its head right in when the water is too deep for dabbling. But when at last the mud is finally covered all the birds fly to roost – on nearby fields or salt-marsh, sometimes (like cormorants and herons, for example) in waterside trees.

Feeding time for these birds is governed strictly by the availability of the mud and so, whether day or night, they must feed when the tide is out. The same regime dominates the life of the inhabitants of the mud itself which must rest (and hope not to fall prey to a bird) when the tide is out and feed (hoping not to be caught by a fish) when the tide is in. Because of the coming and going of the tide the inhabitants of the mudflats are always on the move; either up and down in their burrows, or away to roost. The habitat, hidden from us as it is for half the time, is also a place of change. Change is a natural part of the natural world. Left to themselves the mudflats will grow high enough to support plants and succession will lead to a salt-marsh. But problems for wildlife begin when these relatively slow changes are exchanged for giant schemes for reclamation, airports or water barrages. When internationally famous wildlife sites like the Wash or the Ribble Marshes come under threat of development, it is rightly the birds which are highlighted by conservationists, but the birds, which flock to these deserted places in countless thousands, just represent the top of the chain of plant and animal life which makes up the complex community of the mudflats.

Apart from the eel-grass, there are few other

plants which can endure the open expanses of mud. The first intimations of a more extensive sward come nearer the high-water levels. Here where the mudbank is exposed to the open air for two or three consecutive days even at high water, in other words during neap tides, the first true salt-marsh plants can gain a foothold. Glasswort is one of the first settlers. Sprouting from the bare mud like a forest of miniature trees, the salt-tolerant little plants trap yet more silt – as much as $1\frac{1}{2}$ inches a year, most of it in the autumn. The fleshy stems and branches, which are well adapted to retain the plant's moisture, are smoothly curved to offer the least resistance to the currents which will try to shift the seedlings from their shallow-rooted anchorages.

Cord grass, the other main pioneer on the lowest level of a salt-marsh, can establish itself where stronger currents prevail. This relative newcomer (which first grew in Southampton Water in the 1870s and has since spread all round the coast) is taking over the role of primary colonist in many places. A vigorous hybrid which can grow from root fragments as well as from seed, it generally accumulates between two and four inches of silt a year although as much as six inches has been recorded. In the pioneer zones of the lower marsh these plants spend much of their time submerged, accompanied by creatures of the mud like molluscs and worms. Fish and shrimps will swim amongst them when the tide is in while birds will feed on the plants when the mud is revealed at low water.

As the silt trappers continue their work the marsh is gradually raised so that the land is not covered so often by water. Spring tides will flood in to deposit seeds and nutrient-rich silt, but neap tides allow a breathing space for germination and the establishment of a greater variety of plants. Sea-lavender, thrift and sea-aster provide summer carpets of pink and mauve amid the grassy turf of the middle marsh.

Given time, and the accumulation of more silt, the oldest part of the marsh will raise itself above the reach of all but the highest spring tides. Here the vegetation is dominated by grasses, reeds and rushes. The topmost levels taste salt water only at the extreme high tides of the spring and autumn equinoxes. The salt-marsh is now well on the way to becoming dry land and will have spent at least a hundred years developing.

At this stage, when nature has already done most of the work, it is an easy matter for man to keep out all tidal water with a sea wall, allow rain to wash away the salt, and so reclaim fertile land for agriculture. This kind of reclamation has been going on – around the Wash, for example – since Roman times. In Morecambe Bay, another of Britain's major salt-marsh areas, a great acreage has been embanked and reclaimed but the resulting land, built mainly of sand rather than silt, is less fertile.

The lower, younger marsh will be inundated by salt water at most tides, with a gradual decrease in flooding towards the upper marsh. The zones of vegetation which reflect these environmental differences are threaded by creeks and channels and dotted with salt pans which form distinct habitats within the salt-marsh. As the tide floods in over the mud it often becomes channelled by small irregularities like stones or clumps of vegetation. The last of the receding tide will leave by this same runnel and so a drainage pattern is begun. The water is deeper and so flows relatively swiftly in the embryo creek, with a scouring action which perpetuates the pattern until deep-cut channels cross a mature plant-rich marsh. The creeks cut across the plant zone, displaying their own particular kind of vegetation. Creek sides are often near-vertical and here algae, like *Vaucheria thuretti*, cling on with a gelatinous secretion. On creek banks the characteristic plant is sea-purslane, a bushy perennial which way-marks the channel course with its neat grey-green leaves and small yellow flowers. Demanding good root drainage, this plant flourishes on the banks which are raised a little above the adjacent marsh because of increased deposition here.

These creeks often become blocked. Banks

may slump and collapse or a vigorous clump of cord grass fill the channel. The creek section above the blockage will probably develop into a salt pan. The cut-off creek gets an extra dose of salt water every time the spring tide, which floods the whole marsh, fails to drain through its accustomed channel. Conditions become more and more saline as evaporation gets to work, until all plant life is banished. On the bare salty mud the tiny snail *Hydrobia* can manage, but few other worms or molluscs of the mudscape. Seasonal changes, rain, will decrease salinity for a while and gradually salt-tolerant plants like glasswort will start the cycle over again – a new salt-marsh succession on the pan. If the pan is first taken over by cord grass, the growth is so quick that the pan may quickly show its identity as an island of this stout grass.

Hardy pioneers of the mudscape, *Hydrobia* snails clustering on glasswort, or marsh samphire (the poor man's asparagus).

Although these distinct sub-habitats emerge in the generalized picture, it is the regular flooding which unifies the salt-marsh. The plants are adapted to tolerate salt water one day, sun and rain the next, but the animals cope by indulging in a variety of movements. Birds, for example, seem the very essence of the remote salt-marsh landscape. It is no place for them to breed (the mute swans which attempt it often find nests washed away or eggs chilled by the rising tide) but in other seasons the salt-marsh is a mecca for feeding and roosting. Waders, curlews and godwits, for example, which feed in earnest when the low-water periods reveal protein-packed mudflats, will roost on the salt-marsh during high water. Herons rest and preen here after fishing. Wild ducks, like widgeon, are sustained in winter by the quantities of seeds which are washed in at high tide to be found and eaten when the tide falls back. Birds may be the most obvious, but all creatures of the salt-marsh must live by the tides. The many insects, spiders, grasshoppers and bugs living amongst the plants are the same species as those of the adjoining land – they have no special adaptations – so when high water threatens they must escape by climbing up stems, swimming, walking or flying, often to be hawked by swallows and martins on fine summer evenings. The bodies of those which don't manage to escape will join the debris washed in and deposited by the tide. Where the debris is concentrated in a strand line it is worth investigating for the many shells and cases – shore crabs abound – seeds, pellets, plant and animal remains of all kinds which tell so much of the life of the surrounding waters. This material will be picked over by scavengers like gulls and rats. Mammals visit when the tide is right. Rabbits are common grazers, eating grass and cutting short the strip-like leaves of sea plantain; foxes, hedgehogs, grey squirrels and mink are not uncommon hunters.

Shipload Bay, North Devon.

Gazetteer
of National Trust Coastal Properties

Compiled by Brian Le Messurier

What follows describes the Trust's coastal properties starting on the south side of the Bristol Channel and following the English and Welsh coastline anti-clockwise to end at Gower, with Northern Ireland being dealt with from north to south. In some cases, where there is a proliferation of units, several properties are grouped together, as for instance on the South Gower coast and the Helford River.

Nearly all the National Trust's coastal sites are included; only a few very small or sensitive properties are omitted. Readers will find the Ordnance Survey 1:50,000 maps helpful for locating access points.

The Gazetteer has been planned to bring out the essential elements of each place, without too much emphasis on acreage or the history of its acquisition. Such information is obtainable in the book *Properties of The National Trust*, published every five years – last edition 1983. Opening times of houses can be discovered by referring to the *Properties Open* booklet, which is published annually, or from the free leaflets distributed widely by individual Regions of the Trust.

A list of the Regions with coastal properties and their addresses, and their geographical responsibilities, is given at the end of this book. Further information about the places mentioned can be obtained from the Regional Information Officers at these addresses.

ENGLAND

AVON **Sand Point and Middle Hope**

A narrow two-mile east-to-west hump of limestone, 190 acres in extent forming the northern prong of Sand Bay, three miles north of Weston-super-Mare.

The steep southern slope dips towards neighbouring marshland, and the northern (Bristol Channel) face exhibits rock outcrops and small cliffs. The vegetation is zoned from exposure-cropped turf at the seaward end of Sand Point to scrub slopes of hawthorn, blackthorn, elder, wild rose and bramble further inland. Sea-campion and rock samphire grow on the rock faces.

The scrub provides a habitat for thicket-loving birds such as whitethroat, greenfinch and linnet, and warm days bring out a variety of butterflies and moths, including gatekeepers and skippers, burnet moths and humming-bird hawk moths.

On the eastern end of the property are some ancient cultivation banks and lynchets. At the other end is Castle Batch, probably a Norman motte. There are also some Bronze Age barrows. At the foot of the ridge are the remains of the mediaeval Woodspring Priory, now the property of the Landmark Trust.

The area is approached from the south by the minor road from Weston, and there is a car park at the road end.

SOMERSET **Brean Down**

A bold 159-acre peninsula 300 feet high, poking a limestone finger over a mile into the Bristol Channel, and forming the southern arm of Weston Bay.

Brean Down's landscape is a palimpsest of history: one culture after another has used its windy acres for a variety of purposes. Bronze Age man buried his dead here; Iron Age man used it as a promontory fort; the Romans built a temple about AD 340; a little later cultivation plots were tilled nearby; in mediaeval times rabbits were encouraged to breed for their flesh and fur.

Then, in 1867, a massive fort was built, one of the Palmerstonian forts, designed to protect the Bristol Channel. A plan to build a pier in the 1860s as the first stage of the Brean Down Harbour Scheme came to nothing, and the work was destroyed in a storm. Various twentieth-century wartime works have added their own scars to the catalogue of human use.

Sedgemoor District Council leases and maintains the Down, which can only be reached by the minor road approaching north through the village of Brean. A large car park is situated at the road end. The Trust publishes an illustrated leaflet about the Down.

Selworthy Beacon and North Hill

The Trust owns four and a half miles of coast between Porlock Bay and Minehead, for here the enormous Holnicote Estate meets the Bristol Channel. Of this vast area of 12,443 acres, 9848 acres were given to the Trust in 1944 by Sir Richard Acland Bt.

The underlying rock here is mostly Devonian slate, but at either end of the property, at Hurlstone Point and Greenaleigh Point, it is made of Foreland sandstone. The land along this strip is prone to landslips and the official line of the South West Peninsula Coast Path (which starts at nearby Minehead and goes right round to Poole Harbour in Dorset) is routed inland to avoid the tortuous ground, steep unstable side slopes and deep-cut combes. However, a new rugged footpath, lower down the coastal slopes, has been provided by the Trust. It is tough going, but popular with experienced walkers. The official coast path passes along an elevated ridge with a generous scattering of Bronze Age barrows, and past Selworthy Beacon (1013 feet), a splendid viewpoint.

This is a breezy upland, separated from the mass of Exmoor by a deep wooded valley. Gorse, ling and bracken are everywhere, and the pretty blue heath milkwort flowers throughout the summer. Tormentil is common, straggling along the path edges. The area was used as a tank training ground during World War II, and the military road can be traced.

The purchase of Greenaleigh Farm by the Trust in 1985 means that the six miles of coastline from Bossington to Minehead are owned either by the Exmoor National Park or the National Trust.

The most obvious birds are meadow pipits, stonechats, whinchats and skylarks. This is not a good coast for sea-birds, since there are few rocky cliffs.

Bossington Hill, an abrupt eminence rising steeply from the fertile Vale of Porlock, is the resort of hang-gliders who soar over this low-lying patchwork of fields like winged dinosaurs.

DEVON [NORTH] **Countisbury, Glenthorne and the Foreland**

Five miles of steep hog's back cliffs east of Lynmouth, rising to 1057 feet at Barna Barrow.

The Foreland – Devon's most northerly point – thrusts a lighthouse-twinkling shoulder into the Bristol Channel. Down the arid, scree-sloped valley known as Caddow Combe (see pages 46 and 47) the Trinity House road follows a hair-raising course, closed to private vehicles, but giving pedestrians a good view of this strange landscape. Away to the east stretch the wooded slopes of Glenthorne Cliffs, perhaps the loneliest length of coast in the South-West. Between the Foreland and Lynmouth lie Sillery Sands, a steep climb down but in demand as a beach on a coast with few bathing places. Above the beach is the testing incline of Countisbury Hill, more than a mile long, and higher still is the Iron Age earthwork on Wind Hill. The Trust's Exmoor Basecamp, which offers hostel-type accommodation to parties of young

The Great Hangman, North Devon, with Water Mouth in the foreground.

The Foreland, from Lynton, North Devon.

people, is in the hamlet of Countisbury. A leaflet map describes the area in detail.

Woody Bay, Heddon's Mouth and the Great and Little Hangman

Four stretches of coastline making up about six miles. The moorland-by-the-sea scenery of the Great Hangman contrasts with the steep tree-covered slopes of Woody Bay. The Great Hangman is one of the characteristic hog's back hills of the North Devon coast. It rises steeply to 1044 feet. The shapely Little Hangman was purchased by the Trust in 1984 and is more frequently visited than its larger relative. The pleasant walk up from Combe Martin passes behind Wild Pear Beach which can be reached down a zig-zag path. Seals are sometimes seen offshore.

To the west of Combe Martin the wooded slopes above Golden Cove are owned by the Trust. The exceedingly steep (213 steps) descent to the shingle beach of Broad Strand is worth attempting at low tide for those sound in limb. At high tide the beach is under water. Heddon's Mouth is the sea end of a very deep scree-sided valley of a particularly stark and primaeval character. Down its length hustles the river

Woody Bay, North Devon—looking through the trees to the Bristol Channel.

Heddon, a rocky watercourse haunted by the bobbing dark brown and white dipper and the sleek grey and yellow-grey wagtail. Trout are to be seen in the clear pools between the rapids.

Woody Bay's many acres of dense woodland (much of it sessile oak) are in complete contrast to Heddon's bare rock. Eighty years ago a grandiose plan to develop an up-market resort here, served by the sharp-prowed Bristol Channel paddle-steamers, collapsed when its sponsor was convicted of embezzlement. A leaflet map describes the area in detail.

Ilfracombe to Croyde Bay

About ten miles of cliffs, dunes and coves, interrupted by small sections of non-National Trust land. Part faces north, and part west.

Two contrasting headlands, Baggy Point (sandstone) and Morte Point (slate) thrust westwards, separated by the two-mile Woolacombe Beach, raked by Atlantic rollers and having as its backdrop the extensive dunes of Woolacombe Warren and the smooth outline of Woolacombe Down.

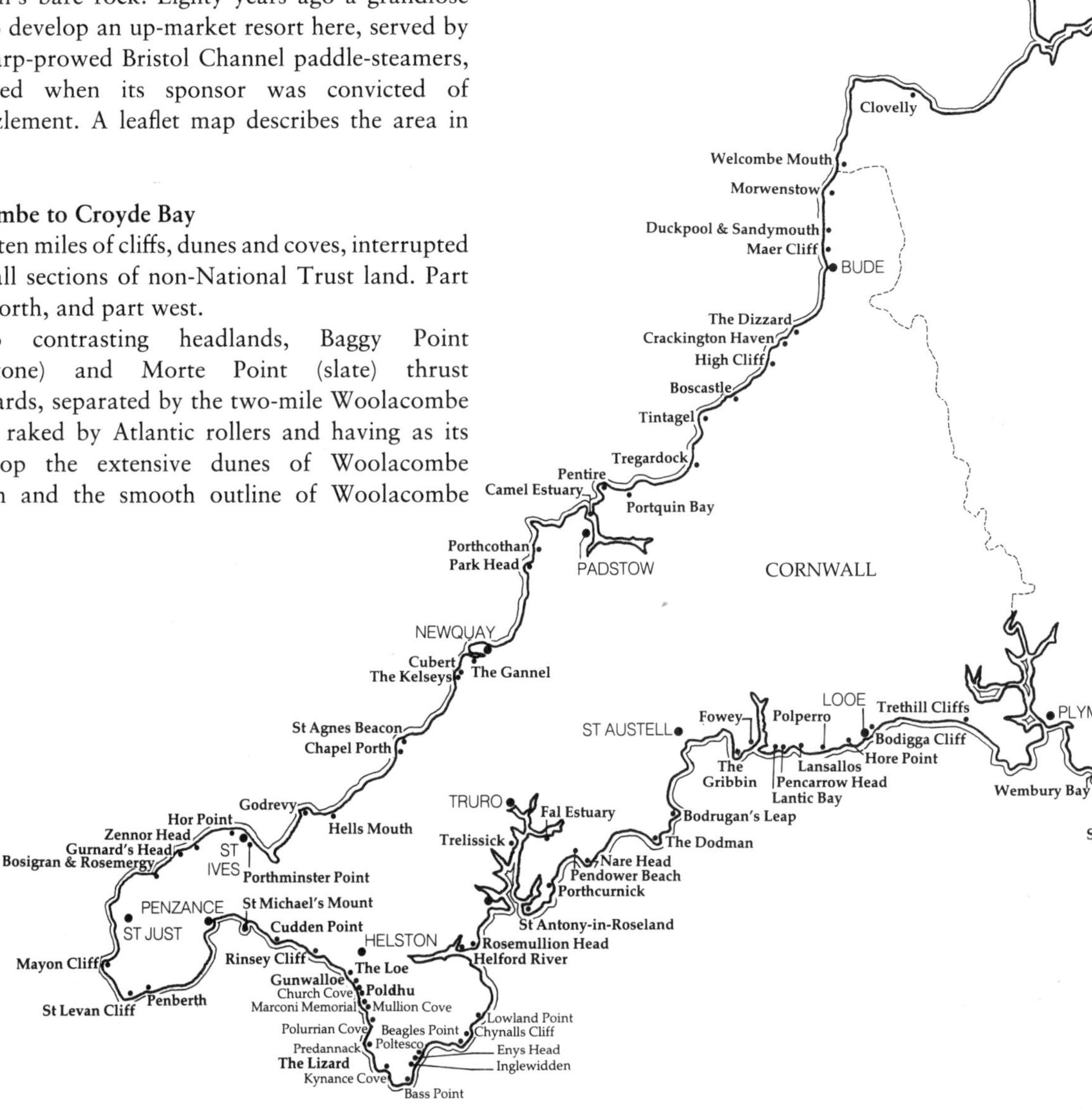

Baggy Point is the best place on this property to observe birds. Vertical cliffs hundreds of feet high are the playground of rock climbers and the haunt of nesting birds, but climbers are asked not to climb between 15 March and 15 June. Gulls, fulmars, shags, cormorants, jackdaws, ravens, kestrels and other birds of prey breed in the locality. Near Croyde Bay the cliffs are colourful in the summer with the flowers of the Hottentot fig, a mesembryanthemum introduced from South Africa.

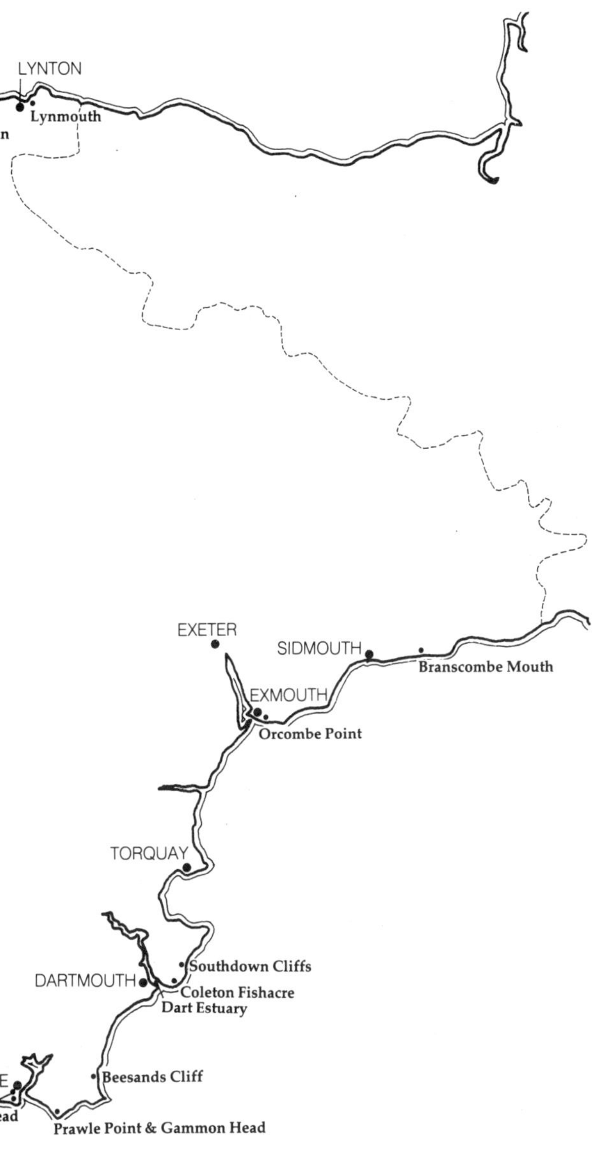

The north-facing coast is ideal for walking; fine paths undulate the grassy sheep-grazed slopes. Damage Cliffs are notable in springtime for the primroses blooming underfoot. In 1984 a new access to Sandy Cove, 300 yards west of Lee, was made possible by the provision of a stout wooden staircase of eighty steps, built on site by Trust wardens and Manpower Services Commission labour, and financed by the Countryside Commission. The coast path reaches Ilfracombe down the Torrs Walk, a well engineered late nineteenth-century path cut out of the slaty rock. Two leaflet maps describe the area in detail.

The Hartland Coast

About three miles of north-facing cliffs between Clovelly and Hartland Point. Shipload Bay (see pages 126 and 127), which marks the western limit of the property, is a delectable beach when the tide is out, but is only reached by a steep descent down 273 steps laboriously manufactured by the Trust's North Devon wardens.

At the other end of the estate Windbury Point and the Beckland Valley, with its coastal waterfall, are open areas of great charm in the spring when primroses and bluebells colour the hillsides. A leaflet map describes the area in detail.

Lundy

A rock-girt three-mile long island in the Bristol Channel, eleven miles from the nearest land, Hartland Point, leased to the Landmark Trust.

Visitors reach Lundy by ship from Bideford or Ilfracombe. There is no harbour, so passengers are ferried ashore to land on the beach.

Bird life is abundant, and there are interesting animals and plants. Human artefacts go back to prehistory and include the remains of crashed enemy aircraft from World War II. Operational lighthouses sweep the Bristol Channel at the north and south ends, and the Old Light stands on the highest point.

A Victorian church, massive in profile and making no concession to its exposed situation, also punctuates the island's skyline. Lundy is Norse for 'puffin island' but sadly few puffins are seen on Lundy at the present time and the breeding colony of gannets deserted the north end when the lighthouse was built there at the end of the last century.

The interior is an elevated plateau, and most of the buildings are clustered at the south end above the landing beach. Cottages, camping, a hostel and a small hotel provide a variety of holiday options. Enquiries about communications and accommodation should be made to the Administrator on Lundy (tel: Woolacombe 870870 during office hours).

Cornwall **Morwenstow**

Morwenstow, just inside North Cornwall, will forever be linked with Parson Hawker (1804–74), that strange eccentric figure immortalized by Sabine Baring-Gould in *The Vicar of Morwenstow*.

The Trust owns half a mile of coastline between Henna Cliff and Higher Sharpnose Point, running back for about a mile. Out on the cliff, and easily

ABOVE: the wooded slopes of the Coombe valley above Duckpool, Cornwall.

RIGHT: the beach at Sandy Mouth, Cornwall.

reached by a signposted path from the church, is Hawker's Hut, a small garden-shed type of building made of driftwood gathered by Hawker, and here he used to compose his once-popular verse, and watch for ships in trouble. For Hawker was the sailors' friend, and he buried more than forty drowned men in the churchyard.

The church and vicarage (not National Trust) bear the stamp of his personality. The vicarage chimneys represent the church towers of the parishes where he ministered before coming to Morwenstow.

Below Hawker's Hut is a rock climb of 150 feet classified as 'very difficult'. Christened 'Hawker's Slab' by the climbing fraternity, one wonders what the old man would have thought of this memorial.

In early 1986 the Trust added to its holdings in the area by purchasing fifty-three acres in the Tidna Valley which are let to a local farmer.

Sandy Mouth, Duckpool and Maer Cliff

The Trust owns about two miles of coast centred on these two beaches, and extending inland for some distance to include Stowe Barton, site of Sir Richard Grenville's Old Stowe House, from where he set out on his famous voyage to 'Flores in the Azores'.

Access to the coast is by narrow lanes from Kilkhampton through Stibb and down the Coombe valley past the Landmark Trust's cottages and mill

to Duckpool, or down the equally traffic-choked approach to Sandy Mouth. Here the Trust has provided a decent tea room and lavatories, and tucked the cars away in a landscape fold. A small waterfall tumbles over the cliff.

The cliffs on this coast crumble and slip and are not much frequented by sea-birds; land-based species favour the thickets and scrub.

A further mile of coastline is owned between Northcott Mouth and Bude, and this is one of the best places to observe the contorted and tormented carboniferous sandstone and shale rock strata comprising the cliffs. A walk at low tide along the beach will open up the prospect of what are known in geological terms as synclines and anticlines (folds in the rocks, with the strata sloping in opposite directions). A leaflet is available about the area.

Dizzard Point

A wild mile of coast where the cliff path is set back at the top of the 491-foot, forty-five degree, tree-covered unstable slope. The trees are oaks and this feature is not found further west. This 130-acre property was given to the Trust by the Duchy of Cornwall as its contribution to the Enterprise Neptune appeal.

Castle Point to Rusey Cliff

A nearly continuous four-mile stretch of coast broken at Crackington Haven (see pages 18 and 19). That part of the property north of the Haven is intersected by the west-flowing Coxford Water, which reaches the sea to the north of Pencannow Point by a thirty-foot waterfall. The remains of an Iron Age cliff castle can be seen to the north of the Coxford Water valley, and this gives its name to Castle Point.

Crackington Haven's buildings are best disregarded. The beach was robbed of its sand and gravel in times past, and there is now little left. Slate was exported from here, and in the 1830s there were plans to develop a new port to be called Victoria. The plans came to nothing.

From the Haven the reptilian promontory of Cambeak can be seen thrusting westerly into the Atlantic; a scramble along its arête is not for the faint-hearted! The views of the North Cornish coast are extensive. The coast path now heads south along the top of land-slipped cliffs above Samphire Rock and a wonderfully wild beach called the Strangles. Sand was fetched from here too, and the old donkey path is still visible in places, though partly carried away. A new path down has recently been completed by the Trust.

Rabbits are numerous, but the unstable cliffs of upper carboniferous rock are not suited to sea-birds.

The path climbs to High Cliff, the highest point (729 feet, 731 feet or 735 feet, depending on your source!) on the Cornish coast. From here also the views are wide, and extend inland to Bodmin Moor. Thomas Hardy used High Cliff for a dramatic episode in his early novel *A Pair of Blue Eyes*. He came to these parts as a young architect in 1870 and married Emma Gifford whom he met while working on the church at St Juliot, two miles south.

This end of the property may be visited from Trevigue where cars can be parked near the solid Tudor farmhouse.

The property ends at Rusey Cliff. Just outside the Trust boundary are several Bronze Age barrows at Newton Farm. A leaflet is available about the area.

Boscastle

The Trust owns both sides of the twisting, tortuous fiord which is Boscastle harbour, a mile of coast to east and west, and several blocks of land up the Valency valley.

Boscastle (a corruption of Bottreaux Castle) is a harbour which is exceedingly difficult to enter because of the sinuous channel. In the days of sail many ships foundered as they attempted to wriggle to safety, only to be dashed to pieces by the surging tide at the harbour entrance.

The inner quay was rebuilt by Sir Richard Grenville in 1584, and the outer breakwater constructed in the 1820s. Though demolished by a drifting mine in 1941, it was restored by Trust workmen in 1962. A blow hole thumps and snorts nearby when the tide is right.

The Trust property begins to the east at Pentargon where a waterfall reaches the sea in several leaps. Grey seals are often seen, even in the harbour mouth. Butterflies are numerous, and include the ringlet, meadow brown and the large skipper. Sea-birds frequent the cliffs on the north side of Penally. In waste places round the harbour the plant known as Russian comfrey (*Symphytum × uplandicum*) grows abundantly. Originally grown as a fodder crop on Forrabury Common to the south, it is now locally a weed.

On Forrabury Common can be seen a Celtic open-field system where the land is divided up into forty-two

Rusey Beach, the Strangles and Cambeak, Cornwall.

stitches – long rectangular plots – which are cropped in summer and grazed in winter. The Trust owns thirty-four.

The earthwork of a promontory fort separates the headland of Willapark from the Common. There is much heather, and many birds. Rabbits appear to be absent.

The Trust runs a summer-only shop and information centre in the old smithy on the east side of the harbour approach where a leaflet about the area can be obtained. A youth hostel occupies the old stables where horses were kept to operate the capstans and haul the slate which was exported from here. Fishermen working the shellfish grounds to the north still use the tiny port.

Bossiney Haven, Tintagel to Tregardock

While the village of Tintagel – originally Trevena – has few claims to distinction (except the Old Post Office, of which more later) the cliffs are largely unspoilt, and the Trust owns about four and a half miles along the stretch given above.

The Trust's first foothold in the area was the purchase of fourteen acres at Barras Nose in 1897, making it one of the first of its coastal properties. This was in response to the proposal to build the massive King Arthur's Castle Hotel just behind the Nose, which still dominates Firebeacon Down like a stranded whale. The hotel dates from 1899, and similar edifices can be seen at Newquay (the Headland Hotel) and Mullion (the Poldhu Hotel).

Bossiney Haven has a good stretch of sand at low tide, and is reached by a footpath from the small village of Bossiney. This was one of Cornwall's rotten boroughs before the 1832 Reform Act, and sent two members to Parliament. On one occasion there was only one voter not disqualified by holding a government office, and he voted in the two members. The name Bossiney was used by John Galsworthy, a writer with West Country roots, as the name of the architect who eloped with Soames Forsyte's wife Irene.

The promontory of Willapark (a name met with also as Boscastle) bears an Iron Age cliff castle. Lye Rock is separated from its eastern flank by a sea-surging gully, and the twin rocks, the Sisters, provide bird perches offshore. The cliffs here are better suited for sea-birds than those in the north, and the now rare puffin breeds on Lye Rock.

West of a small non-National Trust gap comes Barras Nose, mentioned above, then the Island, also non-Trust, but owned by the Duchy of Cornwall.

The sinuous fiord of Boscastle harbour, Cornwall.

Not really an island, it is reached by a stout wooden bridge and a steep climb. A Celtic settlement overlaid by a twelfth-century castle provided the raw material for tales of King Arthur and his knights for which there is little substance in fact. It is difficult to imagine it now, but in the days of sail, small coasting craft laden with coal from South Wales edged on to the beach below the Island at high tide to unload their cargo, and take on slate.

About one mile inland from here, but near enough to the coast to rate inclusion, is the Trust's Old Post Office, standing in Tintagel's main street. This monument to good taste stands confidently aloof from present-day strident commercialism. Although called the Old Post Office, this former use only dates from the 1840s; before that it was probably the house of a local yeoman, perhaps dating from the fourteenth century. The hall is open to the roof – note the smoke-blackened rafters, and there are furnished bedrooms over the two other ground-floor rooms, and a gallery. The building is open to the public from April to October.

South of the Island there are three more miles of Trust cliffland with firstly, Glebe Cliff, which can be approached by the road leading to the church (not National Trust), a large Norman cruciform church rebuilt in the thirteenth and fourteenth centuries. Behind Dunderhole Point is Tintagel youth hostel and a golf course was once laid out nearby, but this has reverted to rough land.

Likewise, traces of the wartime radar station are hard to find. The youth hostel was converted from old slate dressing-sheds, for there used to be slate quarries along the coastline which exported slate by coasting boats, lowering the material to the vessels by horse-whims (windlasses) at Penhallick Point. The remains of other quarries can be found on the cliffs above Trebarwith Strand, a beach of sparkling sand at low tide, but which disappears totally as the tide floods.

Two miles to the south of Trebarwith Strand is Tregardock Beach and Cliff, only reached by footpath, but worth visiting if the more popular beach is crowded. The path reaches sea level round the Mountain, a pretentious name for a smallish bump which nevertheless exhibits certain menacing qualities. A leaflet is available about the area.

Port Gaverne, Port Quin and Pentire

The Trust owns the beach at Port Gaverne, some fish cellars, and isolated sections of cliff to the east. Fish cellars are the storage sheds where fishermen kept their gear, and, in former times, processed the herrings or pilchards they caught.

Port Quin is a tiny inlet, deserted by its inhabitants for reasons unknown (the legend of a lost fishing fleet can be discounted for various reasons) and its buildings have been converted into four National Trust holiday cottages.

On the headland to the west is Doyden Castle, a small eccentric building built about 1830 in the picturesque Gothic style, almost a folly. It was built by Samuel Symons of Wadebridge as a place where he and his cronies could indulge themselves in drinking and dicing. Now also converted to holiday cottage use, it sleeps three. The producers of *Jamaica Inn* used the area in the 1983 television series.

Doyden House, a few hundred yards away, was built by a governor of Wandsworth Prison for his retirement. It is now divided into four holiday flats. A cliff-edge shaft fenced with slate marks a nineteenth-century mine.

After Doyden Castle there is continuous ownership all the way round the Rumps and Pentire to New Polzeath, a distance of about six miles. The rock is upper Devonian slate, but between Pentire and the Rumps pillow lava is found, looking rather like

Tintagel Castle viewed from Barras Nose, Cornwall.

pumice. Fragments can be seen built into the stone walls.

The cliffs show considerable variety of vegetation. On the north-facing slopes, where the wind is less powerful, thick scrub covers the ground giving good cover for thicket-loving birds. Facing west the vegetation is shorter cropped and wind-pruned. Spring squill, and the lesser and least birdsfoot trefoil are found here. Razorbills and guillemots and a few puffins breed along the north-facing cliffs and the Mouls, an offshore island.* The Rumps is a fishtail promontory with easily seen banks and ditches

*The Mouls's claim to fame lies in the story that early in World War I the poet Lawrence Binyon wrote the famous lines used at the Remembrance Day Service after landing there in a small boat. He was very moved by the peace during a time of war:

They shall grow not old, as we that are left grow old;
Age shall not weary them, nor the years condemn.
At the going down of the sun and in the morning
We will remember them.

Port Quin, Cornwall, foreground,
with Pentire in the distance.

running across the isthmus. This was yet another Iron Age cliff castle. Grey seals breed beneath the cliffs.

Looking back to the 1930s from the present time, it seems hard to understand that the Pentire peninsula was earmarked for building. A public outcry led to its purchase by the Trust. Cars can be parked in the Pentire farmyard from whence paths lead to the coast. The farmhouse and cottages at Pentireglaze are given over to holiday lets.

The Trust owns six and a quarter acres facing the Camel estuary between Trebetherick Point and Daymer Bay. Facing the property is the Doom Bar, a treacherous sand hazard across the entrance to the Camel. This is Betjeman country; the poet wrote much about this part of North Cornwall. A leaflet is available about the area.

Porthcothan, Park Head and Bedruthan

In all, this comprises about two and a half miles of coastal land in three blocks. The Trust owns seventeen acres on the north side of the deep inlet of Porthcothan, then a much larger chunk, the whole of Park Head. This fine greenstone promontory, with its farmed hinterland, another Pentire farm, cannot be easily reached without a walk. One of Pentire's outbuildings now serves as Beach Head Basecamp, a hostel-type accommodation taking six males and six females. Its purpose is:

(a) to clear beaches of litter
(b) to enable young people to do a worthwhile job while enjoying a holiday
(c) to demonstrate by example the need to Keep Britain Tidy.

There are Bronze Age barrows on the cliff top, and rabbits are common. The stone walls are laid herring-bone fashion. Fulmars frequent the cliffs.

One mile to the south is the beach known as Bedruthan Steps, after the enormous rocks (stacks) or stepping-stones employed by the Cornish giant Bedruthan to stride across the bay! Diggory's Island, at the southern extremity of the Park Head property, is at one end of the Steps and Carnewas Island is at the other. In fact they represent the more resistant rocks which have survived the onslaught of the sea.

The National Trust car park gives access to a well-engineered rock staircase rebuilt in 1974/5 after the previous way down to the beach was damaged by a landslip. Most of the beach does not belong to the Trust. Visitors are warned that bathing is dangerous at any time; it is easy to be cut off by the tide, and rock falls can occur.

Beside the car park, formed on the site of Carnewas iron mine, is a National Trust shop, café and information centre using the old mine count house, suitably adapted. A leaflet about the area is available in the shop.

The Gannel, Crantock Beach to Kelsey Head and Holywell Bay

About four miles of Trust coastline immediately west of Newquay, Cornwall's largest seaside resort.

Newquay's westerly growth has (fortunately) been stunted in the past by the Gannel, a tidal estuary which narrows to a stone's throw width at Crantock Beach. Here the Trust has acquired the dune backdrop of Rushy Green, preserving it from the threatened caravan invasion.

Westwards, the matching headlands of Pentire Point West and Kelsey Head cradle Porth Joke, a sandy cove, safe for bathing and remote from kiosks and commercialism. This has helped to preserve an interesting flora in the valley 'behind', where marsh and bog plants flourish, near lime-loving species nurtured by the wind-blown calcareous sand. This material is derived from broken shells, and has long been recognized as a valuable commodity for sweetening acid soil. Quantities have been carted inland for centuries.

Kelsey Head bears a promontory fort and Bronze Age barrows, and in an attempt to control smuggling an excisemen's lookout was built on Kelsey Common. Rabbits and hares are found, and grey seals breed beneath the cliffs, and on the island called the Chick. The cliffs give plentiful sites for sea-birds, particularly members of the auk family.

This length of property ends at Holywell Bay, a place named after a site of pilgrimage at Trevornick farm (not National Trust) where a mediaeval well-head marks the venerated destination. Another so-called holy well is a spring trickling into a cave at the north end of the beach.

Bathing at Holywell is possible but may be dangerous. Visitors must follow the life-guard's instructions.

The St Agnes area

The Trust owns St Agnes Beacon (629 feet), a ridge of high land half a mile back from the coast, as well as land on either side of St Agnes Head. The Head itself is owned by the local authority.

Newdowns Head, east of St Agnes Head, is a smallish promontory on the edge of a decayed mining area. The cliffs along here are exciting for birdwatchers, with kittiwakes, fulmars, ravens, black-headed gulls, razorbills and guillemots.

To the south is the much larger Chapel Porth property extending for two miles from Carn Cowla almost to Porthtowan, and inland up Chapel Combe, all wonderful year-round walking country.

This is a fascinating area for the naturalist and industrial archaeologist, second only in interest to the flora in the Lizard region. There is much heather and gorse. Butterflies seen include the common blue, clouded yellow and painted lady, and the lesser spleenwort may be found growing in crevices in buildings. Adders and lizards also live in the area. Basking sharks are sometimes seen offshore.

The remains of tin and copper mine buildings, some of which operated until the 1920s, survive. The preserved engine-house shell of the Wheal Coates mine, Towanwroath shaft, stands half-way down the sloping cliff at the northern end of Chapel Porth beach. This mine closed in 1914. Tubby's Head, not far away, carried a small cliff castle.

Chapel Porth can be reached by a narrow valley road. A refreshment building behind the beach was built by the Trust in 1958 to replace an ugly pre-war building. Cars can park here; Trust members free.

Bedruthan Steps, Cornwall, looking west.

The foundations of a tenth-century chapel can be seen on the cliffs just north of the car park.

At low tide the sands are extensive, but the bather ignores the warning signs at his peril. A local nuisance is the venomous lesser weaver-fish which hides in the sand waiting for prey, sometimes stinging bare-footed bathers.

St Agnes Beacon, the lofty ridge half a mile behind Tubby's Head, affords magnificent views up and down the coast, and even across the county to Falmouth and St Michael's Mount. Bronze Age remains blister the skyline.

Portreath to Godrevy

About six miles of varied coastal scenery, broken only by half a mile of non-National Trust land at the north end of Carvannel Downs. The property is particularly noted for its archaeological remains, its bird life and flora. Access is easy since for much of the distance the B3301 forms the southern boundary.

On Tregea Hill, the first headland west of Portreath, the remains of gun batteries dating from the Napoleonic Wars may be seen. They protected the harbour at Portreath, which, although small, nevertheless imported the large quantities of Welsh coal needed to keep the Cornish beam engines running and thus the tin and copper mines working. The cliffs provide breeding ledges for sea-birds and grey seals frequent a cave beneath Tregea Hill.

The strangely named Ralph's Cupboard is a slab-sided projection from the main cliff of awesome aspect where razorbills and kittiwakes breed. The large field stretching inland from here came to the Trust in 1954 littered with the wartime legacy of a

Chapel Porth beach, Cornwall,
with the remains of Wheal Coates engine house.

military camp. With the aid of the Civic Trust, parties of young people demolished the lot and tipped the rubble over the cliff.

Crane Castle is another Iron Age promontory fort, and Basset's Cove commemorates the long-term landowners here until the 1920s when the great Tehidy estate, just inland, was broken up. Dwarf scrub heath grows healthily and the Burnet rose is abundant.

The Reskajeage Downs give way to the Hudder Downs where the names Deadman's Cove and Hell's Mouth hint at the terrifying nature of the vertical cliffs along this north-facing coast. Nevertheless they were worked for tin in the seventeenth and eighteenth centuries. The royal fern is found in the undercliff, and fulmars, cormorants and shags breed plentifully. The B3301 is very near the cliff edge along here, and visitors must watch children and dogs carefully.

Much of Godrevy Point, which includes the Knavocks, is owned by the Trust and farmed by a tenant. The light sandy soil burns in dry conditions; regular rain is needed for good cropping. Archaeological excavations in the 1950s proved the existence of a farming settlement on Godrevy Towans dating from the first century BC. Godrevy Point itself is demarcated by a linear earthwork, and there are the remains of fields and terraces west of Hell's Mouth.

Grey seals breed below the Knavocks which is also a good place for sea-birds. Stonechats and linnets are the main land-birds, with some meadow pipits and skylarks. A colony of the silver-studded blue butterfly is known in the area.

Offshore is Godrevy Island with its lighthouse, unmanned since the 1930s and one of the first automatic stations in the Trinity House service. Virginia Woolf's novel *To the Lighthouse* remembers her childhood days nearby, and Kilvert's *Diary* describes a fight between a seal and a conger eel in the locality. Cars are allowed on to the Point near Godrevy farm.

Trencrom Hill

Not on the coast, but only two miles from the sea at Carbis Bay, and about half-way across Cornwall's narrow neck between St Ives Bay and Mount's Bay, Trencrom Hill justifies inclusion because of its proximity to the coast and the extensive sea views.

This sixty-four-acre hill is rather like a Dartmoor tor, and the two main granite rock-piles on its 500-foot-plus summit are surrounded by lesser natural rock outcrops which were linked by a defensive wall built *c.* 200 BC. Four large hut circles and possibly several others can be found within the enclosure. The 'fort' may have been occupied in the post-Roman period. Adders are not unknown among the rocky, bracken slopes, and the butterflies include the wall butterfly and the small tortoiseshell. Birds include dunnock, robin, blackbird and wren.

About a quarter of a mile to the north-east the Trust owns the Bowl Rock, a natural rock feature of domed appearance whose presence is justified in folk-lore by ascribing it to a ball bowled by a giant living on Trencrom. A leaflet describes the area.

The Penwith Coast from St Ives to Zennor, Gurnard's Head, Bosigran and Rosemergy

The Trust owns nine separate parcels of land along this twelve miles of coast. Within St Ives it owns a half-mile long narrow strip of twelve acres south from Porthminster Point towards Carbis Bay consisting of small fields and cliffs between the railway and the sea.

Hor Point, one mile west of St Ives, was bought in 1957 to avert a threat by the local authority to use the cliffs as a refuse tip.

The three-quarter mile of Trowan Cliff and Pen Enys Point were bought in 1984. This is good dairy cattle country, and the headland of semi-improved pasture is grazed by a milking herd.

There follows one of the Trust's most recent acquisitions, Treveal Farm, lying on the cultivated shelf between the moorland and the sea. Over a mile of coast and 160 acres in all make this a valuable piece of the Penwith coastal jigsaw. The coast path passes along the cliffs of course, but the property can also be reached by the public right of way running down through the farm and Trevail valley to River Cove. Cars must be left on the B3306. From the cliffs there are good views of the Carracks, the seal islands, a popular destination for boat trips from St Ives, as the animals are usually lolling on the rocks.

Tregerthen Cliff on the west side of Wicca Pool is about half a mile long, then after another gap the splendid Zennor Head is reached, about one mile of bold rocky headland. Some years ago the vegetation which was rich in interesting species caught fire, and the peaty turf burned below the surface for weeks. (This happened on the north end of Lundy in the 1930s, and the turf is only now recovering.)

Tucked in on the west side of Zennor Head is

Pendour Cove where the famous seduction of the squire's son by the mermaid took place. The area is easily reached by the path from Zennor village. The slope of the cliffs does not make it popular with sea-birds for breeding purposes.

Another lesser headland is owned by the Trust, then comes Gurnard's Head, only given to the Trust in 1982, and one of Cornwall's most dramatic promontories. A path from the Gurnard's Head Hotel on the B3306 leads out to the coast, and there is the inevitable Iron Age cliff castle across the peninsula of the Head – two stone ramparts and three ditches protected sixteen stone huts within. A sling-thrower's step behind the inner wall is an interesting refinement. On the edge of the cliff at Treen Cove, to the east, are the ruins of Chapel Jane, a single-

Cove near Zennor Head, Cornwall.

Near Sennen Cove, Cornwall.

chamber structure dated after excavation to the twelfth and thirteenth centuries.

The last property in this group, Bosigran, is the largest – 498 acres, two miles of coast from Porthmeor Cove to Trevean Cliff. Inland the property climbs nearly two miles to the moorland beyond Carn Galver (762 feet).

The cliffs are granite and give rock climbing of a demanding standard. The Climbers' Club has its local headquarters in the old count house of Bosigran mine, for there are mining reminders in the locality. There are two main climbing cliffs, Bosigran Face (300 feet) and Commando Ridge, and they face each other across Porthmoina Cove with Bosigran Pinnacle, a substantial islet, in the cove.

The many rocks in the area make it good reptile country, and mosses, lichens and liverworts are also abundant. Seventy plant species are present, as there is a good variety of habitats among the wet flushes. The royal fern is found here. Kittiwakes and auks breed in small numbers, but climbing activities and sea-bird nesting tend to conflict.

Bosigran Castle (Iron Age) tops the main cliff, and was a univallate (single wall) site. No huts are known inside. In recent years two groups of late Iron Age settlements, including several courtyard houses, have been discovered at Bosigran. The site of a long-disused watermill is known; there is documentary evidence for it in 1627.

This stretch of coast ends along the three-quarters of a mile of Rosemergy Cliff, a rough, bracken-covered slope. The Brandys rocks washed by the sea at the foot of the cliffs are named after the brandis, a three-legged trivet on which cooking pots stood before the open hearth in Cornish kitchens.

In 1985 the Trust acquired the 200-acre tenement of Rosemergy, considerably extending the Bosigran property westwards, and occupying the hinterland of Rosemergy Cliff. A web of drystone walls (called hedges in Cornwall) delineates fields first created perhaps 1000 years ago. This is a truly ancient landscape, a palimpsest of different historic and prehistoric eras.

Levant Cornish Beam Engine

Two Cornish beam engines are open to the public at Pool, near Camborne, one on either side of the

A3047, but there is another owned by the Trust on the cliffs one mile west of Pendeen.

As it is in a delicate condition and work to maintain it is constantly in progress, a visit can only be arranged with the consent of the Regional Office of the National Trust at Lanhydrock, Bodmin.

Polpry Cove, Chapel Carn Brea and the cliffs between Sennen Cove and Land's End

These three properties are the nearest the Trust gets to that most emotive of English promontories, Land's End.

The half mile of Polpry Cove is a recent (1982) acquisition by the Trust. It is about two miles south of Cape Cornwall and represents the sea frontage of a 43-acre property, Boscregan farm.

In the angle between the A30 and B3306 (but best reached from the minor road to the east) is Chapel Carn Brea, a 53-acre hill top reaching 657 feet, and referred to (like everything else round here) as the 'first and last' hill in England. Although two miles inland from Whitesand Bay, it is worthy of inclusion as its position enables it to claim the widest sea view visible from the British mainland. Bronze Age barrows are an added interest, and on the largest stood a mediaeval chapel dedicated to St Michael. Some wartime defence works have left a slight scar on the summit.

The three-quarter mile of Mayon and Trevescan Cliffs between Sennen Cove and Land's End is the most westerly of the Trust's properties in England. (The bid to purchase Land's End itself in early 1982 failed.)

These granite cliffs, especially Pedn men du at the Sennen Cove end, were much used during the war for Commando training. One soldier, Corporal Meddings, fell 100 feet into the sea, and lived.

Kittiwakes, great black-backed gulls and shags nest along these cliffs, and plants include rock samphire, sea plantain, buckshorn plantain, rock sea lavender, rock sea spurrey, spring squill and sea carrot. Lichens are abundant. The wheatear, not common in Cornwall, haunts the area, and snipe are not unknown. Barrows and a cliff castle are evidence of prehistory.

The South Coast of Penwith

The Trust owns about two miles of coast between Pedn-men-an-mere and the point east of Penberth.

The first-named headland which means 'the rocky head by the sea' protects the Minack open-air theatre from the worst of the south-westerlies. This unique and imaginative creation, formed by adapting the naturally concave shape of the cliffs into an outdoor auditorium of great charm is privately owned. Plays are performed here throughout the summer.

Trust ownership begins again beyond Porthcurno, and the main feature here is the headland of Treryn Dinas, almost a replica of Gurnard's Head on the north coast. A series of ditches and ramparts was built in Celtic times across the isthmus to produce the finest cliff castle in Cornwall. The remains of two hut circles stand just behind the inner stone wall.

Painted arrows lead the visitor to the Logan Rock, a naturally balanced boulder weighing sixty-six tons which was displaced in April 1824 by a drunken party of nine sailors led by a Lieutenant Goldsmith, nephew of the poet. The 'locals' rose up as one and insisted on the damage being made good, and the Admiralty ordered Goldsmith to do the work at his own expense. So in November 1824 he returned, and with the aid of sheerlegs and block and tackle reset the stone where it had formerly rested. The holes where the lifting apparatus was attached to the rock can still be seen.

Just to the west of the peninsula is Pedn-vounder Beach, perhaps Cornwall's cleanest beach with the clearest water. It is reached by a rough scramble from the cliff.

Access to the beach, Treryn Dinas and the Logan Rock is across the fields from a car park in Treen village, or over the cliffs from a car park up the valley at Penberth.

This is perhaps Cornwall's most delightful fishing cove; a lively, working place where fishermen pursue their trade, and flowers are grown in narrow sheltered plots. The Trust's policy is to let the cottages to working families with business in the valley. The apparently primitive but eminently practical capstan draws the small boats up the granite slip away from the surging tide, and round the outfall of the stream are the cellars where the fishermen stow their gear, perhaps sitting around making crab- and lobster-pots using withies grown further up the valley. Many years ago there were three watermills along this stream.

Gorse and heather mix attractively on the cliffs, and this is a good stretch for butterflies and moths.

Pedn-vounder beach from near the Logan Rock, Cornwall.

The green hairstreak, small copper, oak eggar and emperor moth may be seen. Porpoises, dolphins and basking sharks are sometimes spotted out to sea.

The Egyptian House, Chapel Street, Penzance
A house of 1830, full-bloodedly decorated in the then-popular Egyptian style, and faithfully restored in the original bright colours by the Landmark Trust to which it belongs. The National Trust has a shop on the ground floor which is open from April.

Trengwainton Garden, Penzance
Set back two miles from Penzance sea front, but with views across Mount's Bay, is this farthest west garden belonging to the Trust. The mild climate, with few frosts, and the south-facing position, mean that trees, shrubs and plants impossible to grow elsewhere in Britain flourish at Trengwainton.

The house (privately occupied and not open) and garden were established in 1814. The estate was bought by the Bolitho family in 1867, and they owned it until 1961.

Special features of the garden are the sloping raised flower beds, tilted towards the sun, the rhododendron bushes and the landscaped stream beside the drive. To the south-west of the house is an enormous specimen of a *Magnolia sargentiana robusta*, a native of China.

See local publicity for opening times. A well-illustrated colour brochure is available.

St Michael's Mount
Shares with Lindisfarne Castle (Northumberland) the romance of tidal disconnection. Nevertheless, it regularly tops the National Trust visitor figures for coastal properties (163,000 in 1982, exceeded inland by Stourhead Garden and Chartwell), probably due to its superb setting in a popular holiday area. A ferry runs from Marazion when the tide is in, otherwise visitors can walk across the causeway, but should watch the tide which floods rapidly.

St Michael is supposed to have revealed himself to fishermen on the Mount in 495, then for 500 years there is silence until we learn from the Domesday

Headlands at Pedn-men-an-mere,
Cornwall.

Book (1086) that during the reign of Edward the Confessor (1042–66) the Mount was held by a priest, Brismar, and dedicated to St Michael. There is some evidence too that there was a religious community on the Mount in Saxon times, no doubt harassed by occasional Viking raids.

The certain history of the Mount begins with the building of the Benedictine Priory in 1135 as a kind of out-station to Mont St Michel off the coast of Normandy and Brittany, a situation that went on into the fourteenth century.

In the fifteenth century the causeway and harbour were built, and houses and fish cellars erected. Payments were collected from boats using the haven. Throughout the Middle Ages pilgrims journeyed to the Mount, and many climbed to the so-called St Michael's Chair, a terrifyingly exposed spot overhanging a 100-foot drop, perhaps to perform a penance, to pray or receive an answer to prayer.

With the Dissolution of the monasteries which began in 1536 the ownership of the Mount was transferred to secular proprietors, and from then on it passed through various hands until the St Aubyn family purchased it in 1659, and it was they who gave it to the Trust in 1954.

Life has not always been peaceful at the Mount. Only part of the island was given over to religious purposes, so aggressors regarded it as a convenient castle. There were occupations and skirmishes in 1193, 1473, 1497, 1549 and the wars with France and Spain meant that a watch had to be kept to seaward as well as to landward. In the Civil War the Mount was occupied by the Royalists from 1642–46, when the Parliamentarians gained control.

From the time the St Aubyns acquired the Mount there was a gradual programme of improvement. With the reduction in the likelihood of pitched battles, the emphasis has shifted from defence to comfort, and a suite of public and private rooms was built over the years. (The higher gun battery comprises cannon captured from a French frigate driven aground nearby.)

The ordinary population of the Mount grew from one in the early eighteenth century to about 300 in

1870. Boats were built, and most of the men were engaged in fishing. In about 1900 a railway was built to carry stores to the house on the top of the Mount. It starts at the south harbour wall and gradually gets steeper, eventually climbing at 1:1¾ at the summit, 650 feet up. The railway is powered by a Crompton Parkinson electric winding engine and works a cable pulling a single four-wheeled wagon.

There is a National Trust shop and café on the island, and an audio-visual presentation introduces visitors to the history, legends and traditions of the Mount. For opening times, see Trust publicity. A well-illustrated colour brochure is available.

Cudden Point

A prominent fifteen-acre headland three miles east of St Michael's Mount which closes the view from that direction. Only acquired in 1979, it protects Piskies' Cove, Bessy's Cove and Prussia Cove from the west. The last two inlets were notorious smuggling sites.

Rinsey Cliff

A half mile of coast enclosing the sandy Porthcew Cove three miles west of Porthleven. The heather and bracken covered cliff is dominated by the engine house and stack of the Wheal Prosper tin and copper mine. The building was built *c.* 1830, and was abandoned in the 1860s. In the years of production it yielded £60,000 of ore.

When the Trust was given the property in 1969 it was decided to retain the engine house which was unsafe, with the chimney leaning over a 600-foot open shaft. The shaft is now capped and the building secure. Cars may be parked at the road end near Rinsey.

St Michael's Mount, Cornwall.

The Trust also owns a quarter-mile length of Lesceave Cliff at the east end of Praa Sands, restricting holiday development in that direction.

The Loe

The largest natural freshwater lake in the West Country was formed, perhaps as recently as the fourteenth century, by great storms piling up shingle across the mouth of the river Cober which flows past Helston, and which was a small port until the Loe Bar cut off communication with the sea. The average height of the lake is now ten feet above sea level and it is about thirty feet deep. A regulatory outfall was built in the nineteenth century to maintain a constant level and prevent flooding in the lower parts of Helston. When violent storms blocked the drain in January 1979 the South West Water Authority sent bulldozers to cut a trench through the Bar. A curious feature of the shingle barrier is that it is composed of eighty-six per cent chalk and flint, and there are no local outcrops nearer than East Devon from which this could be derived.

Wheal Prosper engine house, Rinsey Cliff, Cornwall.

The presence of the lake and its many different habitats has given the area a diversity of interest unique in Cornwall. Trout inhabit the lake, but otters have not been seen since 1959. Where the Cober enters the lake, and at the head of the subsidiary Carminowe Creek, there are marshy, reedy areas, ideal for herons, reed buntings, coots, and moorhens. The list of birds present on the lake, the Bar and the surrounding woods and farmland – and the Trust owns 1554 acres here – is lengthy, and includes pintail, pochard, eider duck, teal, wigeon, shoveler, tufted duck, gadwall, golden eye, firecrest, spoonbill, whimbrel, black tern and common tern. The Trust has built a bird hide capable of accommodating wheelchairs on the north bank of the pool near the boat house, and a five-mile walk right round the lake makes a fascinating day's outing. Four car parks in strategic sites make access easy.

The area is sometimes referred to as the Penrose estate, for a large house, Penrose (privately occupied and not open to the public), is situated on the west side of the pool. The Rogers family lived here from 1770 and Commander Rogers gave this magnificent property to the Trust (along with other land nearby) between 1974 and 1982. He particularly asked that the area should be kept as a place of quiet enjoyment. Boating, swimming and fishing are therefore not allowed. The Trust owns two holiday cottages on the estate.

A memorial above the southern end of the Bar marks the wreck of HMS *Anson* in 1807 when about a hundred crew were drowned. A local man, Henry Trengrouse, was so shocked by the tragedy that he invented the life-saving rocket apparatus which has since saved thousands of lives.

Gunwalloe to Poldhu

From where the large Penrose estate narrows to a 200-yard neck north of Gunwalloe Fishing Cove as far as Poldhu Cove are three miles of cliff and farmland totally different from the property immediately to the north. This diversity of landscape and habitat is one of the attractions of the British coastline and the Trust's holdings along it.

Top: Loe Bar and Pool, Cornwall.

Above: Loe Pool looking seawards across the Bar.

Opposite: Gunwalloe, Cornwall.

Gunwalloe Fishing Cove faces south-west and its quay is now totally destroyed by the sea. A local firm produces building blocks from sand taken from the beach. The unusual six-man winch on the cliff edge is from the wreck of the coalship SS *Brankelowe* which came to grief on the Blue Rock nearby in 1890.

The property swings south round Halzephron Cliff (where there are some Bronze Age barrows) and down to Gunwalloe Church Cove (see pages 78 and 79). This delectable spot is reached by a narrow lane ending behind the beach which is here split by a rocky outcrop, Castle Mound (after the remains of a cliff castle on its flat plateau). The northerly beach is Dollar Cove and the southerly one Church Cove. Behind both are sand dunes, and a stream runs out across the latter. The fourteenth-century church of St Winwalloe with its churchyard is tucked between Castle Mound and the beach. The tower is detached from the rest of the building, and is actually built against the rock. The church has the remains of a screen and attractive tracery.

When the Trust was given the land by Commander Rogers (the same generous benefactor who was responsible for the gift of the Penrose estate to the north) in 1974, cars parked willy-nilly behind the beach causing great damage to the delicate dune system, and enormously detracted from the beauty of

the area. Despite considerable opposition the Trust has built a car park further back behind Winnianton farm and a programme of dune restoration is in hand.

The marshy valley behind the beach is highly thought of as a wetland habitat, and visitors are asked to keep away from its fringes so as not to disturb the species which may be in occupation.

Gunwalloe Towans, the greater sand dune sweep, merges into Mullion Golf Course which has existed here since early this century. Such a use is more in tune with this open coast than a holiday camp, a threat which led to its purchase by the Trust in 1956. Some barrows scattered across the course add prehistoric hazards to a twentieth-century sport. This stretch of land ends at Poldhu Cove, bought by the Trust in 1985. Work then began to solve the erosion problems and tidy away parked cars.

The Marconi Memorial, Mullion and Predannack

The Trust's property starts beneath the large Poldhu Hotel, which dominates Poldhu Cove, and here the Marconi Memorial commemorates part of the history of the site. In April 1901 Guglielmo Marconi transmitted wireless signals to County Cork, and in Newfoundland on 12 December 1901 he heard 'the first but distinct successions of three dots in morse that had crossed the Atlantic from Poldhu', the first wireless message sent across the Atlantic.

The use of the area for wireless purposes continued until 1934, when the cliff was cleared of masts, cables and sheds, the Marconi Company giving forty-five acres to the Trust in 1960 to add to the six and a half acres it passed on in 1937.

South of Polurrian Cove the Trust owns several small but important features of the coast, five acres on the south side of the Cove being the first, and this includes the viewpoint known as Carrag-luz.

About here the rocks change to the distinctive schists, gabbro and serpentine of the Lizard peninsula. The serpentine in particular is unusual, and is supposed to have acquired its name because of the veins of coloured mineral which run through the rock giving it the appearance of snake-skin. Another characteristic is its chemical composition. It contains much silicate of magnesium, and when broken down makes an infertile soil. The hundreds of acres of *Erica vagans* (Cornish heath), a magnesium-tolerant heath, is unique to the Lizard plateau. Yet another quality is its ability to take a shine, so a cottage industry has grown up at Lizard Town of self-employed men making table lamps, lighthouse models and ash trays from the hard attractive stone.

Mullion Cove is owned by the Trust, and the quays have been expensively repaired in recent years. The winch house and fishermen's store are also Trust property, as is the clover-shaped Mullion Island offshore. The Trust also owns two small coastal parcels of land amounting to five acres between Mullion Cove and Predannack Head known as Laden Ceyn, Men-te-Heul and Pedn Crifton.

The mile of Trust land running from Predannack Head to Pol Cornick is only the tip of a vast 674-acre holding spreading inland almost to the A3083, and across the runways of the wartime Predannack airfield. Many types of aircraft from Spitfires to Liberators used Predannack, and Dr Barnes Wallis, famous for his work on the dam busters' bomb, carried out work at the base. Some rock climbing is done at Predannack Head. Biologically the area is one of the two most outstanding properties in Cornwall (St Agnes being the other) and one of the best in the country. This is because of the relatively undisturbed heathland, and the unusual plants associated with the underlying rock. The Cornwall Naturalists' Trust is tenant over part of the property.

Kynance Cove

The best type of Cornish beach – sand, rock pools, clear water and rough-hewn islets offshore. So many people come here in summer that the Trust undertook a major restoration plan in the 1970s to make the approach to the Cove more attractive. Thousands of feet had worn away the turf. Now, with co-operation, expertise and money from the Countryside Commission, some hardened paths have been put in, some of the cliff resown, and the landscape is recovering. Visitors are asked to keep to the paths to preserve the scene.

Bass Point (the Lizard), Cadgwith to Poltesco

Bass Point, one mile east of the Lizard Point, is the National Trust's most southerly property, a three and a half-acre headland carrying a coastguard lookout hut. Here the land turns north up the eastern side of the Lizard peninsula.

To the north of Landewednack (England's most southerly parish) is the half mile of coast owned by the Trust around Parn Voose Cove and the Balk. There is a long-disused quarry on this stretch and the Balk boasts a large day mark for navigation.

This side of the Lizard is much softer than the west side. Fuchsia and honeysuckle thrive, and the lesser butterfly orchid may be found. Hares, lizards (what else!) and adders are present.

North of Cadgwith the Trust owns the one and a half-mile coastal strip to just beyond Poltesco, past Kildown Point and Enys Head. A huer's hut stands between the coast path and the cliff, a reminder of the times when a man was appointed to watch for pilchards. He would then set up a hue and cry (from the Old French *hu*, outcry) and direct the fishermen's attempt to net their catch.

Kildown Point sustains colonies of fulmars, shags and cormorants. Kestrels patrol the cliff top, and the yellowhammer and green woodpecker may be seen. The birds at Kildown may be better observed from Enys Point, the next headland to the north.

A common insect, and one of England's largest, is seen along these cliffs: the great green grasshopper. The female unfortunately lays her eggs on earthy paths, so often gets squashed. If picked up these insects may bite, but no harm is caused and they seem unconcerned at being inspected on the palm of the hand. But be prepared for a rapid take-off!

Poltesco is chiefly notable for the remains of the serpentine factory which made mantelpieces, shop fronts, urns, tables and ornaments for about forty years in the last century. A 25-foot waterwheel provided the power. At the back of the beach is a round capstan house used for hauling fishing boats.

Beagles Point and Chynalls Cliff

One and three-quarter miles of quite unspoilt cliff with a hinterland of flat farming country, 164 acres in all, centred on Treleaver farm, where visitors' cars can be left. They lie round the coast to the south from Coverack, and their comparative remoteness makes them two of Cornwall's least-visited properties.

Beagles Point faces south-west, and Chynalls Cliff looks east to the Dodman and Devon in the distance.

Beagles Point, Cornwall

Above: Kynance Cove, Cornwall.

Opposite: Mullion Cove, Cornwall.

The nearby cliff castle on Chynalls Point is not owned by the Trust.

Lowland Point
An interesting geological curiosity. This aptly named feature barely clears high water, and is an example of a raised beach left over from the Ice Age. The real cliff rises 250 feet a short distance inland. A similar feature can be seen east of Prawle Point in South Devon. The Trust owns half a mile of coast, with a total area of fifty-seven acres. About one and a half miles to the north-east are the Manacles, a much-dreaded reef in the days of sail when ships homed in on Falmouth 'for orders' after weeks at sea. Manacles seems an appropriate name for rocks which trapped ships in a deadly grip, but it is in fact a corruption of the Cornish word *maeneglos*, meaning church rock.

The Helford River
Probably Cornwall's most attractive inlet. It is not an estuary, but a ria or drowned valley. A description is complicated, as Trust ownership is fragmented on both sides and up several of the creeks which grope watery tentacles into the surrounding countryside.

At the mouth of the Helford River a subsidiary reach, Gillan Creek, enters the sea opposite the quarter-mile property of Trewarnevas Cliff and Coneysburrow Cove, acquired in the 1930s. At the head of the Creek the Trust owns two typical Cornish cottages, one of which is let for holiday use. On the north side of the Creek the Trust owns a small wood.

The other properties on the south side of the Helford River are to the west of Helford village, thirty-seven acres at Penarvon Cove, and the wooded bluff of Pengwedhen which almost merge into the $35\frac{1}{2}$ acres of wooded hillside on the east bank of Frenchman's Creek (or Pill, as the Ordnance Survey would have it), and where it becomes part of the main waterway. The scene is one of great beauty, especially at high tide, as the Creek narrows to a channel reminiscent of scenes from *Treasure Island* or a West Indian voyage of discovery, for the trees eventually meet over the water. Maybe we are the victims of the illusion, however, as film-makers use the area when occasion demands. Daphne du Maurier's novel *Frenchman's Creek* is set here. Access is on foot only from the hamlet of Kestle, which is itself signposted from the Manaccan to Newtown road, but the best way to discover the attractions of the Helford River is to travel along it at high tide in a shallow draft boat.

Helford River—north side, Cornwall.

Tremayne Woods are forty-nine acres of mixed woodland on the south side of the Helford River and up the tiny Vallum Tremayne Creek. Tremayne Quay was built by Sir Richard Vyvyan of Trelowarren to receive Queen Victoria in 1846, but the visit was cancelled. Access to the woods is from Mudgeon on the road between Mawgan and Manaccan.

The Trust holdings on the north side of the Helford River are all between Helford Passage and the sea, and include the wonderful garden at Glendurgan, which runs down an inviting valley to the shore at the attractive hamlet of Durgan. Once a fishing village, its catch was sold in Falmouth market, the fishermen's wives leading the pannier-loaded donkeys in a long string through the narrow lanes. Some of the cottages are now let for holiday purposes.

As at Trengwainton, the sheltered position of the garden at Glendurgan has allowed many exotic species to thrive. The Fox family, shipping agents at Falmouth still, began the garden 160 years ago, and with their world-wide connections introduced plants from many overseas countries. The Chusan palm, western red cedars, tree ferns, aloes, deodar cedars, mimosa, swamp cypress and the somewhat sinister *Gunnera manicata* are all importations, and are but a few examples of a vast number of international species.

There are other surprises too. A maze, grown from the somewhat unpromising plant, the laurel, and dating from 1833, survives 150 years later, having responded well to hard pruning, feeding and drainage in 1979/80 after becoming leggy. And on a little plateau above the western valley is the giant's stride, a plaything for children who hang on to ropes hung from a disc at the top of a stout pole. As they run round they become airborne. Such a simple device, like the tree house at Plas Newydd in North Wales, can make a visit to a garden tolerable for energetic youngsters while their parents plod round the grassy sweeps looking at rare bushes and trees.

The house is privately occupied, and not open to the public. For opening times for the garden see local publicity. An illustrated colour brochure is available.

Near at hand are the 270 acres of the Bosloe, Carwinion and Chenhalls properties, which not only include lengths of foreshore, but a considerable area of farmland as far back as Mawnan Smith. Bosloe House is split into three holiday houses sleeping twenty-six people. Other buildings are also available for holiday lets nearby.

At the mouth of the Helford River are $43\frac{1}{2}$ acres of farmland and wooded cliff known as Mawnan Cliff or Mawnan Shear. This was the glebe of the vicar of Mawnan, hence perhaps Parson's Beach which is fringed by ilex trees planted by a former incumbent. Access is from a car park near Mawnan church.

The Helford River at low tide is of great importance to wading birds, and many species over-winter here. Some interesting snails have been found in the area.

Rosemullion Head

About one mile of coast, fifty-two acres in all, on the Falmouth side of the mouth of the Helford River. A prominent but low headland reached either by the coast path or from Rosemullion farm. The foreshore from the Head southwards is nationally important as a site of marine interest. Mining bees and wasps nest in the cliff-head deposits.

Trelissick

It would be unfair to omit Trelissick, tucked away up the estuary of the Fal though it is. The two other great Cornish gardens are included here, Trengwainton and Glendurgan, and although Trelissick is not on the coast proper, it fronts the tidal estuary and superb views down Carrick Roads to the sea beyond are a feature of the estate.

The 376-acre property lies neatly astride the B3289 where it runs down to the western approach of the King Harry ferry, and if Turnaware Point on the east bank is included the total estuary frontage is about three miles.

Within this large estate Trelissick Garden occupies a small part only, the rest being farmland and woods. Nevertheless the Trust has opened a four-mile long circular walk round the fringes of the estate, and this gives ever-changing views, outward through the hanging woods, of the river traffic, the merchant ships tied up in the deep-water channel, and the wading birds probing the muddy verges. The house (privately occupied and not open to the public) was rebuilt in 1825 by the Daniell family who had made a fortune out of the Cornish tin boom. After passing through several ownerships, it came to the Copelands in 1937, and Mrs Copeland gave it to the National Trust in 1955. (Mr Copeland was the managing director of W T Copeland & Sons Ltd, the manufacturers of Spode china, and some of the floral designs used on their china came from flowers grown at Trelissick.)

The Copelands did much of the recent planting and this is now reaching maturity. Sadly, the drought of 1976 and the storm of 16 December 1979 did great damage, but restoration is in hand. A measure of the scope of the garden is the collection of 130 different hydrangea species.

Within the property the old water tower with dunce's cap roof (*c.* 1860) is now redundant as mains water is laid on, and has been imaginatively converted into a staff cottage. Roundwood Quay at the northern end of the estate was the port used by the tin miners at St Day and Devoran, five miles to the west.

There is a restaurant, and shop where plants can be bought. An illustrated colour brochure is available. Four holiday cottages on the estate are available for letting.

The Fal Estuary

The Trust owns a number of small but significant properties on the east bank of the Fal estuary and Carrick Roads.

Up the little-visited creek towards Ruan Lanihorne are two areas of foreshore, Ardevora and Trelonk, totalling fifty-four acres. Then at Turnaware Point, the constriction ending Carrick Roads and marking the start of the Fal estuary, there is half a mile of farmland and woods, a lively place to watch the boats pass by. Access is through Commerrance farm. Down this track came troops embarking for the Normandy beaches in 1944.

With the purchase of Tregear Vean Farm in 1984, the Trust now owns the two miles of cliff fronting Carrick Roads between St Just-in-Roseland and St Mawes.

St Anthony in Roseland

St Anthony Head protects the eastern entrance of Falmouth harbour, and was fortified during the Napoleonic Wars, a military use which continued until 1957 when the War Department abandoned its tenure. The Armada was sighted from here in 1588, and the point was garrisoned by the Royalists (although easily captured) in 1646.

Three years after the Trust acquired the thirty-four acres of the Head in 1959 Vic Heggie was appointed warden, a happy choice, as he had earlier, between 1947 and 1957, been Master Gunner at St Anthony Fort and had served there for a year during the war.

The Fal Estuary, Cornwall.

So, from being in a position of maintaining the Fort, he found himself responsible for clearing away the last of the scars associated with it! He eventually retired in 1982.

Some of the below-ground bunkers remain; they are out of sight, of historic interest, and their removal was physically out of the question. A view-finder helps visitors identify landmarks in the wide-ranging panorama and there are lavatories and a car park. The old guardroom was converted for Vic Heggie into a comfortable home, and planted round with trees. Four small converted military buildings, appropriately named, are available as holiday lets. The lighthouse near sea level dates from 1835. As well as marking St Anthony Head, a red sector in the light serves to warn seafarers of the Manacles reef. When originally built, a bell was rung every minute to warn of fog, but was replaced in 1954 by a nautophone signal. Getting the bell away was no easy task, as it weighed two tons and was thought to be the heaviest bell in Cornwall. A new use in the tower at Penwerris was hoped for, but the belfry stonework proved inadequate, so in 1959 it was melted down in a Leicestershire bell foundry. On a personal note, the mother and grandfather of the compiler of these notes was born in the lighthouse. Ravens nest on the open-sea side of the Head.

In 1984 the Trust bought the half mile of Zone Point, the next headland to the east of St Anthony Head. Since then the redundant and conspicuous red brick coastguard station has been demolished as it was unsafe and unattractive. Bluebells grow right down the sidelands to the cliff edge.

Porthmellin Head and the St Mawes Estuary

The Trust owns several hundred acres extending

Cliffland near St Mawes, Cornwall, looking across Carrick Roads.

from the waist of the St Anthony peninsula at the head of Froe Creek, to the neck of the peninsula at Place, and including 1½ miles of coast and 1½ miles of creek and estuary frontage. Much of the interior is farmland, but the coast path traverses the cliffs round Porthmellin and Killigerran Heads and behind Towan Beach, and a path built by the Trust girdles the property by running along the estuary.

The wooded Froe Creek, where there is a heronry, once had a tide mill at its head. A dam across the creek was filled on the flood, and as the tide fell it operated a waterwheel. This method of milling was utilized where streams were insufficiently powerful to operate a conventional waterwheel, and had the merit of reliability which a windmill cannot boast.

There are several holiday cottages to let in this area.

Percuil

The Trust owns 143 acres of Tregassick farm astride the road leading down from Gerrans to the hamlet of Percuil.

There is a car park and picnic site at the viewpoint on this road and a footpath leads down to the estuary from here and back to Tregassick, a distance of one and a half miles. This beautiful estuary, the Percuil River, now so well used by recreational sailors, was in 1650 the scene of a case of piracy.

Portscatho, Treluggan Cliff, Pendower Beach, Nare Head and Portloe

The Trust owns nearly 900 acres of beach, cliff and farmland, extending inland almost to Veryan and west to Portscatho, and taking up four and a half miles of coast, albeit not in continuous ownership.

Porthcurnick Beach is the northern continuation of Portscatho, and is a popular sandy, family beach as it faces south and provides safe bathing. The property was bought in 1983 together with a number of nearby fields.

The same year the Trust bought half a mile of coastal land – eighty-nine acres – on Treluggan Cliff, thus protecting the attractive willow and blackthorn scrub which might otherwise have been in danger of reclamation. Scramble paths enable walkers to reach some small coves.

Pendower is a family beach, clean and safe, with no steep path for tired children to climb at the end of the day. A recent Manpower Services Commission scheme has restored the badly eroded dunes (the sand was swamping the car park) and a boardwalk suitable for wheelchairs was built. The dune turf contains many flowering plants, including the traveller's joy and lady's bedstraw.

The Trust's land climbs eastwards to Carne (or Veryan) Beacon, where one of the largest barrows in the country makes a superb viewpoint. Tradition relates that it is the burial place of the Cornish saint and king Gerennius, whose body was carried across Gerrans Bay in a golden boat propelled by silver oars which were interred with the body. When it was opened in 1855 a stone cist (burial chamber) was found. Previous excavations had taken place. To the west is an Iron Age hill fort.

Nare Head, cultivated to the cliff edge, can be reached by the coast path or by a track from the car park. In the past few years a major tidying-up scheme at Penare has concentrated the farm buildings in a convenient fold in the ground, and old structures have been removed and a new car park constructed. A wheelchair ramp and picnic area were built overlooking Kiberick Cove, and the whole improvement attracted a Commendation from the Civic Trust in 1985. The judges said '. . . an excellent piece of land management, it benefits the farmer and public alike.' There is much bracken and gorse on the cliff slopes among which rabbits frolic, and the rocky slabs harbour a variety of lichens; the orange *Xanthoria parietina* is the most abundant. Stonechats, rock pipits and linnets frequent the tops, and cormorants and great black-backed gulls breed on the cliffs. Seals bask offshore. Rock climbing is dangerous.

The Trust's ownership includes Kiberick Cove (watch for unstable cliffs) and ends at the Straythe, although a couple of small properties exist south and west of Portloe. There are a number of holiday lets in the area, including a cluster of converted farm buildings at Gwendra.

The Dodman

Probably the finest headland on the South Cornish coast. Trust ownership goes back to 1919 when 145 acres were given, and has gradually been extended until the Trust now has 276 acres.

The name means Deadman, and reflects on the promontory's reputation as a cause of shipwrecks. A reminder of this is the Dodman Cross at the tip of the 373-foot headland, put up in 1896 as a sea-mark, after two destroyers, *Thrasher* and *Lynx*, collided in thick fog and struck rocks on the south-west side. And it was off the Dodman that the pleasure-boat *Darlwin*

Kiberick Cove, near Nare Head,
Cornwall.

sank with all on board in July 1966. A watch-house near the cross was built early last century. The coastguards cultivated a small enclosure.

A ditch and bank, the Baulk or Bulwark, of an Iron Age promontory fort cross the headland; there are barrows, and the remains of an open-field strip system, now largely destroyed by farming activities.

On either side of the base of the Dodman are the attractive Hemmick Beach and Vault Beach. Reed grass grows at Hemmick Beach, eight to twelve feet high, and here also may be found the plant dittander, a tall grey-flowered plant, a crucifer related to the pepperworts, formerly cultivated as a condiment, but now very local. On the cliffs are yellow toadflax, ling, bell heather and golden rod. Kestrels, jackdaws, herring gulls, shags and fulmars are common, but auks are absent. The butterflies include the brimstone and common blue. A car park in the hamlet of Penare serves Hemmick Beach and the headland.

The Lambsowden Cove property, three-quarters of a mile east of Hemmick Beach, extends to seventy acres of farmland. The Cove is reached by the coastal footpath.

To the east, Maenease Point, capped by a coastguard lookout, shelters the attractive village of Gorran Haven from storms. There is a car park at nearby Lamledra.

Half-way between Gorran Haven and Mevagissey is Bodrugan's Leap (Turbot Point on the Ordnance Survey) where Sir Henry Trenowth of nearby Bodrugan, pursued by Sir Richard Edgcumbe of Cotehele, is said to have jumped into the sea and a waiting boat to escape to France during the reign of Henry VII.

Vault Beach and Lamledra Farm, east of the Dodman, Cornwall.

The length of coastline owned by the National Trust in this group of properties is about four miles. Several holiday cottages are available to let.

The Gribbin and the west side of the Fowey River

The 120 acres of Gribbin Head separates St Austell Bay from the approaches to Fowey. It is surmounted by a gaily striped candy-bar navigational day mark erected in the 1830s to distinguish the Gribbin from the Dodman.

Tucked in on the eastern side of the headland is Polridmouth Cove, always called Pridmouth, which is highly thought of as a bathing beach. Cars must be left at Menabilly Barton. Menabilly (the house) was for many years the home of Daphne du Maurier, the novelist, and it is faithfully represented as Manderley in her novel *Rebecca*.

The Gribbin's east and west slopes are clad in a mixture of sycamore, ilex, beech and *Rhododendron ponticum*. The sea buckthorn, not common in Cornwall, grows on the western side. It is a prickly shrub bearing orange berries in the autumn.

On the Fowey side of Polridmouth Cove the Trust owns a further mile of coast with a half-mile gap – once a nine-hole golf course – then the meagre ruins of St Catherine's Castle (*c.* 1540), one of Henry VIII's coast defences, which mark the beginning of the Fowey built-up area.

Upstream from Fowey, and overlooking the china clay quays, the Trust owns the thirty-one acres of woods and meadows of Station Wood.

Pont Pill

This tree-fringed creek, so quiet and unspoilt, is only just across the harbour from Fowey, and is easily reached on foot. The Trust owns much of both banks, about two miles in all, and a circular walk through the property gets the best out of the area. The recommended route is to cross the Fowey river by the Bodinnick ferry, and to follow the Hall Walk through the woods to the hamlet of Pont at the head of the creek, and then to carry on to the pedestrian ferry at Polruan which brings the visitor back to Fowey.

During the Civil War, Charles I just missed decapitation in the woods when a Parliamentary cannon ball from Fowey whistled past. His ultimate fate was but five years delayed.

Hall Walk was a recreational promenade laid out as long ago as the sixteenth century by the Mohun family of Hall, the historic house near Bodinnick (not Trust property). Where it turns up Pont Pill a monument to Sir Arthur Quiller-Couch, who wrote under the pseudonym 'Q', stands looking across at Fowey, where the author lived for fifty years. He was Professor of English Literature at Oxford, and died in 1944.

The woods are a pleasing mixture of oak, ash, hazel, chestnut and sycamore. Squirrels scamper about, and wrens, robins and chaffinches flit among the trees.

At the beautiful hamlet of Pont, the Trust has been busy restoring the old quays and a footbridge. A lime kiln, malthouse and boat sheds can be seen, for this was a busy working place where withy beds provided the material for making lobster-pots and panniers for transporting goods on pack horses. It is not hard to understand that Kenneth Grahame, the author of *The Wind in the Willows*, received inspiration here.

Two holiday cottages are provided at Pont (the occupants share the unusual attraction of a motor-assisted dinghy). The path now swings along the south side of the creek and links up with the foot ferry at Polruan.

On the sea-facing side of Polruan is the small Trust headland of St Saviour's Point.

Polruan to Lansallos

One of Cornwall's most extensive Trust properties, both in terms of coastline owned – about four miles – and the area involved – 1129 acres. It extends from Blackbottle Rock – surely a smuggling reference – nearly to Shag Rock, south of Lansallos, and encloses most of Lantic Bay and Lantivet Bay.

These two indents into the coast are separated by the 447-foot Pencarrow Head, a wide-ranging viewpoint; Bolt Tail (Devon) and the Lizard can both be seen and are about seventy miles apart. Inland are the white tips of the china clay workings near St Austell.

Despite the height of the cliffs, their configuration is not conducive to sea-bird colonies and the impression is not of a rugged coastline. However, the grassy sward of the cliff top is kept trimmed as much by the wind as by the mower operated by the Trust's warden. Tormentil, tree mallow and heather are found, and a patch of early purple orchids grows to the east of Pencarrow Head. Ravens and kestrels haunt the updraught.

Pont Pill, Cornwall.

The sandy beach at the back of Lantic Bay is the finest bathing beach on this strip of coast, although the path down is steep. The sea is particularly clear along here. At West Coombe, near Lansallos, a story considered to be true relates that the miller's wife refused to open the door to succour a half-drowned man. He was found dead on the doorstep in the morning, and his ghost drove the hard-hearted couple away, and the mill fell into ruin.

Lansallos Cove is a well-sheltered inlet, a real sun-trap, reached down a valley where the Trust has planted many hundreds of trees. The final stretch of path to the beach was cut through the rock perhaps a hundred years ago to enable carts to bring up sand and seaweed to the fields.

Access to this coastline is by the South Cornwall Coast Path or by link paths from small car parks at Lansallos, Frogmore and behind Lantic Bay. Several cottages are available as holiday lets.

Polperro

The archetypal Cornish fishing village overlaid with crass commercialism. Around the harbour its character shines through the tawdry trappings of Mammon, especially when the tide is in and the buildings seem to float on the water.

Happily the Trust owns a mile of coast on each side of Polperro, thus preserving the cliffs from unsightly development. Much of the eastern strip came to the trust in 1948 under the will of Miss Angela Brazil, the author of school stories for girls.

The Old Net Loft on Peak Rock overlooking the harbour has recently been converted into a small museum illustrating the fishing life of the village.

Hore Point

About a mile of coast half-way between Looe and Polperro, overlooking the Hore Stone, a vertical slate stack more easily seen from the sea than the cliff above.

Near the Point is one of the Admiralty's measured nautical miles. Two pairs of beacons on the coast provide fixed markers for speed trials offshore.

Looe to Rame Head

The Trust owns three smallish properties on this stretch of coast. Just east of Looe is half a mile of cliff and foreshore given to the Trust by the Metropolitan Railway Country Estates Ltd.

The last Trust properties on the south-facing Cornish coast before Devon is reached front on Whitsand Bay at Trethill Cliffs, Higher Tregantle Cliffs and Sharrow Point, and amount to $1\frac{1}{2}$ miles of coastline. Much of this stretch has in the past been

ABOVE: Lantic Bay, Cornwall.

OPPOSITE ABOVE: Polperro—Chapel Cliff, Cornwall.

OPPOSITE BELOW: the Yealm Estuary, Devon.

degraded by unseemly development, but the Trust holdings have preserved some sections for posterity. Visitors to Trethill Cliffs must not stray on to the Ministry of Defence range at Tregantle Fort when the red flags are flying.

At the foot of Sharrow Point is the cliffside folly known as Sharrow Grot. This artificial cave was hacked out by a Naval lieutenant called Lugger during the American War of Independence as a therapy for his gout. He penetrated fifteen feet deep and the cave is about seven feet high. On the walls and roof he carved many lines of bad poetry. Whatever the quality of his verse, the effort paid off for his gout was cured.

On a fine summer day at high tide young men may be seen diving off Sharrow Point Acapulco-style as the waves surge into a narrow gut between rocks.

DEVON [SOUTH] **Wembury and the Yealm Estuary**
5½ miles of cliffs and estuary-fronting woodland on both sides of the mouth of the river Yealm near Plymouth. The Wembury cliffs extend for 1½ miles eastward from Wembury Beach where there is a National Trust shop and small café in the Old Mill House. The sand tends to come and go, but the beach is the only realistic opportunity for bathing on this property. (Cellar Beach, across the mouth of the Yealm, is not owned by the Trust.) After storms, great piles of seaweed accumulate, to be enthusiastically searched by wagtails and turnstones in search of kelp flies.

The prominent island is the Great Mew Stone, owned by the Ministry of Defence. In the eighteenth and nineteenth centuries it was the home of several strange characters. It is now a breeding place for black-backed and herring gulls, cormorants, shags and buzzards. Even shelducks have nested here.

A grove of Monterey pines is a feature of the cliff walk, and the observant visitor will notice a great deal of lichen growing on the blackthorn bushes. The tangled mass of red threads covering the gorse like a hairnet is the dodder, a parasitical plant living off its host.

The visitor wishing to cross the Yealm should

Rame Head, Cornwall.

establish whether the ferry is running – it tends to be unpredictable – before arriving at Warren Point. A restored sign on the opposite ferry slip reads, *inter alia*:

> Ferriage for every person on weekdays 1d
> The like on Sundays 2d
> For every pony and ass 3d

The estuary woodlands are perhaps best appreciated from across the water. Trust ownership on the south side of the Yealm is not continuous until Cellar Beach is passed, and from here the Trust owns two miles to Saddle Cove. The cliffs are traversed by the Revelstoke Drive, or Nine-Mile Drive, built one hundred years ago by Lord Revelstoke to impress visitors with his property as he drove them round in horse-drawn carriages. Not all of it is in the Trust's ownership.

On Warren Cliffs rabbits were once bred commercially for flesh and fur. One field back from the path is the massive Warren (or Vermin) wall, built to keep the rabbits in their place, on the cliff. At several places there are massive gate buttresses, perhaps the most distinctive feature of the South Devon scene. A leaflet map describes the property in detail.

Bolt Tail to Overbecks

Six miles of rugged cliff land between Hope Cove and the outskirts of Salcombe. The coast path, following the cliffs from end to end, stays high for the most part, only dipping to near sea level at Soar Mill Cove and Starehole Bay where bathing is possible. An Iron Age (about 2000 years old) promontory fort at Bolt Tail consists of a stone bank with traces of a ditch across the neck of the peninsula.

The spiky mica schist rock occurs as tor-like features in the valley behind Soar Mill Cove, and at Bolt Head and Sharp Tor where the Courtenay Walk was cut through the jagged rock by a member of that family in the last century.

A path suitable for the disabled in wheelchairs heads west from the car park at Bolberry Down.

Sea-birds breed on the more inaccessible cliffs, and Bolt Head and Bolt Tail are the best places to view their activity. The 'click click' of the stonechat, a neat black-headed little bird, punctuates the whisper of the sea breezes through the gorse verging the coast path. Secret caves harbour what is almost certainly the only breeding place in South Devon for grey seals.

Overbecks House, at the Salcombe end of the property, contains a museum with maritime connections and is of interest to children. The large gardens provide shelter for plants and shrubs which only grow here because of the mild climate. A youth hostel uses part of the building. A leaflet map describes the property in detail.

Snapes Point

The Kingsbridge Estuary headland of Snapes Point was bought by the Trust in 1985. This unspoilt promontory forms one side of Batson Creek, just north of Salcombe, and will continue to be worked by a local farmer. A small car park is planned, also a two-mile footpath round the waterline. At one time a threat of development hung over the area, and it was used as an embarcation point for US Forces in World War II.

East Portlemouth to Prawle Point

Two and a half miles of beautiful cliffs from Salcombe Harbour to Gammon Head. Signalhouse Point, Prawle Point and Woodcombe Point are detached from the main strip of coastline, and amount to a further mile of sea frontage.

The low cliffs east of Salcombe contrast with the steep, craggy landforms to the west. For one and a half miles round Limebury Point and along Portlemouth Down the high- and low-level coast path options give easy walking. Beyond Rickham Sands the cliffs are higher and more rugged round Deckler's Cliff to Gammon Head, probably the most photogenic promontory on the South Devon coast. Its rearing crest shelters Maceley Cove, a tiny unspoilt sandy beach, only reached by a treacherous scramble (not National Trust). The coast and link paths heading inland have been rebuilt by the Trust using Manpower Services Commission labour. Stone slabs as steps up steep slopes and well-placed stone benches are a welcome refinement.

The thirty-one acres of Signalhouse Point, with a sea frontage of half a mile, were acquired in 1985.

Prawle Point is Devon's farthest south, and is a good vantage spot for birdwatchers, especially during migrations. The Island, nothing more than a rock beyond a wreck-strewn, sea-surging gut, is a noisy gull roost. Scan the lower spray-washed rocks for purple sandpipers in later summer.

Looking east towards Bolt Head along Bolberry Down cliffs, Devon.

Woodcombe Point, one and a half miles east of Prawle Point along a curious two-stage coastline with cliffs set back from the sea, is a mica schist crag of daunting dimensions round which the coast path creeps.

Bathing is possible at Mill Bay, at the western end of the property, and at Rickham Sands, Moor Sands and Maceley Cove, though the latter diminishes to nothing at high tide. A leaflet map describes the property in detail.

Little Dartmouth and Gallants Bower

One and a half miles of cliff and wooded river mouth hill top where the Dart meets the sea. The Trust's Little Dartmouth property, an unspoilt sequence of cliffs and coves, marks the western approach to Dartmouth harbour.

Warren Point, at the western end, is a splendid place for a picnic, with rock and gorse for shelter and views across Start Bay to Start Point lighthouse. At

Little Dartmouth cliffs,
South Devon.

Blackstone Point the path descends to sea level and is carried over a sea-washed gully by a wooden footbridge before ascending northwards up a track built originally to serve a seventeenth-century gun battery.

Several rocks offshore provide perches for cormorants and shags, and kestrels may be seen hovering over the path hoping to spot a small mammal moving in the grass.

Gallants Bower – the origin of the name is obscure – is the lightly wooded hill behind Dartmouth Castle. The Civil War earthwork on its summit was thrown up in 1645 by the Royalists, but it soon surrendered when the Parliamentarians laid siege to the town.

The wooded character of the property has encouraged the kind of bird life not commonly found on the coast: woodpeckers, jays and other woodland birds are often seen. The open glades give views up river and out to sea. In spring, bluebells smother the ground. A network of paths provides good access to all parts of the area and badgers make good use of them. A leaflet map describes the property in detail.

Kingswear to Brixham

Three and a half miles of recently acquired coastline carrying a variety of interest and natural habitats. Despite being so close to the Torbay holiday area this coast has remained remarkably undeveloped, and the path from Old Mill Bay to Man Sands was only cut in early 1983.

The southern (Kingswear) end is dominated by the sea-tolerant Monterey, Corsican and Maritime pines at Inner Froward Point, and an almost complete World War II gun battery, a rare feature, clings to the cliff face, its gun emplacements, searchlight shelters and blockhouses linked by steps and paths. Crowning the high land behind is the Day Mark, a tapering eighty-foot hollow stone navigational aid built in 1864. Ravens and buzzards are common along the cliff slopes.

Offshore is the Mew Stone, often called the Dartmouth Mew Stone to distinguish it from others off the South Devon coast. Herring gulls (mews) and shags nest on its north-facing side, a thriving cormorant colony on top, and grey seals often haul out at low water on its western ledges. The other sea-bird breeding station is at Scabbacombe Head where kittiwakes, fulmars, a few guillemots and even fewer razorbills live in tolerable neighbourliness.

Scabbacombe Sands and Man Sands are the only worthwhile bathing beaches, and both require a walk to reach them. A waterfall tumbles into the former, and a limekiln and a small row of one-time coastguard cottages add interest to Man Sands. A leaflet map describes the property in detail.

Orcombe Point

The Trust owns one mile of open cliff-top land and fields at Orcombe Point, Exmouth, known as the High Land of Orcombe. This prominent red sandstone headland is a special feature of the South Devon coast, and this property is an effective breathing space between the built-up eastern end of Exmouth and the caravans of Sandy Bay.

Salcombe Regis to Branscombe Mouth

Four miles of soft-rock cliff between Sidmouth and Beer. A wide Trust-owned hinterland behind part of the property protects the coast from undesirable development.

The layering of different rock types and the deep-cut valleys have produced a geologically fascinating area. The tendency of the cliff face to slump and slip produces occasional massive land and rock slides. The Pinnacles, chalky crags like crumbling castle keeps, just east of Branscombe Mouth, are the best examples. The westernmost chalk outcrop in England, at Rempstone Rocks, is owned by the Trust, and the alkaline subsoil has produced an interesting and unusual (for Devon) flora.

Evidence of past industries is plentiful. Lime was burnt on the cliff tops, and for hundreds of years potatoes were grown on south-facing frost-free plots, and a short-lived nineteenth-century industry extracted gypsum from the cliffs. The water wheel at Manor Mill is now motionless, but Branscombe's thatched smithy and the nearby bakery operate in the traditional way, the latter using ash faggots to fire the ovens.

The vegetated cliffs are not noted for sea-birds; they provide a better habitat for thicket-loving birds. The steep pebble beaches at Weston Mouth and Branscombe Mouth are unattractive to bathers. A leaflet map describes the area.

DORSET **The Spittles and Black Venn**

A massive slope of collapsed cliff between Lyme Regis and Charmouth, over a mile long and extending to 175 acres.

Mew Stone,
South Devon.

The reason for this instability is the nature of the 'rocks' (they are all sedimentary) and their relationship to each other when waterlogged. Dark clays, shales and limestones are capped by gault and upper greensand giving a kind of layered cake of differing textures. In 1908 a major slippage exposed a band of bituminous shale which caught light and led to stories of a Lyme volcano (see also Burning Cliff).

The wilderness aspect is marked, and the visitor is conscious of a dynamic moving landscape. The area is leased to the Dorset Naturalists' Trust, and managed by them as a nature reserve. A circular path to give visitors the feel of the place has been laid out through the Spittles – access from Timber Hill – but the Dorset coast path goes round the outside. The slope is too unstable to justify laying out a decent path through the reserve when it could be carried away.

Anyone wishing to walk between Lyme Regis and Charmouth at low tide can follow the foreshore, and this will enable fossil hunters to search for ammonites in the exposures where young Mary Anning found the remains of the first Ichthyosaurus, a Plesiosaurus and a Pterosaurus early last century. But be warned of the dangers of insecure cliffs, falling rocks and rising tides.

Among the natural-muddle on the slopes live rabbits, foxes, badgers and roe deer. Butterflies include the small blue, small copper and marbled white, while the peacock, red admiral and clouded yellow are immigrants. Birds are represented by the willow warbler – with its distinctive descending song – the chiffchaff, stonechat, yellowhammer and linnet. In the wet flushes the marsh orchid, brooklime mint and ragged robin grow.

A final word of warning. Don't attempt to negotiate fresh mudflows; they can be deep and dangerous, and walkers sometimes have to be rescued after getting into difficulties.

Golden Cap – Charmouth to Eype Mouth

About five miles of coastline (broken only briefly at Seatown) with a considerable depth of hinterland (1974 acres in all) going back to the A35.

The property takes its name from the distinctive, miniature Table Mountain eminence called Golden Cap, which at 618 feet is the highest point on the south coast of England. The view from the summit is enormous; to Portland one way, to Dartmoor and Start Point the other, and far inland across Dorset and Somerset. A memorial to Lord Antrim, chairman of the Trust from 1965 to his death in 1977, stands near the highest point.

The name *Golden* Cap is sometimes puzzling when one learns that it is composed of *green*sand. The name was first given to the material in the Weald of Sussex and Kent where it contains a mineral which makes it green, but which is missing in Dorset. It was laid down beneath the sea 100,000,000 years ago. Golden Cap is about half-way along this Trust-owned strip.

Much of the cliffland displays similar natural history characteristics to the Spittles and Black Venn mentioned above. In one field west of Seatown a kind of giant's staircase of stepped layers, separated by narrow cracks, makes one think of the upper circle of a theatre.

In places, recent falls have created overhangs, so visitors are warned not to stand on the edge. It's not usually a long drop but likely to be messy! Dogs must be kept on a lead, as animals can easily be panicked over the unfenced edge.

After Golden Cap, the most interesting part of the estate is centred on the hamlet of Stanton St Gabriel where a row of four brick-faced cottages has been converted to holiday letting use. They stand in a gloriously sheltered combe 1½ miles from the A35 at the end of a track, but the Dorchester to Axminster road once passed this way. Badgers visit the cottages

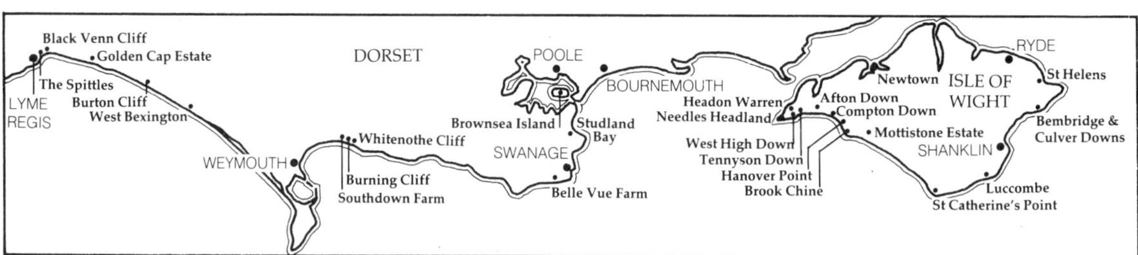

after dark for regular supper handouts. The ruined thirteenth-century church of Stanton St Gabriel stands nearby, and is said to have concealed kegs of smuggled brandy brought ashore on this lonely coast.

Access can be gained to the property at several places. Just east of Charmouth a steep hill signposted 'Stonebarrow' brings the visitor to the top of Stonebarrow Hill where there is parking for hundreds of cars. A summer-only National Trust information centre is in the wartime radar station, and a Trust Basecamp for voluntary work parties occupies the same building. (Not far away, at Westhay, a cottage has been converted into two holiday flats.) The access point for Golden Cap is on the east side of Langdon Hill Wood, above Chideock. Seatown is not Trust property, and has a pub, the Anchor Inn. At the eastern limit, at Eype (pronounced 'Eep'), cars can be parked while this end of the strip is explored. A leaflet map showing the fifteen miles of paths is available.

Burton Cliff

About three-quarters of a mile of 100-foot chalk cliffs sloping down away from the sea to the little river Bride. This stream loops behind the property before entering a reed-grown mere and draining through the pebbles to the sea. The area is good for skylarks, reed warblers, thrushes and finches, and perhaps the occasional water rail. There are riverside and cliff paths and access is from Burton Bradstock, with a car park above the beach.

Lime Kiln Hill

The Trust owns thirty-seven acres on the south side of the B3157 between Swyre and Abbotsbury. It also owns the 225 acres of Labour-in-Vain farm at West Bexington, nearby.

Burning Cliff and White Nothe

About 1½ miles of cliff and foreshore forming the crescent of Ringstead Bay and leased to the Dorset Naturalists' Trust.

The name 'Burning Cliff' is thought to have originated in the 1820s when bituminous shale took light and burnt for several years (see also Black Venn).

White Nothe is a gleaming chalk face with dramatic columnar buttresses on its east side. The views from this high point, south across Weymouth Bay to Portland, or to east and west along the switchback coastline, makes for one of England's finest panoramas. And at one's feet in summer the harebells dapple the chalk grassland.

Gulls and jackdaws nest on the cliffs. Peregrine falcons and ravens used to, but have forsaken the area. Adders and grass snakes bask in the summer sun.

The hair-raising White Nothe cliff path was written into his book *Moonfleet* by the author J. Meade Falkner as the smugglers' escape route.

Cars may be parked at Ringstead, at the hamlet of Burning Cliff, or at the entrance to Southdown farm.

St Aldhelm's Head to Poole Harbour

This considerable length of coastline is taken together, as a number of separate properties along it passed to the Trust under the will of Mr H. J. R. Bankes in 1982. This was part of the Kingston Lacy and Corfe Castle estates, a total of 16,089 acres and the biggest single bequest the Trust has ever received.

West of Durlston Head (where there is a Country Park and information centre – not National Trust) there are two parcels of Trust land amounting to about 1¼ miles of coast. The cliffs here are of limestone, and well furnished with ledges for the varying needs of fulmars, razorbills, guillemots and kittiwakes. Black redstarts are winter visitors.

North of Swanage, practically the whole of Ballard Down, Studland Heath and Shell Bay are now in Trust ownership, all of seven miles of coast if the tidal inlet of Poole harbour is included.

Ballard Down is the western end of the chalk ridge which began westerly around Lulworth and is here interrupted, to surface again at the Needles on the Isle of Wight. The tip of Ballard Down is represented by the stacks known as the Old Harry Rocks, mainland counterparts of their Isle of Wight relations. On either side of the Old Harry prow, Handfast Point as it is called, are deeply sculpted cliffs, the protruding headlands in various stages of stack formation.

Most of Ballard Down is farmed, a practice begun in the war, but the cliff top is prime walking country. The range of butterflies is particularly wide and herring gulls and great black-backed gulls nest on the cliffs.

Once past Studland village the very interesting South Haven peninsula is entered, a complex area of

Looking east from Golden Cap, Dorset
Burton Cliff in the distance.

beach, dunes and sandy meres across which a toll road passes to the Sandbanks ferry.

The whole of this peninsula is under the greatest pressure in the summer, when on a fine day 10,000 people may visit the beach and dunes, to the great detriment of the ecological balance of the area. The Nature Conservancy Council which manages a nature reserve here, has organized a sand-dune nature trail to get the conservation message across. One of the interesting facts is that the heath supports all six British reptiles: the adder, grass snake, smooth snake, slow worm, common lizard and sand lizard. The future management of this property will clearly test the Trust to the limit. A leaflet describes the area in detail.

Brownsea Island

Fortress, pirate stronghold, experimental farm, industrial site, elegant country house, pioneer Scout camp site, recluse's retreat, refugee reception centre, wartime bombing decoy; Brownsea Island has been all these things, and more.

Yet, despite this racy past, and its proximity to Poole and Bournemouth, the 500-acre island with the three-mile coastline is surprisingly demure. To land by the old cottages is to enter another world, where noise, danger, ugliness and technology have little place. The visitor can swiftly lose the other boat travellers as the natural charm of the heath and woodlands swallow them up.

Frequent foot ferries ply from Sandbanks and Poole from April to October, bringing people to swim, sunbathe, picnic, walk the wooded glades, or watch for birds or red squirrels. Two hundred acres of the island are leased to the Dorset Naturalists' Trust as a nature reserve, for on this small island are many different habitats: seashore, salt-marsh, brackish lagoon, freshwater lakes, alder carr,

Brownsea Island beach, Dorset.

heathland, deciduous woodland and coniferous woodland. Sandwich and common terns nest here, as do black-headed gulls and oystercatchers. That there is a large heronry on Brownsea is hardly surprising; the small herd of sika deer is more unusual.

The lagoon is the resort of large numbers of waders in late summer, including dunlin, curlews, common and spotted redshank and greenshank. In winter teal, wigeon, shelduck, pintail and shovelers congregate here, and the smart and distinctive avocet spends the darker months at Brownsea in increasing numbers.

Guided walks are available on summer afternoons. There is a nature trail, and by the quay a cafeteria, National Trust shop, and tuck shop. Some bad weather shelter is available. Private boats may disembark their passengers at the quay on the south-west end of the island only. No dogs are allowed. An excellent illustrated colour brochure is available.

Isle of Wight **Newtown**

A decayed borough and many-tentacled estuary on the north-west coast of the Isle of Wight. The Trust owns about fourteen miles of the estuary and creeks, four miles of the Solent foreshore, some woods, and the old Town Hall and various plots on the site of the ancient settlement.

Sixty families lived here in the fourteenth century on an economy based on oyster-beds, salt pans and the most important harbour on the island, but the place never recovered from an attack by the French in 1377.

Queen Elizabeth gave Newtown two members of Parliament in 1584, perhaps to give it a shot in the arm, and it continued to be thus represented until 1832 when it was declared a rotten borough under the first Reform Act.

The splendid Town Hall of 1699 was rescued from dereliction in 1933 by an anonymous group of benefactors called Ferguson's Gang, and is open to the public between Easter and the end of September. Some relics of the borough are on show, and a shop is on the premises. Occasional concerts are held in the building.

(The colourful Ferguson's Gang operated incognito

Redshank with a worm.

mainly in the 1930s. Money collected, in notes and coin, was handed over by a masked member of the Gang using pseudonyms like Sister Agatha, Red Biddy and the Bloody Bishop. The architect responsible for the restoration of the Town Hall was known as the Artichoke.)

The tidal estuary is a prime site for birds; 4000 waders and 2000 wildfowl have been seen at one time, and 170 different species of birds are recorded. The Isle of Wight Natural History and Archaeological Society has established a nature reserve over 300 acres, including much of the Trust's land.

West Wight—the Needles Headland eastward to Chilton Chine

The Trust owns about eight miles of coastline extending from the Needles Headland to Chilton Chine, as well as large areas of chalk down inland.

The Needles Headland itself, named after the singular chalk stacks tapering seawards to the lighthouse, bears an exceptionally interesting nineteenth- and twentieth-century coastal defence gun site, the Needles Batteries.

Begun in 1861 as one of the so-called Palmerston Forts (for it was Palmerston who had set up the Royal Commission on United Kingdom Defence in 1859) it was fortified continually by a variety of weapons until 1954, and used for 'Black Knight' rocket testing purposes between 1956 and 1971. The Headland was bought by the Trust in 1975, since when a programme of restoration has been carried on, and Prince Charles officially opened the site in June 1982.

None of the guns are *in situ*, of course, though two gun barrels were recovered from Scratchells Bay in May 1983 and one is about to be mounted in a barbette or emplacement. The other lies on the parade ground.

The Needles, Isle of Wight. The Needles Battery can be seen on the apex of the point.

From here a sloping 200-foot dog's-leg tunnel is cut through the cliff to an 1899 clifftop searchlight position at the very tip of the Headland; a wonderful viewpoint.

An exhibition in the magazine gives the site's history. It is open from Easter to the end of October. A twenty-page illustrated brochure is available. Three cottages, once used by coastguards and their families, are available for holiday lets nearby.

Other large Trust properties at this end of the island are Headon Warren and West High Down (459 acres of downland, heath and farmland) and Tennyson Down (155 acres) where the poet walked from his home at Farringford, now a hotel. He lived here from 1853 to 1867, then intermittently until his death in 1892.

The next properties to the east are the downs of Afton, Compton and Brook (there is a golf course on Afton Down), and prehistoric barrows are liberally scattered along this open land, and an ancient ridgeway runs east to west along the elevated crest reaching 666 feet near the prehistoric Long Stone.

Most of the village of Mottistone on the B3399 is owned by the Trust, as is the wooded land above and the farmland sloping down to the cliffs, here traversed by the A3055, known as the Military Road. Many paths cross the property.

At Compton Beach, malibu boards are allowed as the surfing is the best on the island.

OPPOSITE: Tennyson Down, Isle of Wight.

ABOVE: St Catherine's Point, Isle of Wight.

St Catherine's

The Trust owns three areas of land here: St Catherine's Point, Hill and Down. They are situated on a south to north line from the southernmost point of the island. Only the former is on the coast, where about one mile is owned, but the other two properties both command extensive views of the coast.

St Catherine's Point bears an 1840 lighthouse (not National Trust) on its low unstable cliff. Above and behind the lighthouse is an area of landslip where part of the coast road was carried away in 1928. The replacement road was built through Niton. The undulating hummocky scrub of the landslip is a habitat for a variety of flowers and birds, and the Point itself is an assembly area for migratory birds.

St Catherine's Hill (773 feet) is surmounted by the famous St Catherine's Tower, the finest mediaeval lanterned lighthouse in the world. It was built *c.* 1314 together with an adjoining oratory, now gone. The tower (thirty-eight feet high) looks for all the world like a stubby Jules Verne rocket as portrayed in a silent movie; it is in the care of the Department of the Environment. From this high ground both the west and east extremities of the Isle of Wight can be seen.

One mile north is St Catherine's Down, bearing another tower, a pillar topped with a stone ball, the Hoy Monument, or Alexandrian Pillar (not National Trust), built to commemorate a visit by the Tsar in 1815. A Lieutenant Dawes, with a nice touch of irony, added a tablet to the pillar in 1857 to the memory of the British soldiers who died fighting the Russians during the Crimean War.

A holiday cottage at the Point is available for letting.

Ventnor

The St Boniface and Luccombe Downs behind Ventnor include the highest land on the Isle of Wight, 764 feet.

Extensive views stretch eastwards to Selsey and the Sussex Downs, and north across the island to Hampshire. Eight Bronze Age bowl barrows are grouped on Luccombe Down.

Bembridge

A group of several properties at the eastern tip of the island.

Bembridge Down and Culver Cliff are at the eastern end of the chalk ridge which runs across the Isle of Wight from the Needles. Culver Cliff drops sheer to the sea and provides abundant nesting sites for sea-birds. The obelisk is in memory of the Commodore of the Royal Yacht Squadron, the Earl of Yarborough. Bembridge Fort, another 1860 fortification, is owned by the National Trust, but is not open to the public.

Bembridge Windmill, although last used for milling in 1913, was restored after the last war and presented to the Trust in 1961. No other windmill survives on the island. It contains much of the original machinery, and is believed to have been built about 1700.

The windmill is open from Easter to the end of September, and there is a small shop. On each floor there is a display illustrating the machinery to be seen. An illustrated brochure is available.

St Helen's Common and the Duver are pleasant open spaces on the north side of Bembridge (or Brading) Harbour. The Duver (thirty acres) is the sand and shingle spit which stretches almost across the mouth of the harbour. It was once a golf course. The old club house is now a holiday let.

West Sussex **East Head**

A seventy-six-acre spit of land forming the eastern entrance to Chichester harbour. The area is split between dunes and saltings (fifty-three acres) and sandy beaches (twenty-three acres) and there are 1¼ miles of coastline. Bathing is safe, except near the entrance to Chichester harbour. Access is on foot from West Wittering.

East Sussex **Crowlink**

The National Trust acquired this two-mile length of chalk downland in several blocks. It is one of the few unspoilt and undeveloped stretches of coastline in the south-east and fortunately is bounded to the west by the County Council's Seven Sisters Country Park, to the north by land owned by the Forestry Commission, and to the east by the open space owned by Eastbourne Borough Council. The farm is managed as an extensive grassland farm and there is a good network of public rights of way allowing access fairly readily to visitors, especially as there is a Trust car park near Crowlink and another at Birling Gap.

In 1982 the Trust acquired the Birling Gap Hotel, car park and four of the seven coastguards' cottages, together with the White Horses bungalow. It will be necessary to replan the whole of this area to provide screened car parking, a simple tea room and information point, and lavatories. The cliffs erode at about three feet a year, so any future ideas must take this into account! Work will not be completed for some years as the hotel is tenanted.

Kent **Dover, Great Farthingloe**

This one-mile length of cliff top and some agricultural land was acquired as part of the appeal for the White Cliffs of Dover. The Trust does not own the cliff face – this has been retained by British Rail who need it for the maintenance of the railway line beneath, said to be one of the most expensive lines to keep in repair.

The area is well endowed with wartime relics. Gun bases can still be seen, while there are buildings which housed observation posts and living quarters. One of the OPs was also a radar station – its scanner discovered and tracked the German battle cruisers *Scharnhorst* and *Gneisenau* and the heavy cruiser *Prinz Eugen*, during their Channel dash in 1942.

Dover, St Margaret's Bay

The 274 acres of Bockhill farm were bought in 1974 and an additional fifteen acres were acquired by gift from Kent County Council and Dover District Council in 1985. As part (one and a quarter miles) of the White Cliffs of Dover they are emotive and historic.

Near St Margaret's Bay St Augustine landed and the Roman conquest began. Dover was a gathering point for knights departing for the crusades and Henry VIII sailed from here for the Field of the Cloth of Gold. In both World Wars the harbour was the base for the Dover Patrol whose monument is just to the west of the property, and where there is a car park. Between 1940 and 1944 the cliffs were known as Hell Fire Corner.

The cliffs give refuge to fulmars and (with luck) peregrine falcons, now making a comeback. Being the nearest point to mainland Europe, many migrant species arrive and depart from these cliffs.

The flora is of interest as this part of south-east England remained as grassland after the last Ice Age when the rest of the British Isles was covered in forests. So certain species have remained local to the district. A network of footpaths dissects the farm.

ESSEX **Northey Island**

Northey Island, its 300 flat acres criss-crossed by a web of tidal creeks, sits astride the Blackwater Estuary. Except for two hours on either side of high water the island can be reached by a causeway from South House Farm – also owned by the Trust – on the outskirts of the ancient town of Maldon, well known for its sailing traditions.

The interesting bird species, together with the saltmarsh flora, led to the island being designated a Grade 1 site by the Nature Conservancy Council. Access to the island is by appointment with the warden only. A nature trail helps the visitor appreciate the wealth of bird and plant life.

Ray Island

Near the mouth of the Blackwater, up the Strood, the tidal creek separating Mersea Island from the mainland, is the long narrow sliver of Ray Island, an unspoilt salting, cut off at high tide.

SUFFOLK **Dunwich Heath**

Dunwich is a melancholy place. Its dwellings and churches have been collapsing into the sea through coastal erosion since records began, and from being a substantial town in mediaeval times, it is now little more than a village.

About two miles to the south is Dunwich Heath, a 214-acre Trust property with a mile of sea frontage immediately adjacent to the very important Royal Society for the Protection of Birds reserve of Minsmere.

The Heath was a rifle range in World War I and a battle-training area and radar station site in World War II. Until 1968 it was owned by the Dunwich Town Trust and acquired from them in that year with the help of a grant from H J Heinz & Co. Ltd.

Management in the last fifteen years has been towards preserving the essential character of the area – a heathland habitat with bracken and silver birch, and most colourful when the heather is in flower. Marram grass on the cliffs is anchoring the sandy soil. Public car parks just behind the low cliffs give access to the shingly beach down flights of steps or to paths through the property. An information centre and small shop share a building with the site warden at the north end. A tea bar and lavatories stand near the coastguard cottages at the south end.

Fire is a risk in dry weather and Docwra's Ditch between the Heath and the Minsmere Reserve was dug to provide water and to act as a firebreak. Rudd, roach and carp fishing in the Ditch is a bonus. Sea fishing off the beach is often practised, particularly in the winter.

Birdwatchers will probably concentrate on Minsmere where public hides are available, but the nightjar is known to frequent Dunwich Heath. A leaflet map about the area is available.

NORFOLK **4 South Quay, Great Yarmouth**

A visitor could be deceived by the sash windows, iron balconies and the white porch into thinking this is an early nineteenth-century house. But once inside its true antecedents are apparent.

This is a late Elizabethan house of 1596 refaced in the Georgian style. The sixteenth-century panelling, two chimneypieces and a fine moulded plaster ceiling make this interesting building ideally suited to its present use. It is leased to the Norfolk Museums Service as a Museum of Domestic Life. See local publicity for opening hours, but it is normally open throughout the year except for certain Bank Holidays.

Horsey

The Trust owns 1734 acres here, including Horsey Mere, and it is perhaps as a Broadland site that the property is most important. Nowhere else do the Norfolk Broads come so near the coast. This topographical convenience was used by smugglers 200 years ago. Ships brought goods to the coast, and after a short carry inland the contraband was loaded into Norfolk wherries (shallow-draft inland sailing craft) and moved to Norwich by waterway. There are those who say that Nelson learned to sail on Horsey Mere.

A mile in from the coast is a drainage windmill built in 1912 on the foundations of an older mill which operated until struck by lightning in 1943. It has now been restored, though it no longer works the pumps, and is open at a small charge during the summer. The Mere can be used by small craft without permit, but access to the surrounding marshland is restricted because of its natural history importance. There is a car park and lavatories and a talking post to tell visitors about the Mere and its various access points.

There is much Trust farmland in the area, which is also a breeding ground for marsh birds, insects and plants. The coast is undeveloped and unspoilt, the nearest road being some distance back from the dunes which line the coast.

Bockhill Farm, Kent, and the White Cliffs of Dover looking east.

Horsey windmill,
Norfolk.

Gramborough Hill

At Salthouse, east of Cley, the Trust owns sixty-eight acres of marsh and two-thirds of a mile of foreshore, and this includes Gramborough Hill, once the site of a Roman signal station. Many migrant waders visit the area.

The marshes are leased to the Norfolk Naturalists' Trust and entry is by permit only. Gramborough Hill is not part of the reserve.

Access is by car along the track that leads from the coast road just east of Salthouse. There is a car park near the shingle ridge.

Blakeney Point

Pebbles, shingle, sand and the sparse vegetation of wind-swept dunes and beaches, sea to the north and west, a shingle ridge stretching miles to the east, salt-marshes and muddy creeks to the south – such is Blakeney Point. And over all, the sky. Perhaps nowhere else in Britain is one so aware of the sky.

Since 1912, when the Point was declared a Nature Reserve and given to the National Trust, it has been the focus of much valuable scientific research carried out by generations of students and staff of University College, London.

The Point covers 1335 acres and can be approached either along the shingle bank from Cley, three miles away, or by boat from Morston Quay or Blakeney. The ferries operate in the season on the tides, and will both drop visitors off on the Point near the Lifeboat Station and take them round the sand bars to the west of the Point on which common seals are often seen resting.

The shingle banks and dunes attract many breeding birds such as the shelduck, oystercatcher, ringed plover and three species of tern. Migrants come in the spring and autumn, giving chances to birdwatchers who congregate in the hope of spotting rare visitors. They are seldom disappointed.

The Lifeboat House, painted blue-grey, and the summer headquarters of the warden and his assistants, is a landmark at the end of the Point. The lifeboat was last launched in 1923, since when the harbour has continued to silt up. The building now accommodates an informative graphic display about the Point and a small shop. Nearby are lavatories, one of which is equipped for disabled visitors. A wooden walkway 400 feet long links the building with the main observation hut on the seaward side of the dunes. Illustrated guidebooks and checklists, including a guide for young visitors, well describe the flora, fauna and geological history of the Point.

Stiffkey Marshes,
Norfolk.

Morston and Stiffkey Marshes

The network of creeks and salt-marshes that forms the coast opposite Blakeney Point and along to the Holkham Nature Reserve is invaluable as a largely undisturbed habitat for the specialized flora and bird population. The 487 acres of Stiffkey Marshes to the west are the oldest and lie behind shingle ridges that provide ideal nesting sites for terns. Brent geese winter here, and otters hunt over the marsh. Morston on the east is larger with 555 acres and is a popular access point to the coast, especially Blakeney Point. On the quay there is free parking for cars and dinghies and a public lavatory. A two-storey boathouse and information point is also on the quay, and from the gallery there is a superb view of the marshes and the Point. A new coastal footpath skirts the two marshes and links with a small car park at the Stiffkey end.

Scolt Head Island

Nearly four miles long, the island is about 1500 acres of sand dune and salt-marsh, surrounded by shingle and mud, all constantly changing in shape as the tides and currents course around the coast. The sand is washed up and down the beaches and stabilized above the high-water mark by a wide variety of grasses and plants such as glasswort, sea-blite and sea-aster. In summer the sea-lavender covers the marshes with a mauve carpet of blossom.

The Trust has owned most of the island since 1923 when it was purchased from the Holkham estate of Lord Leicester and designated a Nature Reserve. In

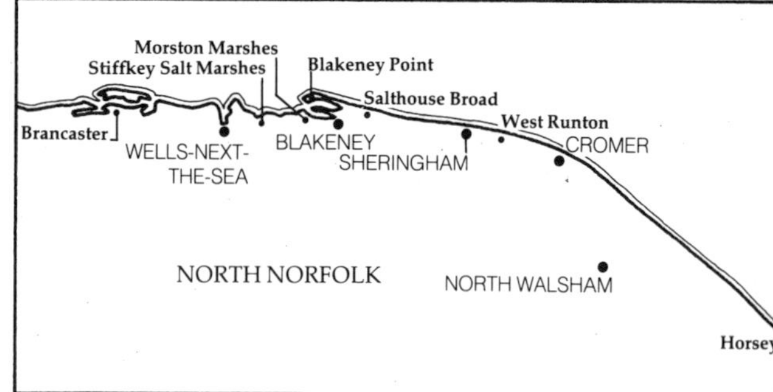

1953 it was leased to the Nature Conservancy Council, and the extreme eastern end, which had not been sold in 1923, was handed over to the Norfolk Naturalists' Trust.

There are nesting colonies of the sandwich and common terns on Scolt Head. Together they number over 3000 pairs in the breeding season. Wigeon and brent geese winter in large numbers, feeding on the eel- or wigeon-grass on the salt-marsh.

Access to the island is from Brancaster Staithe from where the boatmen run a ferry during the season April to September. The ferry operates two hours either side of high water. On the staithe (the hard) can be found the necessary information about the tides and the launching of boats. During the winter the boatmen dig bait on the marshes for this is in great demand by fishermen. There are mussel 'lays' or beds in the creeks, worked by the boatmen who use an old line of sheds for their equipment and storage on the east side of the harbour. These are owned by the Trust.

The Nature Conservancy Council warden for Scolt Head lives at Brancaster Staithe as does the National Trust coastal warden whose base is the Dial House, opposite the sailing club house. The barn next door has been converted into an information point and bicycles can be hired from here throughout the season.

Brancaster

Over 2000 acres of wide beach, backed by high dunes and some salt-marsh that stretches for miles from the golf club round to Brancaster Staithe. The Trust has held this coastline since 1967 when it was acquired through a local appeal and Enterprise Neptune. The reclaimed marshland now used as a golf course is not owned by the Trust, which likewise does not operate the car park at the approach to the beach by the club house. Experiments have been made to anchor the shifting sand dunes by planting grasses and controlling access.

NORTH YORKSHIRE **Newbiggin Cliff**

Filey Brigg pokes a boulder clay finger into the North Sea just north of Filey, and here the Cleveland Way begins its ninety-three mile route up the east coast to Saltburn-by-the-Sea, then inland to Helmsley. In 1983 the Trust bought about half a mile of dramatically steep cliff on the first stretch of the Way, north-west of Filey Brigg, with Enterprise Neptune funds and a grant from the Countryside Commission.

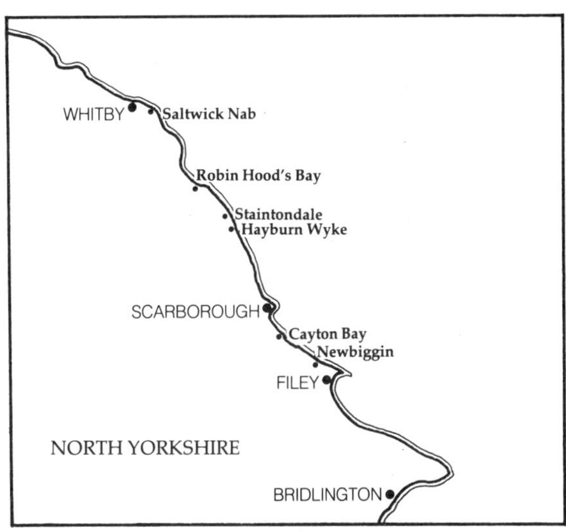

Cayton Bay and Knipe Point

Two miles south of Scarborough the headland of Knipe Point acts as the northern pincer-like promontory of Cayton Bay, a broad beach with low-tide sandbanks which can be dangerous to the careless bather.

The Trust bought Knipe Point in 1984 with land on either side. The one mile purchase included wooded undercliff and rock exposures of interest to geologists. It is proposed to route the Cleveland Way through the undercliff. Enterprise Neptune funds and grants from the Countryside Commission and Scarborough District Council enabled the purchase to be made.

Hayburn Wyke and Staintondale

The Trust owns nearly two miles of cliff top above the remote and beautiful undercliff of Beast Cliff at Staintondale, together with the small but very attractive bay at Hayburn Wyke. Hayburn Wyke provides the visitor with attractive walks through woodland and beside a dashing stream before the splendour of this little bay is revealed. The stream descends the last step of the cliff in a waterfall falling to the boulder beach. The bay is enclosed within cliffs. These are of geological interest because of their exposed strata, and the vegetation on them is of interest to the naturalist.

Access is on foot from the Cleveland Way long-distance footpath. There is car parking nearby by arrangement with the Hayburn Wyke Hotel. A charge may be made.

Robin Hood's Bay

National Trust ownership within this magnificent bay

Morston Creek, Norfolk.

includes most of the southern headland at Ravenscar, and all the northern headland beyond the village of Robin Hood's Bay. Some recent purchases have extended the Trust's ownership within the Bay and the hinterland, so essential to preserve the atmosphere of the place as a whole.

Apart from the spectacular beauty of this coastline, there is considerable interest, both natural and man-made. The cliffs are designated as a Site of Special Scientific Interest, and with the wave-torn rock ledges beneath, provide a textbook example of the evolution and erosion of sedimentary rocks. They are also a mecca for fossil hunters who can find fossil oyster (*Gryphea*), the fossil cuttlefish (belemnites) and the coiled ammonites.

The old and overgrown quarries beyond the cliffs which so enhance the backdrop to the bay provide another slice of cake for the geologist. They produced shale for the alum industry which was active here for nearly 300 years until the mid nineteenth century. The alum was lowered over the cliff to schooners tied up in

ABOVE: Brancaster marsh, Norfolk.

BELOW: Brancaster dunes—invaded beach huts, Norfolk.

a dock cut out of a rock ledge. Cannon on the cliff top were evidence of the cargo's worth to piracy. The chemical was extremely valuable for fixing dyes in textiles and in the tanning of leather. The remains of the old alum refining works at Low Peak are important industrial archaeology relics and are today being surveyed and preserved by the Trust.

The Trust owns the sixteen acres of Ravenscar brickyards, a fascinating feature reached on foot along the line of the disused Whitby to Scarborough railway. In the middle of the Bay is Boggle Hole, a famous cave, and here the Mill Beck has cut deeply into the cliffs to form one of the few ways down to the shore.

Ravenscar is known locally as 'the town that never was'. From the late nineteenth century to World War I, a company struggled to fulfil its dream of creating a second Scarborough here. They laid down sewers and roads and plots for housing, but the people never came. The high winds on this exposed cliff top dissuaded buyers and the project was never realized.

Trust ownership at Robin Hood's Bay extends over 400 acres and almost three miles of cliff. There is a Trust information centre and shop at Ravenscar open during the summer.

Saltwick Nab, Whitby

A small (seven and a half-acre) property which includes a rocky point (or nab) jutting into the sea one mile east of Whitby. This is a very well known local feature. Access is from the Cleveland Way.

NORTHUMBERLAND **Druridge Bay and Buston Links**

The gleaming five-mile golden sweep of Druridge Bay is in contrast to the scene of devastation associated with the open-cast coal mines a mile or two inland. The Trust acquired ninety-nine acres with about a mile of dunes and coast in the centre of the bay in 1972.

The Trust owns a similar though smaller property to the south of Alnmouth – eighteen and a half acres of sand dunes at Buston Links, amounting to half a mile of coastline. The rest of the dunes and saltings at Alnmouth have been leased to the Trust by the Duke of Northumberland. Sand quarrying in the 1950s and 1960s had threatened the existence of the dunes, but the fencing of vulnerable areas, the planting of marram grass, and the laying of paths have saved the situation.

Dunstanburgh, Low Newton and Beadnell

The Trust owns the awesomely dramatic ruins of Dunstanburgh Castle, perched on one of the eastern outcrops of the Great Whin Sill, the basaltic backbone of this part of Northumberland.

The evidence of Romano-British occupation in the form of Samian ware and broken imported millstones has been so overlaid by subsequent disturbance that conclusions about early habitation are difficult to draw. The structure we see today was begun in 1313 on the orders of Thomas, Earl of Leicester, and enlarged and strengthened by John of Gaunt in 1380. For ninety years it suffered a turbulent history as the Wars of the Roses ebbed and flowed across the land, punctuated by Scottish raids from the north. Then, with its capture after a damaging siege, the castle's usefulness – except as a quarry for materials: stone, timber and lead – was at an end. What a tribute therefore to those original builders 600 years ago that the walls still stand on this exposed site.

Considering how long it is since the castle was occupied, the remains on this ten-acre site are considerable. The keep was originally the gatehouse, and consists of two drum towers separated by an arched entrance passage. Long lengths of wall survive with various gateways and towers, notably the Lilburn Tower, so well seen if the visitor approaches the castle across the golf course from the west. A guidebook to the castle can be purchased from the small hut on the site.

The castle's main defence, the craggy basalt cliff, is a fine habitat for sea-birds. Several hundred pairs of kittiwakes breed here, their cacophony audible from far off, and the quieter fulmar is here too. Eider ducks, oystercatchers and rock pipits nest in the castle grounds, and visitors are asked to use the mown paths during the breeding season.

Although the Trust owns the castle, it is under the guardianship of the Department of the Environment. For opening times, see local publicity.

The Trust owns Embleton Links, the dunes and foreshore including the golf course, extending round the back of Embleton Bay. The calcium-rich sand provides ideal conditions for such plants as bloody cranesbill, burnet rose and pyramidal orchid.

At the north end of the links is Newton Pool, a freshwater lake behind the dunes protected as a nature reserve. Breeding birds include the black-headed gull, mallard, teal; coot, mute swan, dabchick, sedge warblers and reed buntings. Two hides for birdwatchers are provided, one specifically for disabled visitors.

Saltwick Nab, North Yorkshire.

Low Newton by the Sea is practically all owned by the Trust. A leaflet about the area is available at the Trust's information centre in Craster, one mile south of Dunstanburgh Castle.

A few miles to the north, at Beadnell, the Trust owns the group of huge eighteenth-century lime kilns, stoutly built of sandstone, right by the harbour, and used now by the fishermen to store their lobster-pots. Standing on the tops of the kilns one gets a good view of life in this little fishing harbour where the traditional East Coast coble is still the boat used by the working boatmen.

The Farne Islands
A group of barren, treeless rocky islands, famed in history, and beloved by naturalists, lying between two and five miles off the coast. They can be reached by motor boat from Seahouses, weather permitting, from

Dunstanburgh Castle, Northumberland, from the south.

April to the end of September, but access is restricted during the sea-bird breeding season, 15 May to 15 July. See local publicity for details.

There are about thirty islands altogether, covering eighty acres, and they are in two main groups, the Megstones to the west, and the Crumstones to the east. Each group has a lighthouse; the Longstone (1826) well out into the North Sea, and the Inner Farne light (1811), which replaced others nearby. It was from the Longstone in 1838 that Grace Darling and her lighthouse-keeper father rowed to the Big Harcar rocks to rescue survivors from the wrecked *Forfarshire*. She became a national heroine, but lived for only four more years, dying of tuberculosis in 1842.

Inner Farne was the home of the ascetic St Cuthbert in the seventh century. Here he lived and died, and after his passing his prestige encouraged a succession of anchorites to share the sparse existence of life on a windswept rock sixty feet above sea level. A

Embleton Bay, Northumberland.

Benedictine monastery was built in the thirteenth century and survived until the Dissolution.

The present-day anchorites are the ornithologists, botanists and wardens who guard the islands and record its wildlife, for the group of islands has one of the most varied and largest colonies of sea-birds in the British Isles. Puffins, guillemots, razorbills, shags, cormorants, oystercatchers, fulmars, terns (four species), eider duck, kittiwakes, and other gulls. Some of the cliffs are white with accumulated droppings. One of the largest colonies of the grey seal can also be found here. The Trust publishes a handsomely-illustrated guide to the Farne Islands in full colour.

St Aidan's and Shoreston Dunes

This six-acre stretch of coastline between Bamburgh and Seahouses is very popular with visitors, with the result that litter clearance is a time-consuming task. There are good views out to sea to the Farne Islands. On a still day they may seem to be floating.

RIGHT: Farne Islands, Northumberland—Inner Farne, with kittiwakes and guillemots.

OPPOSITE ABOVE: Farne Islands—eider duck with young.

OPPOSITE BELOW: Farne Islands—kittiwake with young.

Lindisfarne Castle

Lindisfarne, or to use its modern name, Holy Island, is joined to the mainland by a metalled causeway which is under water at high tide.

The Trust owns $37\frac{1}{2}$ acres of the south-east corner of Holy Island. Here, on a high natural cone of dolerite, the ruins of a Tudor fort were built upon by Sir Edwin Lutyens from 1903 to produce a small domestic-scale twentieth-century castle of great romantic appeal. The building was commissioned by Mr Edward Hudson, the founder of *Country Life*.

The only approach to the castle is on foot up a shallow-stepped ramp which brings the visitor to the lower battery. Once inside and beyond the entrance hall, the grandest part of the castle, the rooms and corridors take on a more homely aspect. Perhaps the most interesting rooms are the ship room and dining room; both are vaulted, and Lutyens probably utilized the magazines of the Tudor fort.

The views from both the higher and lower batteries are widespread, inland to the Cheviots, and for a vast distance up and down the coast. Out to sea are the Farne Islands. On the crag itself fulmars breed. A few hundred yards to the north is Gertrude Jekyll's small walled garden, now restored to its original plan as the result of the discovery of the 1911 plans in a collection of Jekyll papers in Berkeley University, California. To the east are the well-preserved limekilns.

Also on Holy Island are the monastic remains of Lindisfarne Priory (not National Trust). There is a Trust shop and information centre in the main street of the attractive village. Visitors must note that it is

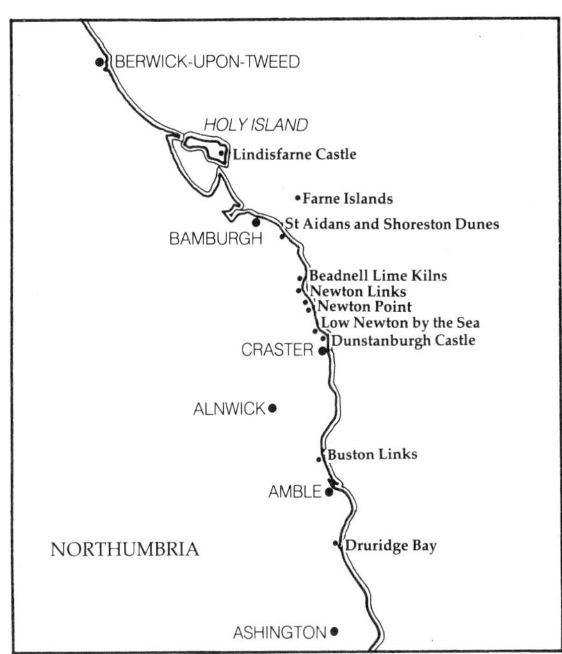

impossible to cross to the island from two hours before high tide to three hours after. Tide tables are printed in local newspapers.

CUMBRIA **Solway Commons and Burgh Marsh**

Not owned by the Trust, but held on a long lease granted by the 7th Earl of Lonsdale at a peppercorn rent.

The area consists of 1483 acres of common land in two blocks fronting the Solway Firth, and extending to ten miles of coastline. A coast road runs round the Cardurnock Peninsula above the saltings which characterize the shoreline. Inland is Bowness Moss, a peaty fen, white with cotton grass in early summer, across which the railway engineers of the last century had the greatest difficulty in constructing a line. Eventually the track was laid on bundles of faggots. The railway led to a viaduct over the Firth more than a mile long, but it was damaged by ice in 1910 and never rebuilt.

Sandscale Haws

The 651 acres of sand dunes and marsh at the mouth of the Duddon Estuary just north of Barrow-in-Furness were bought in 1984 with Enterprise Neptune funds and grants from the Countryside Commission and Nature Conservancy Council.

Miles of sand are exposed at low tide, but bathing is only safe near high water when the dangerous river currents are kept in check by the incoming tide.

Cars may be left in the local authority car park at Roanhead, and access is by public footpath and along the foreshore.

LANCASHIRE **Bank House Farm**

A fifty-seven-acre property on the northern fringe of Silverdale village overlooking the salt-marshes of the Kent Estuary (now owned by the Royal Society for the Protection of Birds) which here merges imperceptibly into Morecambe Bay.

Neat limestone walls enclose a patchwork of small fields and spinneys. Low limestone cliffs mark the shore line, and a much-used coastal footpath crosses the property through fields golden with wild daffodils in the spring.

ABOVE: Lindisfarne Castle, Northumberland.

LEFT: St Aidan's Dunes, Northumberland.

This property was given to the Trust in July 1983 when the deeds were handed over to the chairman of the North West Region, Mr Stafford Howard, by the donor, Mr T B Bright. In 1985, George's Lot, a cliff field in Silverdale previously belonging to Gibraltar Farm, was acquired extending the length of foreshore open to the public.

Jack Scout Land

Jack Scout Land, sixteen acres of cliff and foreshore on the fringe of Morecambe Bay, was acquired in 1982. It is the first coastal property north of the Ribble to be owned by the North West Region of the Trust, and is on the edge of the Kent Estuary marshes about two miles south of Silverdale. It is of high landscape value and scientific and historic interest, and highly regarded by naturalists as the limestone pasture and scrubland are the home of rare plants and birds.

There are extensive views from the top of the cliffs of the bay to the hills of the Lake District across the Kent Estuary. The foreshore path winds amongst slabs of exposed limestone. Above the path is a belt of oak, ash and thorn and the foreshore is gashed by dangerous tidal channels.

The protection of Jack Scout Land by the Trust will ensure the preservation of this unusual landscape with its strong contrast of aspect according to the tide, limestone outcrops and rich wildlife. The Giant Seat, made of limestone, with its view across the bay, will be maintained, and seasonal grazing will be continued. Most importantly though, protection will remove the danger of land improvement, with its possible destruction of rock outcrops to facilitate the use of agricultural machinery, the killing of rare plants by modern fertilizers and disturbance of wildlife.

MERSEYSIDE **Formby Point**

Formby Point is on the extreme western tip of what is historically Lancashire, though now termed Merseyside for administrative purposes. The Trust's property extends to one and a half miles of coastline and 493 acres of sand dunes, pine woods and foreshore which remain surprisingly unspoilt despite their closeness to large urban areas and increasing recreational pressure. The centre of Liverpool is only ten miles away.

Formby Point is an excellent example of duneland, for it demonstrates the process of dune succession from the beach via the mobile dunes to the mature fixed dunes of the hinterland.

Further inland where older dunes are more protected they have become fixed, and it is here in the early 1900s that Corsican and Scots pine were planted. Many trees have suffered badly from salt spray and sand blasting and at sixty years of age are very stunted and distorted in shape. Later plantings in the 1960s of lodgepole pine have also suffered in the same way. Erosion by the sea is an increasing problem, as is coastal pollution and litter.

The vegetation at Formby can be divided according to the dune succession. The pioneer marram grass is followed by sea spurge and sea-holly. The fixed dunes support woody shrubs such as buckthorn, dewberry and creeping willow. In damper spots silver birch, sycamore and alder are established and give a natural cover of deciduous woodland.

Asparagus has been an important crop in the district since the eighteenth century, and is still grown today. The fields are levelled out of the older dunes by hand, and are cropped for about fifteen years, after which it is necessary to rest the land and move on to another patch. The fields are small and well protected from the wind by barriers of brushwood. Another man-made feature is a large dump which was used for nicotine waste until 1977. The dump is high in organic matter which promoted vigorous nettle growth and also acts as a host to a variety of butterflies and birds.

A popular rarity with the many visitors to Formby are the red squirrels in their pine-wood reserve. This attractive animal was introduced many years ago and thrives here, untroubled by squirrels of the grey variety. The natterjack toad is also found here.

A car park is sited 200 yards behind the beach and paths and boardwalks radiate from here to all parts of the property. The Trust publishes an excellent leaflet describing the area, pointing out the habitat succession from the beach back to the pine woods.

The Wirral

Several properties owned by the Trust are grouped together on the western side of the Wirral.

Forty acres of meadow and arable land front the Dee Estuary near Heswall, and access is via the Wirral Country Park.

Caldy Hill and Thurstaston Common are both slightly inland, but have wide-ranging views across the sand bars and spits of the mouth of the Dee to the mountains of North Wales in the distance. Thurstaston Common is a tumbled gorsey wilderness of sandstone rock and sandy trails, much loved by children and used for orienteering. Thor's Stone, a twenty-five foot rock pinnacle, is said to have been used by the Vikings for pagan sacrifices.

WALES

GWYNEDD **Aberconwy House, Conwy**

The last mediaeval house (*c.* 1500) in Conwy, owned by the Trust since 1934, and now housing on its three floors a well-stocked shop, an exhibition about the history of Conwy, and an audio-visual presentation on the same topic. Mussel-fishing was one of the local pursuits and examples of the pearls extracted are on show. A leaflet about the house is available.

Conwy Suspension Bridge

Thomas Telford's famous bridge over the river Conwy below the castle of Edward I was constructed in 1826. When the new road bridge was built in 1958 Telford's bridge was at risk of demolition, but after an appeal for funds the Trust acquired it in 1966. The bridge sympathetically echoes the architecture of the castle, and the original toll house at the east end is retained and operates as a National Trust information centre and Telford exhibition in the summer. An illustrated brochure gives the full history of the bridge.

Penrhyn Castle, Bangor

Standing in large grounds at the north end of the Menai Strait is this monumental neo-Norman country house built by the architect Thomas Hopper for his client Mr G. H. Dawkins-Pennant between 1820 and 1845.

The cyclopean 'keep' towering over the drive catches the eye as the visitor approaches, but the rest of the castle is seen to advantage from the other side. Once within and having passed through several fortress-like timber doors, and along a low entrance passage, the first of the rooms is the largest, the Great Hall. The scale is enormous, and it has been compared to Durham Cathedral. Everywhere the round Norman arch dominates, and a gallery passes round about twenty-five feet up. Hot air ducts brought heat into the Hall through brass floor grilles, and one can imagine the thrill a wide-skirted lady, a stranger to Penrhyn, would experience when walking over the welcome warmth for the first time!

Apart from the sheer scale of the house, the feature which is most evident is the quality of the materials used and the craftsmanship employed. Most of Hopper's original furniture is still in the house, but the large plants shown in contemporary prints have gone.

The visitor must allow at least 1½ to 2 hours to see the house, for besides the downstairs rooms there are several bedroom apartments to see, the extensive domestic quarters, as well as a display of dolls, a natural history collection, and an industrial railway museum containing eight locomotives. A spacious shop and a light and airy tea room in the old kitchen complete the attractions of this very grand property.

Several English language guides and brochures are available, and the visitor who can only read Dutch, German, French, Welsh or Braille is catered for. A children's questionnaire keeps school parties busy.

From the grounds Anglesey and Puffin Island can be seen to the north; the Great Orme and Llandudno to the east; while Snowdonia rises southerly.

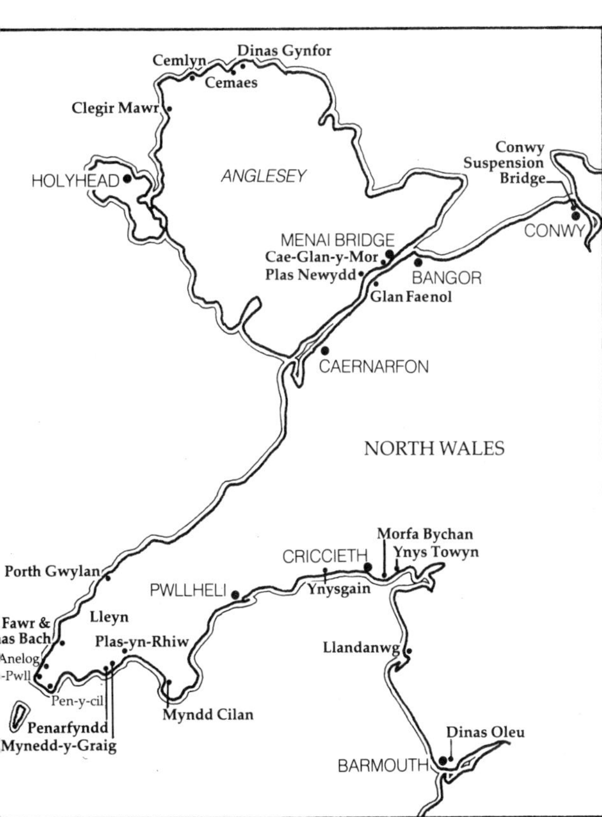

Dinas Gynfor, Anglesey

Only a small property, 4½ acres, but a remote lofty and rocky headland, and the northernmost point of Wales, it was given to the Trust in 1913 through the efforts of the Commons, Footpaths and Open Spaces Preservation Society. An Iron Age fort crowns the highest point, and choughs and fulmars breed on the cliffs. The remains of a copper mine will be seen on the approach walk to the property from the nearest road.

Cemaes, Anglesey

About 1½ miles of low rocky headlands backed by grassy sheepwalks on the side of Cemaes Bay. This is a Hebridean landscape. At the north end of the property is the old church of Llanbadrig, dedicated to St Patrick and having legendary links with him. If the visitor can get past the pigeon-populated porch he will find Islamic motifs worked into the restoration, a condition imposed by the benefactor, Lord Stanley, a Muslim by faith and uncle of Bertrand Russell. Wylfa Nuclear Power Station bulks menacingly across the bay.

Cemlyn, Anglesey

About two miles of the north Anglesey coast, it includes the parabolic pebble beach, Cemlyn Bay, thrown up by the cataclysmic storm of 1859. This is sometimes referred to as the *Royal Charter* storm after that steamship which went down with the loss

Cemaes, Gwynedd.

of about 500 lives. Over 200 ships were sunk or driven ashore. The beach became a dam with a lagoon of brackish water impounded behind, and the area is now a nature reserve managed by the North Wales Naturalists' Trust. Arctic terns, common terns and black-headed gulls nest here, and visitors are asked not to walk along the shingle barrier between April and July, so as not to disturb breeding birds. Hen Borth, at the western end of the property, is a small, quiet shingle and sand beach. Nearby is the small twelfth-century Llanrhwydrys church.

A recent acquisition is the thirty-three acres of Trwyn Pencarreg and Felin Gafnan, half a mile towards Wylfa. It includes a rocky headland and an attractive old mill building with half its machinery intact.

Clegir Mawr (Mynydd-y-Garn), Anglesey

This property consists of only half a mile of actual coastline at the north end of Church Bay, Anglesey, but $151\frac{1}{2}$ acres of land on this prominent hillside, including the summit of Mynydd-y-Garn which rises to 560 feet and is topped by a stone monument to the Thomas family. Extensive views across to Holyhead Mountain, and out to sea where the Skerries reef bears a prominent lighthouse. A forerunner of the present tower was allowed to exact a toll from passing ships, but evasion was too easy and its builder died a broken man.

Plas Newydd, Anglesey

This late eighteenth-century house designed by John Wyatt for Lord Paget stands on a splendid site beside the Menai Strait, looking across to Glan Faenol and the mountains of Snowdonia beyond. The grounds are extensive, and include formal and informal gardens, and a rhododendron garden some distance from the house. An attractive way to reach Plas Newydd in the summer is to take a launch excursion from Caernarfon.

The visitors who arrive by car, however, will first pass through the shop and reception area occupying the original dairy building. The tea room was imaginatively converted from the tiled milking parlour of 1810. A pleasant five-minute walk down to the house past a cricket ground with extensive views across to Snowdon and along the Strait to the two Menai bridges prepares one for the beauties of the house. Beyond the cricket ground are the stones of a Neolithic cromlech (burial chamber), one of Anglesey's finest prehistoric monuments.

The Hall is one of the best interiors surviving in Wyatt's Gothic style. A gallery and plasterwork fan-vault carry the eye upwards, and the paintings demand attention. From here the Music Room is entered, the largest room in the house, also hung with many important paintings.

The visitor moves upstairs, then down, and eventually enters the Rex Whistler exhibition room. The painter, who was killed in 1944, had a long association with Plas Newydd and executed the 58-foot long *trompe l'oeil* mural in the next room, so the exhibition and the mural should perhaps be taken together. The mural is a masterpiece. Undoubtedly inspired by the view across the Menai Strait to the mountains beyond, it employs Italianate themes and Renaissance elements to effectively create a sunlit scene of great beauty and charm.

The visitors now move into the Cavalry Museum, centred round the exploits and campaign relics of the 1st Marquess of Anglesey. The story of how he lost his leg at Waterloo, provoking the exchange between himself and the Duke of Wellington – 'By God Sir, I've lost my leg.' 'By God Sir, so you have.' – is often recounted as an example of British phlegm. One of his articulated artificial legs, a pioneer attempt at making good a limb deficiency, is also on show.

Before returning to the car park (or the dock if the arrival was by launch) parents will find that their children will enjoy the imaginative tree house in the garden.

The Marquess and Marchioness of Anglesey continue to live at Plas Newydd, and parts of the estate are used by Cheshire County Council's Education Department for short-term courses. The house is closed on Saturdays when the Music Room is often used for wedding receptions and other functions. Guidebooks about the house are available in Dutch, German, French, Welsh and Braille.

Cae Glan-y-Mor, Anglesey

The National Trust owns an eleven-acre field facing the Menai Strait between Telford's road bridge and Stephenson's railway bridge (now also carrying road traffic). The bequest has preserved this open vista, and a small lay-by enables people to pull in and see the view across to the mountains of Snowdonia.

A half-acre rocky islet in the Menai Strait, Ynys Welltog, was given to the Trust in 1982.

Glan Faenol

Lying directly across the Menai Strait from Plas Newydd on Anglesey, Glan Faenol comprises about one and a half miles of shore and 336 acres of open parkland and woodland. The parkland is currently let to graziers, whilst the woodland is managed by the National Trust.

Car parking facilities and waymarked walks are being established. The estate has a number of interesting features which will gradually be incorporated into the walks, including limekilns and a mausoleum, and it has superb views over the Menai Strait to Plas Newydd and beyond.

Segontium

The Roman fort of Segontium is about half a mile from the coast, on the outskirts of Caernarfon, but qualifies for inclusion by reason of its status as *fons et origo* of the town and because the sea can be seen from it.

Although the site is owned by the Trust, the excellent small museum is a branch gallery of the National Museum of Wales and the remains are under the guardianship of the Ancient Monuments Branch of the Welsh Office. Admission is free.

The fort was established in AD78 to protect the northern flank of Wales from Irish pirates and to guard the nearby mines, and was garrisoned until 390. Little remains except low walls marking the outline of the buildings.

Porth Gwylan

About half a mile of low cliffs between the coves of Porth Gwylan and Porth-y-Chen, on the north-facing coast of the Lleyn. The cliff top is a flattish sheepwalk, and the dark water-washed gullies give nesting sites for shags, ravens, fulmars and kittiwakes. Rusting capstans at Porth Gwylan tell of beach-launched fishing craft in the past, but no one puts to sea from there now.

The tip of the Lleyn

The Lleyn ('peninsula') is not like any other part of Wales. Its flattish plateau of croft-like farms punctuated by shapely mountainous features and almost surrounded by sea makes one think of the Assynt part of Sutherland. The Lleyn exudes that same Celtic fringe atmosphere to be found in Ireland, Anglesey, the St David's part of Wales and Cornwall. Many of its people use Welsh as a first language.

The interrupted Trust ownership of about four miles begins just to the south of Porth Oer, often called the Whistling Sands because of the strange noise emitted as you walk across it. Similar beaches in Scotland are known as Singing Sands. The effect is caused by the shape of the sand grains. The rocks along this coast are schists and gneisses of the Mona complex. Two tiny islands, Dinas Fawr and Dinas Bach are owned by the Trust.

Mynydd Anelog, a 626-foot hill of moorland character, has some hut circles on its slopes, and is worth climbing to take in the view back up the peninsula to Snowdonia, across to Anglesey and south to St David's Head, seventy miles away.

Braich-y-Pwll is the real end of the Lleyn, where the road ends at the Trust car park, and there is a coastguard lookout on the highest point. Here there used to be a chapel to St Mary – the ruins can be picked out in the dip below the car park – where pilgrims could wait and pray before making the perilous crossing to Bardsey. Pious people in the Middle Ages understood that three trips to Bardsey equalled one to Rome.

Any coastal viewpoint is greatly enhanced by islands, and Bardsey is well shaped and commands attention. As you look at it, the left side is a sheer 500-foot drop to the sea. To the right the land is flat with the striped lighthouse at the south end.

Choughs breed on Braich-y-Pwll, and if the time of year is right you will find the gorse and thrift providing a startling visual counterpoint.

Two further holdings occupy the headlands at Mynydd Bychestyn and Pen-y-Cil at the southern tip of the peninsula.

The Plas-yn-Rhiw Estate

This is centred on the small manor house of that name at Rhiw on the south coast of the Lleyn. This house, partly late Tudor, and enlarged in the eighteenth century, was rescued from dereliction between the wars by the widowed Mrs Constance Keating and her three daughters, and subsequently this and several other properties in the area were given to the Trust by the daughters. The house and gardens are a surprise, as the Lleyn is not known for architectural pretensions or tree cover. Flowering shrubs, box hedges and rooks are the memories one takes away from the garden.

Around the headland to the south of Plas-yn-Rhiw is about three miles of Trust land. Access to the two small beaches at Porth Ysgo means leaving cars back from the cliff top. From the 800-foot high Greigiau Gwineu there are spectacular views across Porth Neigwl (Hell's Mouth) to another property Mynydd Cilan on the headland opposite where the Trust owns a quarter of a mile of coast and open land reached from Abersoch.

Tywyn-y-Fach

A nineteen-acre patch of scrub and sand dunes between the A499 and the sea acting as a kind of green belt or *cordon sanitaire* between the hotels of Abersoch and the caravans of the Warren.

Ynysgain

Foreshore and farmland facing south across Cardigan Bay just west of Criccieth.

This is a simple place. There are no majestic cliffs, no stately homes, though Criccieth Castle can be seen along the pebble beach eastwards. It is a place of East Anglian skies and small incidents like a heron fishing at the mouth of the Afon Dwyfor or the lines of wreckage blown ashore during the last storm. And across the eastern skyline are the mountains, with Cader Idris claiming the crown.

Y Maes, Llandanwg

A recent acquisition of twenty-four acres of land surrounding the mediaeval church of St Tanwg, which is said to have served Cantre'r Gwaelod which was inundated by the sea in the seventh century. The Trust allows free access at all times. Some dune stabilization work will have to be carried out. A local authority car park adjoins the property.

Dinas Oleu

Although this property only extends to four and a half acres it has the distinction of being the first land acquired by the Trust, having been given in 1895 by Mrs F Talbot. A further twelve acres adjoining Dinas Oleu, and known as Cae Fadog, was bought in 1980. The area, of steep rocky hillside, is above the southern end of Barmouth, and can be reached up the many slate steps of Idris Lane or St George's Lane near the Barmouth Hotel, or by toiling up the very steep Dinas Oleu Road opposite Woolworths.

Dinas Oleu, Gwynedd—the National Trust's first land acquisition—above Barmouth.

DYFED **Coybal, Cwm Soden, Cwmtydi**

A group of small properties stretching for about one and a half miles along the coast just 'round the corner' westerly from New Quay, and amounting to about 180 acres. The Cwm Soden valley is well wooded and contrasts with the more open land on either side. Access is by footpath or along tortuous lanes. Enterprise Neptune funds and a grant from the Countryside Commission helped towards the purchase of this land.

Lochtyn, Llangranog

About one and a half miles of dramatic cliff, including an island, six miles south-west of New Quay, with a considerable depth of property inland. The flat-topped but elevated hill rising from the spine of the headland, Pen-y-Badell, possesses an ugly Government installation, with two lines of electricity poles leading to it (which are being transferred underground at the present time). The ten-acre island, Ynys-Lochtyn, projects beyond the headland.

Penbryn

The Trust owns the north end of Penbryn Beach. Before the Trust bought the property in 1967 comercial interests were removing the sand, but this has now stopped, and conservation of the dunes is taking place. Enterprise Neptune funds assisted by donations from the Goldsmiths' Company and Mr N C Barford helped towards the purchase of the property.

Mwnt

The Trust owns about one mile of coast here, including the conical hill known as Mwnt (mound), a prominent feature on this coast four miles north of Cardigan. On the sheltered side of the hill is a late thirteenth- or early fourteenth-century church, whitewashed and alone. Simple within, it nevertheless once had a rood screen, of which fragments remain, as well as the door leading up through the wall thickness to the rood loft. On one side of the peninsula a sandy cove is easily reached by gentle steps past a limekiln. On the north side a stream plunges into a sea-washed chasm. Offshore I have seen a school of porpoises undulating past the point. Southwards two and a half miles distant, is Cardigan Island.

Ceibwr Bay

In 1984 Mr and Mrs Wynford Vaughan Thomas gave six and a half acres to the Trust on the west side of Ceibwr Bay. The Pembrokeshire Coast Path passes along the cliffland, but parking is very limited and visitors are recommended to park in Moylegrove and walk down.

Barry Island Farm

Between Aber-eiddy and Porthgain the Trust has acquired Barry Island Farm (not in fact an island) with a coastline of two miles. The Pembrokeshire Coast Path runs along the cliffs, and in the spring this is a good place to see fulmars. The geology draws field parties to visit the Blue Lagoon quarry to search for fossils of 'tuning-fork' graptolites in the Ordovician rocks.

The land was purchased by the Trust in 1985 with help from Enterprise Neptune funds, the Countryside Commission and the Pembrokeshire Coast National

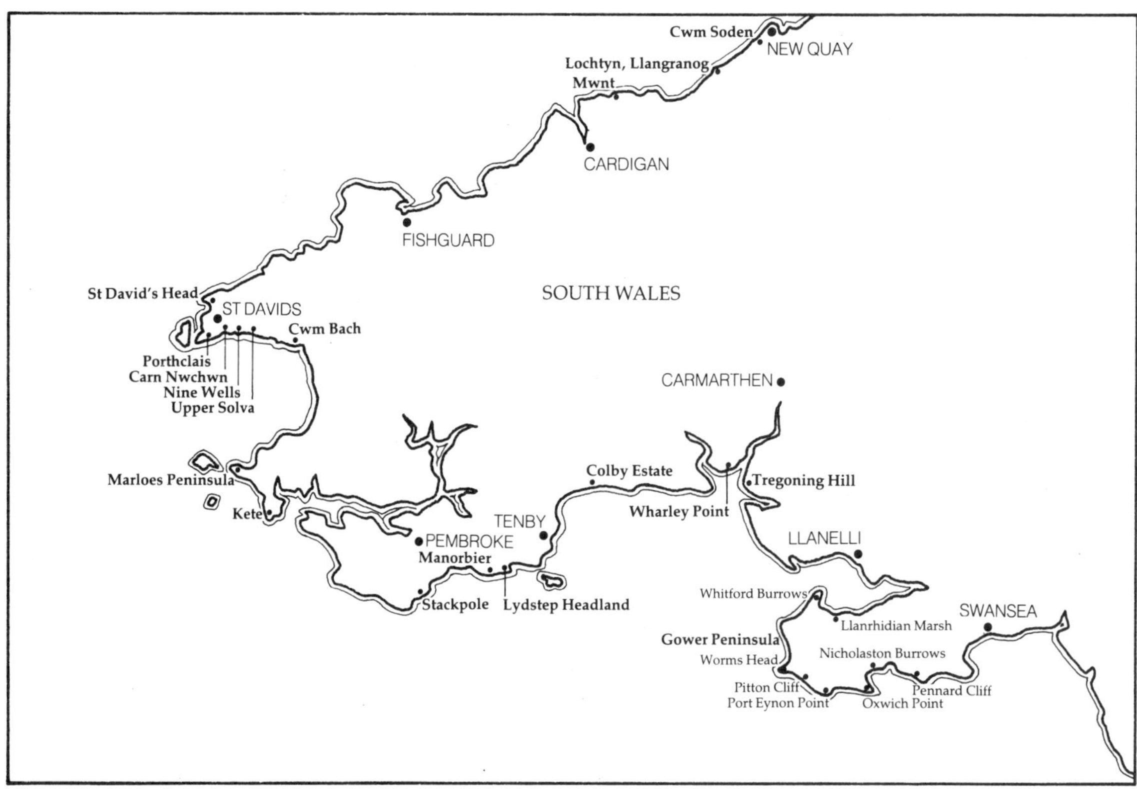

Park Authority. The Trust, assisted by the Manpower Services Commission, is starting a programme of restoration of the Pembrokeshire hedge banks.

St David's Head

The Trust owns several miles on what is probably the most emotive coastline in Wales, as well as the prominent hill tops of Carnllidi and Penbiri. Its property begins half a mile north of the Porth Mawr or Whitesand Bay local authority car park, and choughs may be seen near the boundary cairn.

The tip of the Head was defended by an Iron age rampart known as the Warriors' Dyke. In front of the main stone 'wall' – traces of original stone wall can still be seen – were two small earth banks and ditches. Within the promontory fort are a number of hut circles, the stone footings of round huts. The vegetation here is mostly grass and heather, and outcropping rock of the lower Ordovician type is everywhere.

Offshore are many small islets and reefs, the largest island, to the south, being Ramsey. The South Bishop lighthouse is to the right of Ramsey, and on a very clear day the slender tower of Douglass's rock light on the Smalls reef can just be made out to the left of the South Bishop. (Incredibly, the first Smalls lighthouse was constructed on a framework of wooden piles through which the sea washed, nevertheless standing for eighty years.) In the other direction, the limit of visibility is Strumble Head, also bearing a lighthouse.

A walk of three or four miles along this remote and craggy coast is well worth while. Ravens, buzzards (perhaps being mobbed by other birds), and kestrels are the larger birds to be seen, while the stonechat and yellowhammer are much in evidence. Seals are often seen a short distance away from the foot of the cliff looking back at the coast path walker.

To the right of the path soon after leaving St David's Head are the remains of a Neolithic (3000BC) burial chamber known as Arthur's Quoit. The capstone is

OPPOSITE ABOVE: Lochtyn, Dyfed.

OPPOSITE BELOW LEFT: looking south from Mwnt to Cardigan Island, Dyfed.

OPPOSITE BELOW RIGHT: St David's Head, Dyfed.

Sea-shore view at Marloes, Dyfed.

thirteen feet long. An eighty-foot high waterslide near Penbiri where a stream plunges to the sea is a rare sight on these cliffs.

Trust ownership ends north of Penbiri's summit, and the short climb to the top gives a view out of all proportion to the effort involved. At 573 feet it is but a modest hill, but its craggy shape, and the way it rears up from the surrounding flat country gives it the character of a small mountain.

Carnllidi, twenty-two feet higher, is also worth a climb on the way back. From this vantage point can be seen Iron Age fields to the north, and the ruins of a radar station which used the site of a World War I hydrophone installation. Underwater detectors are said to have led to the destruction of fifteen German U-boats. On exceptionally clear days the Irish Wicklow Hills are just discernible across St George's Channel.

St Bride's Bay (north side)

A great deal of the south-facing arm of St Bride's Bay, perhaps nine or ten miles, is owned by the Trust. This stretches from the northern end of Newgale Sands with two breaks to Porthlysgi Bay. Additionally the Trust now owns Lower Treginnis Farm and the headland opposite Ramsey Island, the westernmost mainland promontory in Wales. The Pembrokeshire Coast Path follows the unspoilt cliffs. The purchase of this property in 1984 was made possible by Enterprise Funds, the Wales in Trust Fund and grants from the National Heritage Memorial Fund and the Countryside Commission. There is no parking on Lower Treginnis Farm, but pedestrian access can be achieved through the farm itself. Westerly, there are views across the tidal race of Ramsey Sound to Ramsey Island which may be reached from Porthstinan, and round here the Trust owns several other small properties.

Most visitors will be introduced to this coast where the A487 drops down to the attractive village of Solva. A National Trust information centre is open in the village during the summer months.

Geographically, the winding, steep-sided channel is a ria or drowned valley. Historically, this tortuous sea loch gave protection to the community which developed there, both from the weather and the Viking attempts at rape and pillage. That some of these may have succeeded is evidenced by the name Solva, which is Danish for samphire, a plant still found locally.

Solva was a busy little shipping port until the end of the last century; its steamship was sunk by a German U-boat in 1915. Limekilns, warehouses and a quay attest to this past activity, and you could get a single ticket to the USA for £4 in the 1840s.

A gentle climb to the cock's comb crest of Gribin Point above the limekilns will unfold the landscape. An Iron Age promontory 'fort' straddles the seaward end. Beyond Gribin Point the path descends steeply to an attractive pebble beach called Gwadn (the Trust is not responsible for the unsightly bulldozed tracks up the valley; they are outside its land) and climbs again to Penrhyn where it stays high for some distance.

Near enough to the coast – half a mile – to be considered in this book is Pointz Castle, a Norman motte named after one Ponce, an eleventh century tenant of the Bishop of St David's. A car park here gives access to a secluded beach, Porthmynawyd.

Another access point to this coast is from the cliff-top car park above Caer-fai where there is a fine stretch of sand at low tide. Much of the stone for St David's Cathedral came from here. Going eastwards, practically every headland carries an Iron Age earthwork. The cliffs show massive folding in the Cambrian rocks.

Further west, the tiny inlet of Porth Clais is a similar place to Solva, though smaller. A breakwater at the entrance keeps out the worst of the tidal surge. The limekilns have been restored; they operated from 1650 to 1900.

The Marloes Peninsula

About four miles of spectacular coast, plus two islands, Midland Isle and Gateholm. The former is half a mile offshore across turbulent six-knot waters and a kind of giant's stepping-stone between the mainland and Skomer. Gateholm is reached by a low-water scramble, and on its flat plateau is evidence of a considerable settlement in the Dark Ages.

The tip of the property is called the Deer Park, as during the Edwardes period of ownership they built (in about 1800) a deer-proof wall across the neck of the peninsula, but there is no evidence that deer were ever introduced. Iron Age people had built a defensive bank across the same narrow point about 2000 years earlier. Another earthwork of this era is on the cliff top just west of Gateholm.

The attractive small inlet of Martin's Haven at the road end is the starting place for boat trips to Skomer (enquire locally for details), and above the cove is the Lockley Lodge Interpretive Centre run by the West

Wales Naturalists' Trust which leases Skomer from the Nature Conservancy Council.

A walk round the cliffs of the Deer Park, taking in the coastguard lookout on the highest point, gives good views of the islands – Skokholm with its lighthouse is three miles south-west – and the abundant bird life. Fulmars and choughs breed on the west-facing cliffs, and seals have their pups in certain caves. Grassholm, the home of many thousands of gannets, lies ten miles west, and is only seen as the walker progresses south-east along the peninsula towards Gateholm, as initially it is hidden behind Skomer.

The two coasts of the peninsula – north, rocks more rounded, slopes gentler, with much blackthorn and gorse, while the south exhibits jagged rock and little vegetation – are due to the different rock types – silurian on the south, and the Skomer volcanic series on the north. The red crags of Gateholm show it to be of old red sandstone. The stronger winds on the south side keep all vegetation pruned low to the ground.

Kete

A mile of old red sandstone coast on the west side of the Dale peninsula, the site of HMS *Harrier*, a naval air direction centre which closed in 1960. Concrete foundations remain from this installation, and the Trust car park, one mile north of St Ann's Head, uses hard-standing dating back to the war. When the Trust took over the site the area was littered with ugly huts and fences. Mesolithic flints – about 10,000 years old – were discovered on this stretch of coast.

Freshwater West

The National Trust owns about a mile of sea frontage, and a sand dune hinterland of a similar depth protects this scenic area from despoliation.

Warning notices and flags inform visitors that currents and quicksands render the beach too dangerous to use, but at low tide, when the waves are creaming in over the golden sand, the sight is spectacularly beautiful. The south-westerlies have carried the sand 200 feet up and well back from the road giving a well developed dune system.

On the southern headland the Pembrokeshire Coast National Park has restored a seaweed drying hut, the last of twenty or so such thatched structures where families used to dry the purple laver seaweed after collection and before cleaning and despatching to market for human consumption.

Stackpole

One of the National Trust properties with the greatest variety of interest and beauty on the whole of the coastline of England and Wales. Not only is there a superb sequence of cliffs and beaches, but three long wood-bordered lakes reach to the sea through fertile farmland.

The name 'Stackpole' comes from the Norse *stac*, an isolated rock, and *pollr*, a small inlet, and this well describes the scene around Stackpole Quay, about half-way along the eight miles of cliffs. Eastward from the Quay is perhaps the least interesting stretch – maybe it's something to do with the fact that the rock here is old red sandstone – and this reaches as far as Freshwater East. Stackpole Quay, where there is a Trust car park, was one of many small ports in West Wales. As the roads were so poor the sea was the natural means of communication. The hinterland was owned by the Earls of Cawdor (who had married into the Lort family whose land it then was) and they kept their yacht at Stackpole Quay. The buildings nearby are now holiday cottages let by the Trust (details from the South Wales Regional Office). For its conservation work at Stackpole the Trust was given the Prince of Wales Award.

Over the cliffs to the south is Barafundle Bay, a beach of sublime quality backed by dunes and untainted by cars. The coast path leads out to Stackpole Head where the limestone cliffs provide homes for razorbills, guillemots, kittiwakes and a few puffins and choughs. Blow holes in various stages of development punctuate the cliff top, so care is necessary. Alas, the irritating Milford Haven chimneys can be seen poking their tips over the intervening country, and a north wind will waft sulphurous fumes even to Stackpole.

After rounding Saddle Point the spacious sands of Broad Haven, the second of Stackpole's great bays, come into view, backed by dunes stretching north-east high across the Warren to link up with Barafundle's own dune system. Broad Haven is another access point for cars.

Behind the beach the three lakes come together. They were formed between 1790 and 1840 by damming three narrow valleys, two of which were formerly tidal. Thus a freshwater habitat was added to the area. Paths provide walks along the water's edge and across causeways giving a variety of circular options. From these routes you may see reed-warblers, coots, kingfishers and herons. Water lilies

Lydstep Headland,
Dyfed.

float on the surface, and roach, tench, pike and eel live under water. Otters live in the lakes too. The Pembrokeshire Coast National Park publishes a leaflet about the routes round the lakes which are based on the National Park car park at Bosherston, one mile inland.

The National Trust and the Nature Conservancy Council jointly manage the designated National Nature Reserve, and wardens of both these organizations are based at Stackpole Home Farm where there is also a National Trust Basecamp. Parties stay here while doing voluntary work in the neighbourhood. This is currently being developed as an educational centre for parties of up to thirty who will study geographical, geological, ecological and historical topics while leaving time for orienteering, swimming and canoeing.

The former mansion of the Cawdor family, Stackpole Court, was demolished in 1967 and the property came to the Trust in 1976.

Lydstep Headland and Manorbier

A bold limestone promontory protecting the sandy beach of Lydstep Haven (and, it must be said, its associated caravan sites) from the south-westerlies.

Trust members are allowed, on production of their membership cards, to drive to the Headland car park. At low tide the cavern (signposted) is worth seeing. A limestone quarry on the tip of the Headland which once sent loaded sailing ships across the Bristol Channel to Devon and Somerset and up to Cardigan has gone attractively back to nature. Choughs may be seen on the cliffs. This is a good vantage point for the island of Caldey.

Two miles to the west is the 48-acre Manorbier property. Its vertically striped sandstone cliffs are noteworthy.

The Tudor Merchant's House, Tenby

A narrow, three-storey mediaeval house standing in Quay Hill above the harbour. Believed to be a fourteenth-century house with fifteenth-century alterations, it was beautifully restored, and is well appointed with furniture which, though later than the house, fits the character of the dwelling admirably.

Wall paintings discovered in the 1960s under about twenty-eight coats of limewash are contemporary with the house. A small shop is sited in the entrance hall. A colour brochure is available.

The Colby Estate, Amroth

Amroth is the southern terminal of the Pembrokeshire Coast Path, and is a small seaside resort with steep wooded hills running up behind the beach. Much of this hinterland was given to the Trust in 1980, and includes the woods and gardens of Colby Lodge which are open to the public. The house is not open. In the formal gardens is an attractive gazebo and a fountain in the form of a recumbent woman. An illustrated brochure is available.

West Glamorgan **The South Gower Coast**

The Gower peninsula has miraculously escaped the worst ravages of rampant commercialism despite being so close to the Swansea conurbation.

The Trust owns the three boldest headlands west of the Mumbles, with much of the finest cliffland between, as well as the deep, narrow limestone cleft, the Bishopston valley, which pokes inland for a couple of miles, its river disappearing below ground, but emerging to flow into the sea at Pwlldu Bay. The total length of coastline owned from east to west is about twelve miles.

Access to the first strip of coastal land starting at the east end is easy. A good car park at Southgate enables the walker to go in either direction along a track above and behind the cliffs. High Pennard, the lofty hill top on Pwlldu Head bears an Iron Age fort. There are a number of caves in the limestone rock. Much horse-riding is practised along the cliff top.

The next beach partly owned by the Trust going west is Three Cliffs Bay, which merges at low tide with Oxwich Bay to the west to form a south-facing three-mile beach of exceptional beauty. The sands have blown inland and upwards for some distance to form Pennard Burrows, to the east of Three Cliffs Bay, and Nicholaston Burrows to the west. Among the dunes is a stone burial chamber (Neolithic) and not far away the motte of a Norman motte-and-bailey fortification. The single most dramatic feature along this coast is Great Tor, a vertical cliff of skyscraper proportions, best seen from below at low tide. Most of Oxwich Bay is not owned by the Trust, but is a National Nature Reserve managed by the Nature Conservancy Council which has a Reserve Centre behind the beach at Oxwich. The Centre sells leaflets about the area.

The National Nature Reserve extends into National Trust property where it begins again near Oxwich Point. This next property is about three miles long and reaches nearly to Port Eynon.

The last Trust-owned section begins at Port Eynon Point, and is about five miles long, as far as Kitchen Corner. At Port Eynon Point a mediaeval dovecote has been restored. This length of coastline, being more remote than the others, and having higher, more precipitous cliffs, has a larger sea-bird population. Fulmars and kittiwakes breed. The earthworks of three more Iron Age promontory forts may be seen at Paviland, the Knave and Fall Bay. East of Tears Point there are several sandy beaches at low tide. And so Worms Head is reached.

The West Gower Coast

In an area where there is so much beauty it is almost invidious to pick out some sites above others as 'special'. But the gleaming scimitar of Rhossili Bay, with its backdrop of Rhossili Down and the dramatic Worms Head and Burry Holms framing the picture, gives the whole scene a theatrical completeness seldom found in nature.

The Trust has established a summer information centre in the row of coastguard cottages at Rhossili near the car park, and it is from here that most visitors will start their exploration of this corner of Gower. The twelfth-century church has a memorial to Petty Officer Edgar Evans who was born in the parish and who was one of Captain Scott's party which reached the South Pole in 1912 but died on the way back.

At low tide the black timbers which can be seen sticking out of the sand below the village are the ribs of the *Helvetia* which was driven ashore in 1887. Her crew was saved. The beach is used by surfers.

The summit of Rhossili Down is the Beacon, at 632 feet the highest point in Gower. It is much favoured by hang-gliding enthusiasts. To the north is an ancient burial site of about 2500BC. The Viking chief here interred is supposed to be one Sweyne, who gave his name to Swansea.

The visitor thinking of scrambling across the rocks (it is referred to on signs as 'the causeway', but no man-made surface exists) to Worms Head must first establish that he has time to accomplish this 'walk' between tides, and a visit to the Trust Information

Fulmar spitting oil.

Centre will tell him this. The crossing can safely be done 2½ hours either side of low tide. The name 'Worm' is derived from an Old English word meaning dragon, and seen from certain angles the humps and bumps of the Head's components do look like a sea serpent. At bird breeding time the visitor is asked not to go right out to the best nesting places.

The North Gower Coast

The Trust owns nearly 2000 acres of sand burrows, commercial forest and salt-marsh centred on Whitford Burrows and Llanrhidian Marsh. The area has not got the same appeal to visitors as the two other Gower coastlines, but these two areas are of the greatest importance floristically and for birds. Wading birds are attracted to the salt-marshes in large numbers, and the site is managed by the Nature Conservancy Council and the West Glamorgan Wildfowlers' Association.

NORTHERN IRELAND

CO. LONDONDERRY **Mussenden Temple, Black Glen, Bishop's Gate, Downhill Castle ruins and Bar Mouth**

Remarkable for the elegant Mussenden Temple (1785), perched on a high cliff top above the gleaming scimitar of Downhill Strand. Not far away there once stood Downhill Castle (1770) on a similar site, positioned to catch the coldest winds, and making no concession to comfort. Only its ruins remain.

The Temple is a Corinthian-columned rotunda inspired by the Temple of Vesta at Tivoli. The domed roof carries a large urn contrived to serve as a finial. Its builder, Frederick Hervey, the Earl-Bishop of Derry, placed his library inside, and allowed the estate's Roman Catholic servants to celebrate mass in the undercroft. He named his expensive, ashlar-built whim after his cousin, Mrs Mussenden.

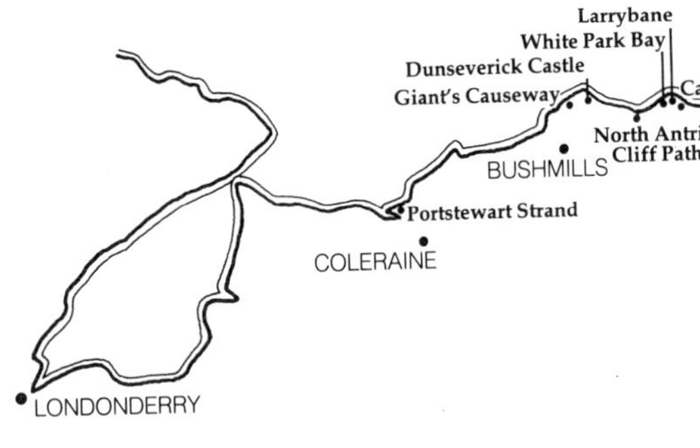

The Bishop's Gate survives at the entrance to the demesne, its environs cheerful with roses and shrubs in the summer. The Black Glen leads to a pond and spectacular views along the Donegal and Antrim coasts.

A short distance to the east is Bar Mouth wildlife sanctuary at the mouth of the river Bann. It has an observation hide with illustrations inside it of the birds which may be seen from it.

Co. Antrim **The Giant's Causeway and the North Antrim Coast**

For convenience, the Trust properties between the mouth of the river Bann and Ballycastle to the east are considered together. They are described from west to east.

Portstewart Strand (actually in Co. Londonderry) is 185 acres of duneland over a three-mile length of coast to the west of Portstewart. Cars may park on the beach at low tide, but motorcycles are not allowed. There is a shop, refreshments and lavatories.

Beyond Bushmills the Causeway Coast begins, from Runkerry round to Dunseverick, a distance of five or six miles. Of this sharply indented cliff, only about a quarter of a mile is the Giant's Causeway proper, between Port Ganny and Port Noffer, and this is itself split into the Grand, Middle and Little Causeways.

This feature, which has aroused so much curiosity for centuries, is composed of vast numbers of curiously symmetrical basalt columns which seem to match up with the similar geological structure at Fingal's Cave on Staffa in the Hebrides. The material is formed from the cooled lava which erupted about sixty million years ago. Most of the columns are hexagonal, but there are pentagons, and four-, seven- and ten-sided columns.

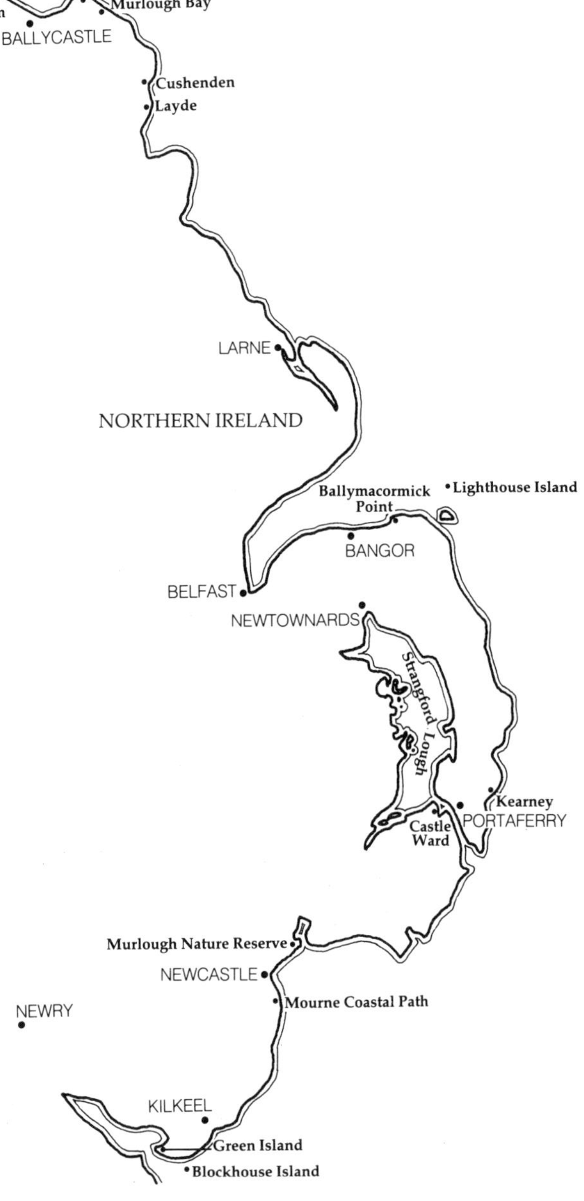

Each little cove has a name, and the Celtic attribution Port-na-Spaniagh has obvious connections with the wreck of the Armada galliass *Gerona* in 1588. In 1969 a large quantity of coins, jewellery and weapons was recovered from the sea here.

The beauty and interest of the coast are not concentrated into this one section. The whole coast-

The Giant's Causeway, Co. Antrim.

line is a succession of rugged headlands and beautiful bays. Sea-birds frequent the area in large numbers and the botanist will find plants such as the sea-spleenwort, sea-fescue and the vernal squill. Grey seals are frequent visitors to the quieter bays.

The Trust does not own all this stretch of coast, but much of the cliff path is maintained by it. In places there is a high and low path, and six old kelp kilns and drying walls can be seen from the paths.

In the last century the Giant's Causeway was the focus for guides competing for the tourists' custom, and small trading shacks proliferated beside the approach path. The Trust removed all these, but provides a shop, information office and refreshments.

Dunseverick Castle and harbour occupy five acres, but little remains of the castle except a single tower. After a lively history it was demolished by Cromwell's army.

The Trust's Whitepark Bay property extends to 179 acres of sandy shore, flanked by white chalk cliffs, a contrast to the brown basalt of the Causeway Cliffs to the west. This beautiful beach is backed by dunes, pasture and arable land, and a youth hostel is sited behind the bay. The small village of Portbradden shelters under a cliff at the western end of the bay. Man has lived here for thousands of years; finds of a Neolithic date have been made. A nature trail is laid out, and an eight-page booklet describes the route and what there is to see.

Larrybane and Carrick-a-Rede are the last two properties on this strip of coast, eighty-eight acres altogether. Larrybane was acquired only in 1979, and

Whitepark Bay, Co. Antrim.

the Trust has now completed a major tidy-up job—clearing away disused and unsightly quarry buildings. Carrick-a-Rede is a different kind of site, and is famous for its sixty-foot long rope bridge. This is needed by the fishermen to reach the small island from which they catch salmon, and is only in position from May to September. It is also a tourist attraction; the eighty-foot deep chasm has the capacity to thrill those bold enough to test it. The bridge is also useful for birdwatchers, and offers excellent views of seabirds going about their business, including the unusual sight of razorbills and guillemots swimming under water in pursuit of small fish, a spectacle assisted by the shallow water and sandy bottom between the rocks.

The views from Carrick-a-Rede are magnificent. Offshore is the island of Rathlin with the Hebrides beyond, and eastwards stretch more cliffs with Fair Head in the distance.

Fair Head, Murlough Bay and Torr Head

Fair Head (over 600 feet high) can justly claim to be the north-east corner of Ireland, and its unspoilt beauty is appropriately superlative. Choughs are present though their numbers have declined in the past thirty years or so. Gannets can often be seen diving offshore, and a herd of wild goats lives on the cliff slopes. The Mull of Kintyre is often visible across the North Channel.

Two farmhouses and a cottage in the local vernacular style are sited at the foot of the wooded slopes of Murlough Bay, and contribute to the scene as traditional buildings moulded by time.

The Trust owns approximately 500 acres of this splendid coastline of cliffs, woods and grassy, sheep-grazed slopes.

In the section on Golden Cap (Dorset) mention was made of a memorial to Lord Antrim (Chairman of the Trust 1965–77) set on its summit. Another reminder of his service is a memorial set in the wall beside Benvan Cottage.

Cushendun and Layde

The small village of Cushendun is situated at the mouth of Glen Dun, one of the beautiful Glens of Antrim. The surprise here is the houses built in 1912, 1923 and 1925 by Clough Williams-Ellis for Lord Cushendun. Some of them, the Maud Cottages, were built in the Cornish style in honour of Lord Cushendun's first wife, a Cornish lady.

The Trust also owns land at nearby Layde. A path leaves a car park and heads down to a small beach, passing the ruins of the twelfth-century Layde Church, a wonderfully peaceful and atmospheric spot.

Murlough Bay, Co. Antrim.

BELFAST **Crown Liquor Saloon, Great Victoria Street**

The acquisition of this establishment illustrates the Trust's recognition of the value and rarity of a richly ornamented Victorian pub, and it gets into a book about the coast for the very good reason that Belfast is a port.

Bass Ireland manage it still and have carried out a meticulous programme with the Trust to restore authentically the extravagant nineteenth-century interior with its mirrors, tiles, carvings, mosaics and ceramics. Of course it provides full bar facilities and snack lunches.

CO. DOWN **Belfast Lough**

The Trust owns three small properties at the mouth of Belfast Lough.

Lighthouse Island One of the Copeland Islands, this 43-acre island is managed as a bird observatory. The remains of an interesting old lighthouse (*c.* 1711) may be seen, but the present operational light is on neighbouring Mew Island.

Cockle Island A half-acre island near Bangor. No public access during the bird breeding season of May to July.

Ballymacormick Point A 44-acre promontory of rough land reached from the east end of Bangor promenade or from the Watch House, Groomport.

Kearney and Knockinelder

Two slivers of coastline, two miles in all, but including thirteen houses in the village of Kearney. An additional large area of covenanted land adds to the importance of this coastal strip.

Strangford Lough Wildlife Scheme

This enormous tidal inlet bites twenty miles into County Down from its narrow channel between Portaferry and Strangford. (The name 'Strangford' is a corruption of the Viking *strang fjord*, and refers to the swift tidal current at its mouth.)

Under a conservation scheme launched in 1966 the Trust manages the foreshore, and brings together in its Strangford Lough Committee representatives of everyone interested in the Lough—sailors, divers, landowners, farmers, ornithologists, wildfowlers and fishermen, and this body works together for the preservation of all that is special about Strangford, its landscape and wildlife.

This initiative, with the Trust as pilot, was necessary for several reasons. Fears that wrong developments could damage the Lough (its northern tip is only fifteen minutes from the outskirts of Belfast) were complicated in Northern Ireland by the lack of those statutory bodies, such as the National Parks and the Countryside Commission, which might have triggered a protective process in England and Wales.

Cushendun,
Co. Antrim.

The Lough is shallow and the thirty-five or so islands are drumlins of boulder clay left over from the last Ice Age; these features can also be seen in the country round about.

The wildlife which uses the Lough is prodigious in its variety. Tens of thousands of wildfowl and waders and forty per cent of the world's population of pale-bellied brent geese come to Strangford Lough in the winter. Four different kinds of terns nest here, and the underwater life entices marine biologists to probe its secrets.

Common seals inhabit the smaller islands giving birth to their pups in late June. Porpoises and killer whales are also known to negotiate the narrow entrance. Foxes haunt the tidelines at night and otters are not unknown.

In the past fishing and a shell fishery have operated commercially, but over-fishing and more competitive catches elsewhere have made it uneconomic now, though it is done recreationally.

The Trust owns several islands and Ballyhenry Island, Darragh Island, Gibb's Island, Taggart Island,

Salt Island and Green Island can all be visited by boat. Flowers and butterflies abound. Certain other islands are preserved for their ornithological interest.

Car parks, viewpoints and hides are available for visitors, and a booklet describing the Lough is available locally.

Mount Stewart (the house, garden and Temple of the Winds)

The complicated building history of the house dates from 1744 but owes most of what is seen today to the early nineteenth century, and it was completed in 1828. Its south front, the side which faces down Strangford Lough, is long and low and two storeys high, with a loggia supported on four Ionic columns.

The somewhat squat exterior does nothing to prepare the visitor for the hall in the centre of the house. The height extends through two floors to a glass dome with a first-floor gallery overlooking the striking checked floor, probably originally intended for the display of sculpture. In contrast to this heavily classical room, the music room in the centre of the west front has a lightness and delicacy appropriate to its function, though it was not designed as such.

The contents of the house are as memorable as the architecture. A full-sized Stubbs masterpiece showing Hambletonian, the racehorse, is pre-eminent, but there are numerous other splendid paintings, as well as furniture and fittings of many styles.

Until 1921 the garden at Mount Stewart was one mile away, and the house was shaded and screened by trees. Edith, the energetic Marchioness of Londonderry, changed all that. She laid out a series of terraces, avenues, enclaves and theme gardens so that one can happily wander here all day, guidebook in hand, noting the numerous varieties and marvelling at their sculptural and colourful composition.

To the east of the house is the Temple of the Winds, a neo-classical two-storey eyecatcher set on a promontory to give spectacular views across the Lough. Designed by James 'Athenian' Stuart for the 1st Marquess of Londonderry between 1782 and 1785, it served as a banqueting house, belvedere and estate pavilion, but might be regarded by present-day pragmatists as a folly, though of the most utilitarian kind. The first-floor room, reached by a spiral staircase housed in an apsidal tower at the rear, is decorated with a plasterwork ceiling and marquetry floor of exquisite beauty. Beneath this stunning little building, a vaulted basement gives access to a passage with wine cellar and scullery which led to domestic rooms hidden from view by the contours of the hill.

There is a shop at the house and a tea room in the east wing. Two guidebooks describe the house and the garden.

Castle Ward

There can be no more beautifully sited house in Northern Ireland than Castle Ward, nor one which so captures the interest of the visitor. Perhaps more than most country houses one needs to 'read it up' beforehand and walk round the exterior to appreciate the duplicity of architectural styles which contributes so much to the attraction.

Castle Ward is not a fortress but a delightful dwelling looking across the entrance of Strangford Lough. Its builders were Bernard Ward and his wife Anne; Ward had been MP for County Down for many years. No doubt the house was a material manifestation of the prestige he acquired when created Baron Bangor in 1770. But the couple could not agree on the architecture, so an unknown architect designed one front in the classical Palladian style for Lord Bangor and the other in the fashionable Gothic taste for his independently minded wife. The interior reflects the exterior from basement to attic. This incompatibility must clearly have caused problems in the marriage, or may have been a symptom of a deeper difficulty. At all events Lady Anne Ward deserted the quiet shores of Strangford Lough for the livelier spa waters of Bath.

One of the curiosities of Castle Ward is the domestic arrangements. The servants occupied quarters round a courtyard linked to the house by an underground passage, and only a valet or lady's maid slept in the house. The laundry, employing late nineteenth-century equipment, has been restored by the Trust.

The garden, sheltered by giant oaks and beeches, grows azaleas and rhododendrons, and swathes of daffodils and bluebells delight the eye in the spring. The climate is mild enough for palms to thrive. A 1610 three-storey tower house built for defensive purposes stands in the farmyard.

Beyond here and approached by a lime avenue is the Temple Water—currently being restored—a long, straight-sided lake. Two ponds nearby carry a collection of wildfowl, and the object is to introduce the visitor to the Trust's Strangford Lough Wildlife Scheme. Above is the Temple, a large summer pavilion in the classical style.

Also on the estate is Audley's Castle, a fifteenth-century tower house on a rocky bluff overlooking the entrance to Strangford Lough, and the view from the top is well worth the climb. Near here, a Neolithic burial chamber dates the occupation of the area back to several millennia BC. Thirty-four skeletons were found during a 1951 excavation. Throughout the estate there is a variety of opportunities for walks along the coast and through woodland. A hide gives visitors a view over the birds which visit Audley's Bay.

Elsewhere on the property is a caravan site, holiday cottages and a Basecamp for young people. In bad weather, an audio-visual show describing the history and architecture of the house is given in the theatre, a large converted barn in the stable yard. Concerts and exhibitions are also held. The estate sawmill and cornmill have been restored and are open to the public. The old slaughterhouse is an information centre and shop. Teas are served in the season. A guidebook describes the estate, and a history pack has been prepared for children. In 1981 Castle Ward received the Sandford Award for Heritage Education.

Management by the wardens and their staff includes the monitoring of the sea buckthorn, protecting the dunes, maintaining the paths and interpreting the reserve to visitors.

Dundrum Inner Bay is a vastly important area for birds, particularly as a feeding ground. The breeding birds are shelduck, mallard, heron and moorhen. During the winter there may be 4000 to 5000 waders in Dundrum Inner Bay, of twelve different species.

Beside the car park near the A24 Belfast to Newcastle road is an information and interpretation centre where visitors can discover the wealth of interest as it changes with the season. From here paths head for the beach a short distance away, and a programme of guided walks is provided in the summer. This positive policy was responsible for Murlough being given a Certificate of Distinction in the British Tourist Authority's 'Come to Britain' Award Scheme in 1981.

Leaflets describing the reserve can be obtained from the information centre. Access to those parts of the reserve away from the paths is by permit only. The area is managed with Queen's University, Belfast.

Murlough Nature Reserve, Dundrum

This large (938 acres) promontory of sand dunes and heathland occupies one side of the tidal channel leading into Dundrum Inner Bay. Its south-east-facing sea-shore is sandy and in demand for public recreation, while the inland aspect of the sand-bar is mud, much loved by birds. In between are the hundreds of acres of massive sand dunes for which the area is famous, some of them 5000 years old, and there are 'young' ones near the sea 120 feet high. The Mourne Mountains provide a theatrical backdrop.

Prehistoric man lived here, and his occupation sites are occasionally uncovered by wind erosion when they are examined by archaeologists. Rabbits were culled for flesh and fur until fairly recent times.

During World War II Murlough was a Services training ground and aircraft dispersal area, and it was later planned to turn the dunes into a coniferous forest, and a trial plot of 1000 Corsican pines was planted at the south end of the reserve. But Murlough came to the Trust, and since 1967 a programme of landscape and nature conservation has gone forward, to preserve its special character and manage and develop its potential for wildlife while allowing public access.

The Mourne Coastal Path

The Trust owns and maintains two paths south of Newcastle. One gives access to the Mourne Mountains up the Bloody River, and the other runs for 1½ miles along the coast south of Bloody Bridge. Both were made by local men under job creation schemes, primarily Enterprise Ulster, and the acquisition of land was made possible by donations and Enterprise Neptune.

The area is rich in geological interest. Especially notable are a ring dyke, interesting forms of granite, and benches or platforms from before the Ice Age. It is also a storehouse of legend and ecclesiastical history. The river crossing was consecrated by the founding of the church of St Mary, and its remains can still be seen. Armor's Hole is here too; a deep cave worn by wave action, into which it is said an old man named Armor was thrown by his son in the eighteenth century. His body was found the next day on the opposite side of Dundrum Bay.

Bloody Bridge gets its name from the best known incident in the wars of 1641. Although the facts are now lost, tradition has it that a group of Protestant prisoners was being brought under escort from Newry to Newcastle in exchange for Irish prisoners.

The Irish commander, Russell, hearing that he was to be attacked at Newcastle, or, as another version puts it, that his prisoners had been hanged there, slew about fifty of his charges on the rocks.

There is a car park at Bloody Bridge which is the most convenient access point.

Co. Down **Blockhouse Island and Green Island**
These two small islands, totalling only two acres in all, lie in the narrow strait at the entrance to Carlingford Lough, and just on the Northern Ireland side of the channel.

They are important nesting sites for common, arctic and roseate terns, and have therefore been leased to the Royal Society for the Protection of Birds from whom permits to visit have to be obtained.

HEADQUARTERS AND REGIONAL OFFICES HAVING COASTAL PROPERTIES

Headquarters:
36 Queen Anne's Gate
London, SW1H 9AS (01 222 9251)

Membership:
PO BOX 30, Beckenham,
Kent BR3 4TL (01 650 7263)

ENGLAND

Cornwall:
Lanhydrock Park, Bodmin, Cornwall
PL30 4DE (Bodmin 4284)

Devon:
Killerton House, Broadclyst,
Exeter, Devon EX5 3LE (Exeter 881691)

East Anglia (*Essex Cambridgeshire, Norfolk, Suffolk*):
Blickling, Norwich, Norfolk NR11 6NF
(Aylsham 3471)

Kent & East Sussex (*includes south-eastern Greater London*):
Scotney Castle, Lamberhurst,
Tunbridge Wells, Kent
TN3 8JN (Lamberhurst 890651)

Mercia (*Greater Manchester, Merseyside, Shropshire, most of Cheshire and Staffordshire, part of West Midlands*):
Attingham Park, Shrewsbury,
Shropshire SY4 4TP (Upton Magna 343)

Northumbria (*Durham, Northumberland and Tyne and Wear*)
Scots' Gap, Morpeth
Northumberland NE61 4EG
(Scots' Gap 691)

North West (*Cumbria and Lancashire*):
Rothay Holme, Rothay Road,
Ambleside, Cumbria LA22 0EJ
(Ambleside 3883)

Southern (*includes Hampshire, the Isle of Wight, south-western Greater London, Surrey and West Sussex*):
Polesden Lacey, Dorking,
Surrey RH5 6BD (Bookham 53401)

Wessex (*Avon, Dorset, Somerset, Wiltshire*):
Stourton, Warminster, Wiltshire
BA12 6QD (Bourton, Dorset 840224)

Yorkshire (*includes North, South and West Yorkshire, Cleveland and North Humberside*):
Goddards, 27 Tadcaster Road,
Dringhouses, York YO2 2QG
(York 702021)

WALES

North Wales:
Trinity Square,
Llandudno, Gwynedd
LL30 2DE (Llandudno 74421)

South Wales:
The King's Head, Llandeilo,
Dyfed SA19 6BN
(Llandeilo 822800)

NORTHERN IRELAND

Rowallane House, Saintfield,
Ballynahinch, County Down BT24 7LH
(Saintfield 510721)

Acknowledgements

We acknowledge with warmth the many people who have helped us to compile this work.

In particular Hilary Soper helped unravel the complexities of geomorphological process at the coast. And Peter Crookston kindly allowed use of material from an *Observer* magazine article on speciation. Regional Directors, Information Officers and Wardens of the National Trust offered nuggets of great value relating to the coast in their care, to say nothing of tea and sympathy.

We remember with gratitude many sunbaked days, and not a few wet and windy ones, which allowed us a measure of insight into the nature of our precious coastal assets. And most of all we salute the National Trust, which holds such a significant part of the coast and manages it with practical understanding. We believe that joining the Trust is one of the most powerful ways in which as individuals we can safeguard our coastal heritage.

T.S.
B. Le M.

The authors and publishers would like to thank the following who supplied illustrations:

Colour

Heather Angel 35, 59(above and below), 92/3, 101, 122, 123(left); **Ardea** 92 (centre), Bob Gibbons 34, John Mason 92(below); **J. Allan Cash** 14, 100; **Noel Cusa** 22/3, 38/9, 50/51, 62/3, 88/9, 104/5; **Eric and David Hosking** John Hawkins 27; **Frank Lane Agency** Desmond Dugan 123(right), M. Nimmo 30/31, W. Wisniewski 75; **Jim Greenfield** 58(above); **Simon McBride** 11, 96/7, 148, 149; **The National Trust** 108(above), 152(below), John Bethell 145, BKS Surveys 181, John Gollop 134, R. Hillgrove 152(above), 164/5, 169(below), Alan North 3, 19, 46/7, 78/9, 131, 135, 153, 177, 200, 205(below left), C. M. Radcliffe 126/7, 130, 205(above and below right), V. D. Shaw 209, Skyfotos 184/5, Tim Stephens 54, Charlie Waite 31(below), 74, 84/5, 92(top), 197, Andy Williams 169(above), Mike Williams 6, 15, 138, 139, 142, 143, 156, 157, 172, 173, 176, 180, 188, 189(above and below), 192, 193, 196/7, 213, 216, 217; **Natural Science Photos** 43, 84; **Seaphot** Keith Scholey 67(above), Peter Scoones 58(below); **J. C. Ticehurst** 66/7; **Woodfall Wildlife** Mary Breeds 108(below), Peter Corkhill 31(above), 67(below), 109, 115(above), Alan Potts 70/71, David Woodfall 1; **Peter Wrigley** 168.

Black and white

Aerofilms 150; **Heather Angel** 12, 13(right), 57(above), 61, 116(above and right), 125; **Aquila Photographics** 21, 44, 178, R. J. C. Blewitt 55, R. T. Mills 81(below), D. A. Smith 81(above); **Ardea** J. B. and S. Bottomley 116(left), David and Katie Urry 28, 36/7, 76, 87; **Noel Cusa** 20, 25, 29, 35, 49, 53(above and below), 56(above and below), 57(below), 60(above and below), 65(above and below), 68, 112(above and below), 113(left and right), 115(below), 118(left and right), 119(above, left and right), 120; **Mary Evans Picture Library** 94; **David Hosking** 33; **Eric Hosking** 36, 83(below), 121, 211; **Simon McBride** 99, 137, 146; **The National Trust** 203, Ray Bishop 151, Brian Bradbury 179, Peter Burton 191, Clifford R. Clemens 161, Enterprise Neptune 16, Leonard and Marjorie Gayton 158, Harry Graeme 167, A. F. Kersting 163, 170, Jeremy Taylor 185, Nicholas Toyne 17, 129, Charlie Waite 195(above and below), Mike Williams 140, 171, 186, 194, 206, 214/5, Charles Woolf 155, 160; **Natural Science Photos** F. Greenaway 72, **Portsmouth and Sunderland Newspapers Ltd** 13(left); **Seaphot** Menihin 83(above); **Derek G. Widdicombe** 102.

Index

Figures in italic refer to illustrations.

A
Abbotsbury 176
Aberconwy House 199
Admiral, red 20
Ailsa Craig 107
Albatross 77
Alderney 44
Anemones *60*
Asparagus, poor man's *125*
Auks 41, 113
  flight 73
Avocet 121, *121*

B
Badger 32
Baggy Point 132
Bank House Farm 198
Barmouth 203
Bar Mouth 212
Ballard Down 178
Barna Barrow 129
Barnacle, acorn *112*
  goose 114, *115*
Barras Nose 138
Bass Point 155
Bass Rock 44
Basset's Cove 144
Beach, sandy *62–3*
Beadnell 191
Beagles Point 158, *158*
Beaulieu River *116*
Beckland Valley 133
Bedruthan 141, *142*
Beer 174
Belfast Lough 217
Bembridge 182
Bempton 44, 45
Berry Head 30
Bio-luminescence 48
Bishop's Gate 212
Blackcap 21
Black Glen 212
Black Venn 175
Blakeney Point 33, 53, 186
Blockhouse Island 220
Bloody Bridge 220
Bockhill Farm *184*
Bolberry Down 25, 171, *171*
Bolt Tail 171
Boscastle 137, *138*
Bosherston 53
Bosigran 147
Bosloe 160
Bossiney Haven 138
Bossington Hill 129
Brancaster 189, *189*, 190
Branscombe Mouth 174
Brean Down 128, *129*
Brownsea Island *177*, 178
British Trust for Ornithology 80, 113
Brixham 30
Bugloss, viper's *31*
Bunting, cirl, 25, *25*
Burgh Marsh 197
Burning Cliff 176
Burton Cliff 176
Buston Links 190

C
Cabbage, sea 31, *31*, 92, 95
Caddow Combe 47, 130
Cadwith 155
Cae Glan-y-Mor 202
Cambeak 137
Camberwell Beauty 20
Campion, red 32
  sea 92, 95
  white 32
Cape Clear 80
Carbis Bay 146
Cardigan Island 107
Carlingford Lough 220
Carrot, sea *31*
Carwinion 160
Castle Point 134
Castle Ward 218
Cattle 107
Cemaes *200*, 201
Cemlyn 201
Channel Islands 44, 110
Chapel Carn Brea 147
Chapel Combe 144
Chapel Porth *143*, 144
Charmouth 175
Chenhalls 160
Chesil Beach 34, 56, *100*
Chichester harbour 123
Chideock 176
Chiffchaff 21
Chiton *57*
Chough 26, 27, *27*
Clegir Mawr 201
Coastguard 91, 94
Cockle, common 116, *117*, 118, 120
Colby Estate 209
Coleton Fishacre 25
Conwy Suspension Bridge 199
Corfe Castle 178
Cormorant 28, 72, *72*, 73, 113, 123
Corophium 118
Countisbury 129, 130
Crab, edible *57*
  fiddler *56*
  hermit 68, *68*
  porcelain 112
  shore *57*, 119, 125
  spider *56*
Crackington Haven *19*, 134, 137
Crane Castle 144
Crantock beach 142
Crest marine 32
Cricket, scaly 56, *56*
Crow 114
Crowlink 183
Crown Liquor Saloon 217
Crustaceans 65
Cuckoo 31
Cudden Point 151
Curlew 120, 122, 125
Cushendun 215, *217*
Cuttlefish 49, 113, *113*

D
Dab 69
Dartmouth 29
Dartmouth, Little 25, *172*, 173
Deadman's Cove 144
Deer, red 109, *109*
Dinas Gynfor 201
Dinas Oleu 203, *203*
Dinoflagellates 48
Diver, black throated 86
  great northern 86
  red-throated 86
Diving birds 73
Dizzard Point 134, *136*
Dodman, the *164*, 166
Dogfish 113
  lesser-spotted *114*
Dolphin 91
Downhill Castle 212
Doyen Castle 141
Drag fold *14*
Druridge Bay 190
Duckpool 133, *134*
Dundrum Bay 219
Dune, sand *50–51*, *115*
Dungeness 80
Dunlin 120
Dunstanburgh 191, *192*
Dunwich *16*
Dunwich Heath *54*, 185
Durlston Head 178

E
East Head 183
Egyptian House 149
Embleton Bay *193*
Erosion *12*, 13, *13*, 98ff.
Estuary *88–9*
Exmoor Basecamp 130
Exmouth 123
Exploitation, of fish stocks 77
  of seabirds 45
Eype 175, 176

F
Faeces, bird 30
Fair Head 215
Fal estuary *160*, 161
Farne Islands 36, *85*, 194, *194*, *195*
Farthingloe, Great 183
Fennel 32
Fertilizer, seaweed 114
Fescue, red 32
Fig, Hottentot 31, 133
Fishes, Royal 91
Fishing boats *66*, 68
Flamborough Head 98
Flounder 119, *120*
Fly, kelp 114
Foreland, the 129, *130*
Formby Point 199
Foula 43
Foulness 123
Fowey river 166
Fox 49, 125

Freshwater West 207
Froward Point, inner 173
Fulmar 43, 73, 80
  at nest *211*

G
Gallant's Bower 173
Gammon Head 172
Gannel estuary 142
Gannet 44, *44*, 69, 73, *75*, 77
Giant's Causeway 212, *213*
Glasswort *84*, 124, 125, *125*
Glendurgan 159
Goat 107ff.
Goby, rock 60, *60*
Godrevy 144
Godwits 120, 122, 125
  black-tailed 80
Golden cap 175, *176*
Goose, barnacle 80, 81, *81*, 82
  brent 123
Gower 209–12
Gramborough Hill 186
Grass, cord *84*, 124
  couch 114
  eel *122*, 123
  lyme 114
Green Island 220
Greenaleigh Point 129
Gribbin, the 166
Gribble 49
Groynes 102, 107
Guernsey 107
Guillemot *37*, 41, 42, *42*, 74
Gull, black-headed 45, 69, *70*
  herring 69, 95, 114
  lesser black-backed 32
Gulls 32
  flight 73
Gunwalloe 79, *152*, 154
Gurnard's Head 147

H
Hall Walk 167
Halophytes 29
Handfast Point 178
Hangman, Great 130, *132*
Hayburn Wyke 190
Heddon's Mouth 130, 132
Hedgehog 49, 125
Helford Passage 159
Helford River 158, *159*
Hell's Mouth 144
Heron 123, *123*, 125
Holderness 98
Holkham 53
Holly, sea 53
Holywell Bay 142
Hope Cove 171
Hore Point 146, 168
Horsey 186, *186*
Hudder Downs 144
Hunstanton 101
Hurlstone Point 129
Hydrobia 119, 120, 121, 123, 125, *125*
Hydroids 49

I
Ice-plant 31
Islay 80

J
Jack Scout Land 198
Jackdaw 26
Japweed *122*

K
Kearney 217
Kelp flies 49
Kelsey Head 142
Kete 207
Kiberick Cove *163*
Kingsbridge 25
Kingston Lacy 178
Kingswear 173
Kittiwake *35*, 41, 42, 73, 80
Knavocks, the 144
Knockinelder 217
Knot *87*
Kynance Cove 155, *157*

L
Labour-in-Vain Farm 176
Ladybirds 20, *20*
Land's End *93*, 147
Langmuir circulations 48
Lantic Bay 167, *168*
Layde 215
Leadenhall Market 45
Levant Beam Engine 147
Lichens 94
Lihou 107
Lime Kiln Hill 176
Limpet 60, 65, 112
  blue-rayed 49, 112
Lindisfarne Castle 195, 197
Lizard, common *53*, 95
Lizard, the 155
Lleyn 202
Lobster 65, *65*
Lochtyn 204, *205*
Lockley, Ronald 107
Loe Bar 152, *152*
Logan Rock 148
Longshore drift 15
Looe 170
Lowland Point 158
Low Newton 191
Lugworm 118, *118*, 120
Lundy 76, 107, *108*, 109, 133
Lydstep Headland 208, *209*
Lyme Regis 175
Lynmouth 129
Lynton 130

M
Maceley Cove 172
Maer Cliff 133
Mallow, tree 30, *31*, 95
Manorbier 208
Man Sands 173
Marconi Memorial 154
Marloes *206*, 207
Martello towers 27
Martin's Haven 26, 207
Martin, sand *36*, 41
Marram 13, 31
Mermaid's purse 49, 113
Mewstone, Dartmouth 173, *173*
Mewstone, Great 170
Middle Hope 128
Migration 20
Minack 148
Mink 125
Minsmere 121
Monarch butterflies 20
Montagu, Colonel 25
Morecambe Bay 124
Morston 187, *188*
Morte Point 132
Morwenstow 133
Mourne Coastal Path 219
Mouse, Rhum 110
  St Kilda 110
  wood 110
Mottistone 181
Mount's Bay 26
Mount Stewart 218
Mudflats 117
Mullet 84, 119, *119*
Mullion 155, *156*
Murlough 215, *216*, 219
Mussel *61*, 120
Mussenden Temple 212
Mwnt 204, *205*

N
Nare Head 163
National Trust, The 17, 25, 27, 33, 36, 53, 98, 122
Needles, the 181, *182*
Newdowns Head 144
Newtown, I. of W. 179
Newtown estuary *15*
Nine-mile Drive 171
North Hill 128

O
Oarweed *112*
Old Harry rocks 178
Old Mill Bay 173
Orache 114
Orielton 107
Orkney 107
Osprey 82, *83*, 84
Otter 111
Overbecks House 171
Oystercatcher 33, 53, 121

P
Park Head 141
Pebbles 48
Pedn-men-an-mere 148, *149*
Pedn-vounder 149
Penberth 148
Pencannow Point 134
Pendour Cove 147
Pendower Beach 163
Penguins 41
Pennant, Thomas 45
Penrhyn Castle 200
Pentire 140
Percuil 162
Peregrine 42, 43, *43*
Petrel, storm 41
Piddock 65, *65*
Pigeons 95
Pine, Monterey 29
Pipit, rock 27, 49
Plankton 32, 48
Plants, coastal 28, 29
Plas Newydd 201
Plas-yn-Rhiw 203
Plantain 102, 125
Plover, grey 121
  Kentish 55
  ringed 33, 55, *55*, 84
Plovers 120
Poldhu 154
Polperro 168, *169*
Polpry Cove 147
Polridmouth Cove 166
Polruan 167
Poltesco 155
Pont Pill 166, *167*
Pony, Rhum 109
  Shetland 110
Pool, rock 56, *58*, *59*
Poole 178
Porlock, Vale of 129
Porpoises 91
Port Gaverne 140
Port Quin 140, *140*
Porthcothan 141

Porthcurno *148*
Porth Gwylan 202
Porth Joke 142
Porthmellin Head 162
Porthtowan 144
Portlemouth, East 172
Portloe 163
Portreath 144
Portuguese man o'war 115, *115*
Prawle Point 172, 173
Prawn *59*, 68
Predannack 155
Puffin 41, 42, 73, *74*, 76, *76*, 77, 102

R

Rabbit 25, 32, 95, 107, 125
Rabbit warrens 110
Ragworm 68, 118, *118*
Ralph's Cupboard 144
Rame Head 170, *170*
Rare Breeds Survival Trust 107
Rat, brown 110
Raven 25
Ravenglass 45
Ray 113
Razorbill 41, 42, 113
Receiver of Wreck 91
Red admiral 80
Redshank 120, *179*
Redstart, black 25
Rempstone Rocks 174
Reskajeage Downs 144
Rhum 44, 109, *109*
Ribble marshes 123
Ringstead 178
Rinsey Cliff 151
Robin 49
Robin Hood's Bay 98, 190, *190*
Rocky Shore *104–105*
Ronaldshay, North 107
Rosemergy Cliff 147
Rosemullion Head 160
Royal fish 91
RSPB, The 83, 121
RSPCA, The 113
Rusey Cliff 134, *136*

S

St Agnes 144
St Aidan's Dunes 195, *196*
St Aldhelm's Head 178
St Anthony in Roseland 161
St Bride's Bay 204, *205*
St Catherine's Point 181, *181*, 182
St David's Head 204, *205*
St Kilda 43, 45, 107
St Margaret's Bay 183
St Mawes 162, *162*
St Michael's Mount 21, 26, 150, *150*
Salcombe 171, 172
Salcombe Regis 174
Salinity 117
Salt 48
in seabirds 73
Saltmarsh 123ff.
Saltwick Nab 190, *191*
Saltwort 53
Samphire, marsh, *see* glasswort
Samphire, rock 32, *34*, *92*, 95
Sand 49
Sandbanks 178
Sanderling *81*, 86
Sandhopper 49, 114, *118*
Sand-mason 113
Sandpiper 49
purple 80, 86
Sand Point 128
Sandwort, sea 53
Sandy Mouth 113, *135*
Scabbacombe 173, 174
Scilly, Isles of 31, 41, 110
Scolt Head Island 187, 189
Scorpion, sea 60, *60*
Sea-aster *123*, 124
Sea-beet 31, 32, 99, 114
Seabirds 32, 69
Sea-blite 114
shrubby 56
Sea holly 34, *34*, 114
kale 31
lavender 124
mat 49
pink, *see* thrift
potato 113
purslane *84*, 124
urchin 113
Seals 48, 86
Seal, common 48, 86
grey 48, 85, 86, 91
Seaweed 29, 112
Segontium 202
Selworthy Beacon 128
Sennen *146*, 147
Sharrow Point 170
Shag 28, *28*, 72, 73, 113
Shearwater, Manx 44, 69
Sheep 107
Soay 107
Shetland 41, 77
Shelduck 120, 123
Shell Bay 178
Shell, peppery furrow 118, *118*, 120
Shingle banks 56
plants 34
ridge *40–41*
Shipload Bay *126*, 133
Shipworm 49, *115*
Shoreston Dunes 195
Shrew 110
Shrew, Scilly 110
white-toothed 110
Shrimp *58*
Sidmouth 174
Sillery Sands 130
Skate 113
Skokholm 80, 107
Skomer 44, 107, 110
Soar Mill Cove 171
Solva 207
Solway Commons 197, *198*
Sparrow 49
Spartina, see grass, cord
Spinach 32
Spittles, the 175
Splash zone 29
Spleenwort, sea 29, *29*
Sprat 69
Spring 22–3
Springtail 57, *59*
Spurn Head 98
Squirrel, grey 125
Squirt, sea 49, *49*, 112
Stackpole 208
Staintondale 190
Starehole Bay 171
Starfish, common 65, *65*
Starling 49
Start Bay 173
Start Point 173
Stiffkey Marsh 187, *187*
Stonechat 21
Stonecrop 102
Strandline 49, 111, 113, 114
Strangford Lough 217
Studland Bay 53
Studland Heath 178
Swallow 21
Swallow, sea *31*
Swan, mute 125
Swanage 178
Swyre 176

T

Tamar estuary 122
Tellin, Baltic 118
Tenby 209
Tennyson Down *181*
Teredo 49
Terns 32, 73, 80
Tern, arctic 80
black 80
common 53
little 34, 53
sandwich 33, 53, *53*
Thornwick Bay *99*
Three Cliffs Bay *210*
Thrift 30, *35*, *93*, *95*, 102, 124
Tintagel 138, *139*
Torcross 99
Torr Head 215
Torrs Walk 133
Transpiration 53
Tregea Hill 144
Tregerthen Cliff 147
Trelissick 160
Trencrom Hill 146
Trengwainton Garden 149
Treveal Farm 146
Trey n Dinas 148, 149
Treyarnon *97*
Tube-worm 113
Turnstone 49, 86, 114, *116*
Turtle, loggerhead 115, *115*
Tywyn-y-Fach 203

V

Valerian, red *31*
Vault Beach *164*
Ventnor 182
Vole, Orkney 110

W

Waders 86, 120, 125
Wagtail 49
Warren cliffs 171
Warren Point 173
Wash, The 48, 123, 124
Water Mouth *132*
Wembury 170
Weston Mouth 174
Whales 91, 94, *94*
Wheal Prosper *151*
Wheatear 21, *21*
Whelk, common 49, 113
dog *112*
Whimbrel *82*
White Nothe 176
Whitepark Bay *214*
Whiting 69
Widgeon 125
Willapark 138
Wind Hill 130
Windbury Point 133
Winkle 49, 60
Woodcombe Point 172, 173
Woody Bay 130, *131*, 132
Woolacombe 132
Wreck 111

Y

Yealm estuary *169*, 170
Yellow-horned poppy 34
Y Maes, Llandanwg 203
Ynysgain 203

Z

Zennor 145
Zennor Head 147